UNIVERSITY OF WINCHESTER
LIBRARY

Martial Rose
Tel: 01

Literature, Theory, History

Literature, Theory, History

Jonathan Hart

LITERATURE, THEORY, HISTORY
Copyright © Jonathan Locke Hart, 2011.

First published in 2011 by
PALGRAVE MACMILLAN®
in the United States—a division of St. Martin's Press LLC,
175 Fifth Avenue, New York, NY 10010.

Where this book is distributed in the UK, Europe and the rest of the world,
this is by Palgrave Macmillan, a division of Macmillan Publishers Limited,
registered in England, company number 785998, of Houndmills,
Basingstoke, Hampshire RG21 6XS.

Palgrave Macmillan is the global academic imprint of the above companies
and has companies and representatives throughout the world.

Palgrave® and Macmillan® are registered trademarks in the United States,
the United Kingdom, Europe and other countries.

ISBN: 978–0–230–11339–8

Library of Congress Cataloging-in-Publication Data

Hart, Jonathan Locke, 1956–
    Literature, theory, history / Jonathan Hart.
        p. cm.
    ISBN 978–0–230–11339–8
        1. Literature—History and criticism—Theory, etc. 2. Literature—
    Philosophy. 3. Literature and history. 4. Comparative literature. I. Title.

PN50.H365 2011
801—dc22   2011012941

A catalogue record of the book is available from the British Library.

Design by Newgen Imaging Systems (P) Ltd., Chennai, India.

First edition: October 2011

10 9 8 7 6 5 4 3 2 1

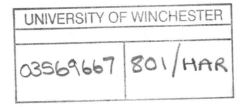

For Philip Ford
si placeant, librum, si non, amplectere, mentem;
maius erit voto, si sit utrumque, meo.

Contents

Preface and Acknowledgments

In this book I have tried, as in *Interpreting Cultures*, to discuss related topics in literature, theory, and history. The origins of this volume occurred long ago informally in my interest in literature, history, geography, and philosophy, and formally in the 1980s and 1990s in writing about poetry, history, empire, theory, and Comparative Literature. In some ways, this context, which was a crucial time in debates over theory and literature and their relation to history, is a key as it allows for some distance as well as a dialogue between past and present. Here, I have revised earlier work, some of which has appeared in journals and volumes in France, the United Kingdom, India, Brazil, Canada, and the United States. Some parts appear here in print for the first time. The body of the book begins with a discussion of Comparative Literature and ends with a similar debate in a new but earlier context. History, theory, and literature move backward and forward in different movements, in the act of living, reading, and writing. Interpretation involves sequence, a looking forward and back, a consideration of events, arguments, and stories as they happen, and an overview and retrospection. This book moves forward in a linear fashion but also circles back with different patterns in between. Criticism and theory, like the Bible, epic, and history, involve such patterns. The chapters contain work written from the late 1980s to about 2007, while the introduction and conclusion are very recent. There is an internal movement to the volume that is not based on the chronology of the writing but on the relation of one part to the next.

Comparison is at the heart of the book whether it is in connection with topics of literature, empire, culture, self, other, New Historicism, feminism, poetics, theory, history, editing, translation, conquest, or globalization. The range of the subjects focuses on fictions and poetics, ways of seeing, and historical representation and context. The book begins with a debate on the current state of Comparative Literature in North America and beyond, something I conceived first for a European audience. The second chapter compares the travel or encounter narratives of various empires at key moments—particularly in connection with "discovery"—and itself grew out of something written for an international audience of comparatists. In the third chapter, I consider some theoretical questions about writing and critical theory while discussing systems, law, theater, teaching, learning, and scholarship. Bartolomé de Las Casas and William Shakespeare, so key in the sixteenth and seventeenth centuries, make brief appearances here and elsewhere in the book. These were crucial times in the recovery and reconsideration of the classical past and in the shock of discovery—the advent of modernity. The question of comparison is also part of this chapter.

A central comparison between self and other, author and reader, occupies the fourth chapter. Otherness and the representation of the New World are, more specifically, a principal focus. Self and other also relate to historicism, feminism, and difference in the fifth chapter. In particular, in the 1980s and early 1990s New Historicism and feminism were particularly strong in departments of literature in North America. The work of theorists, like Stephen Greenblatt and Barbara Johnson, were central to the time and have historical significance still. The sixth chapter examines poetics and poetic worlds, calling attention to discovery and recognition in the fragile world of poetry, which is a possible world in an actual world. These worlds interact. W. B. Yeats and Seamus Heaney join the irrepressible Shakespeare to provide examples of poetic worlds. The relation between literature and the world is another recurrent comparison. In the connection between self and other, there is also stereotyping, something I analyze in the seventh chapter. Here, I also ask about the possibility of being after theory in a discussion of Terry Eagleton. If theory is a way of seeing, can we ever get beyond it? In the eighth chapter, I return to a longtime preoccupation in my work—the relation of history to poetry. I speak about the genres of history, including epic in the Renaissance, and about the rhetoric of history, as well as the connection between early modern and postmodern in the context of the modern. Here, I relate theory and history through literary and dramatic works like those of Shakespeare.

The ninth chapter returns to Las Casas and shows the power of translation in the way French and English texts use him to construct an image or stereotype of Spain. The typology of the Old World and the New World, of Europeans and Natives, provide the key comparisons in this chapter. I circle back in the tenth chapter to various topics that were vital in Comparative Literature in the late 1980s and early 1990s—World Literature, signs (semiotics), readers, narrative, literary history, the arts, translation, the notion of the "Third World," and East-West. The chapter ends with globalization and the War of 1898, when power was shifting from Britain to the United States, and then I move to a wider context of conquest. This background puts into focus some of the forces behind globalization that link past and present, and the age of colonization and decolonization. But Jean-Paul Sartre opted for the term "neocolonialism" rather than "decolonization." Both put pressure on the other. Books teach, and in this volume I concentrate on teaching explicitly in discussions involving the translation and reception of Las Casas and the question of the lesson of masters put by George Steiner in the third and ninth chapters respectively.

This book I dedicate to Philip Ford—friend, scholar, teacher—whose generosity and kindness have been exemplary. His work in Neo-Latin and the Renaissance and his literary sense have been an inspiration.

As in other prefaces and acknowledgments, I have thanked many, and here I express my gratitude to all those and concentrate on a few people, institutions, and agencies that have made specific contributions to the book or my wider research in the period in which I wrote it. Many thanks to those who have generously lent intellectual support to my research and writing over the years, including Jeremy Adelman, Anne Barton, Catherine Belsey, Jean Bessière, Ross Chambers, J. Edward Chamberlin, Tom Conley, Margaret W. Ferguson, Philip Ford, Thomas Healy, Roland Le Huenen, Linda Hutcheon, J. Hillis Miller, Kenneth Mills, Christopher Norris, Anthony Pagden, Paul Perron, Elizabeth Richmond-Garza, Andrew Taylor, Gordon Teskey, Mario Valdés, and Michael Worton. My thanks to students and colleagues at the University of Toronto, Trent University, Harvard University, University of Alberta, University of Cambridge, Princeton University, and the Sorbonne-Nouvelle, and to colleagues, hosts, and students at other universities during shorter appointments and visits. My particular thanks to Gordon Teskey—a talented painter who happens to be a leading teacher, scholar, editor, and critic of poetry and of the Renaissance—for allowing me the honor of having his painting, *The End of Language*, on the cover of this book. In this case I do hope the reader will judge the book by its cover.

My thanks to friends, hosts, and colleagues as I have set out in earlier prefaces, and here I mention particularly Alfred and Sally Alcorn, E. D. Blodgett, Terry Butler (in memory), Milan Dimić (in memory), Isabel Gil, Timothy Kilbourn, María Felisa López Liquete, Stephen Mobbs, Ricardo Gutiérrez Mouat, Juliet McMaster, Robert Merrett, Jane Moss, Kenneth Munro, Lenore Muskett, Donald and Cathleen Pfister, Ricardo Quinones, Josef Raab, Wilfried Raussert, Peter Sinclair, Irene Sywenky, Pauline Thomas, John Herd Thompson, and Linda Woodbridge. I would like to remember my old friend, Shelagh Agnes Heffernan, a schoolmate, dedicated teacher, and distinguished economist who died—with great courage and after years of chronic illness—on December 14, 2010, while I was in the final stages of this book. My thanks also to Cindy Chopoidalo and Jane Wong at Alberta for help with the technical matters of the manuscript. To the librarians at Toronto Reference Library, Toronto, Harvard, Alberta, Princeton, the John Carter Brown Library, Cambridge, Oxford, the British Library, Bibliothèque Nationale, Bibliothèque Sainte-Geneviève, and elsewhere, I offer my thanks. To the editors and publishers of *Ariel, Canadian Review of Comparative Literature/Revue Canadienne de la Littérature Comparée, European History Quarterly, Harvard Review, Journal of Literary Criticism, The Historian, Renaissance Quarterly, University of Toronto Quarterly,* Aeroplana Editora, Palgrave Macmillan, and The Modern Language Association of America, my thanks for publishing my work and for permission and the courtesy to reprint earlier versions of material in the chapters (specific debts occur in the notes). These editors at the time of the original writing included Santa Arias, Kees Boterbloem, Brian Corman, Eduardo F. Coutinho, Milan Dimić (in memory), Francis King, Pamela McCallum, Eyda M. Merediz, Daniel Pageaux, Sheila J. Rabin, Rajnath, Victor Ramraj, Richard Spall Jr., Christina Thompson, and Shaobo Xie. My editor at Palgrave Macmillan, Brigitte Shull, deserves praise and thanks. I also wish to express gratitude to Rohini Krishnan at Newgen and Joanna Roberts and Ciara Vincent at Palgrave. It has been a great pleasure to work with Palgrave Macmillan on so many of my books.

Many thanks also to members of my family: my father George and my mother, Jean (in memory); my brothers, Charles and Alan; my sisters, Gwendolyn, Deborah, and Jennifer; my wife, Mary Marshall; and our twins, Julia and James.

So this study of written texts, the letters left in works, and their relation to ways of seeing or theory and past and present of history is something that ranges from ancients to contemporaries, but I often discuss critics, theorists, and historians working in the past two or three decades, paying close attention to their words and analysis as I do to literature. Sometimes, in the wrestle of time, it is not simple to undo the twists and holds, and in pursuit of fictions, truth, method, and history itself, it may be that we are part of the scene that the speaker describes in Jean Toomer's "Her Lips Are Copper Wire," which begins: "whisper of yellow globes / gleaming on lamp-posts that sway / like bootleg licker drinkers in the fog."

Introduction

Poetics and rhetoric, representation and the art of persuasion, are keys to *Literature, Theory, History* and share a concern with the relation between speaker and audience, writer and reader. These three disciplines in my title describe the focus of my writing as poet, critic/theorist, and historian. Working in the three areas for some time, I have long seen them as connected through language and, more specifically, in the use of stories and argument and figures of speech to related word and world. Rhetoric and poetics share this ground, and these three fields are all rhetorical to a greater or lesser extent. Plato seems to have mistrusted poetry as overwhelming reason with emotion, whereas Aristotle saw poetry as a means of purging feeling through catharsis. Figures and tropes for one may mislead, whereas for the other they lead to equilibrium and knowledge. The language of poetry, philosophy, and history is controversial. Expressions may be explicitly or implicitly metaphorical, and metaphor, which identifies one thing with another (this man is an island), is one of the centers of language. Metonymy, which is also a key to language, is a displacement or something that stands in for something else. Literary theorists, like Jonathan Culler, acknowledge the importance of tropes, but so do historians like Hayden White, who uses four tropes—metaphor, metonymy, synecdoche, and irony—to examine "emplotment" or historical explanation. Synecdoche has the part representing the whole, and irony generally means, in its rhetorical guise, meaning the opposite of what is said (or saying the opposite of what is meant).[1]

Literature is made of genres or codes of expectations, something that goes back to Aristotle but that Northrop Frye set out more than fifty years ago.[2] Poetry, for instance, is often mediated through a voice, a speaker or a narrator, who lies between the poet and the reader or listener. Poems can be oblique and indirect, and this obliquity and indirection complicates, particularly in lyric, the relation between author and reader. The poem is itself and part of a larger body of poems in a genre and of literature as well as a moment in literary history, so that the text also has a context. It also has rhythm, rhyme, and poetic qualities that are formal and do not have to do directly with meaning or the semantic element. The poem is individual but it is also part of a collective. It relates to other poems and to the world, and it comes from a poet through a voice to the reader or listener. A poem is of poetics and the possible world of fiction while using the language of the everyday plainly or in an elevated fashion. Longinus wonders whether there is something like an art of the sublime and connects sublimity with the greatness of the soul.[3] Plotinus's idea of intellectual beauty, although as a Neoplatonist, derived from Plato, is connected with the beauty of divine intellect and may be revealed through contemplation.[4] Literature is made up of the matter of the world and of other literature.

The legacy of the Sophists and the classical rhetoricians has called into question the notion of essential meaning or ideas. The work of Kenneth Burke, Wayne Booth, Mikhail Bahktin, Wolfang Iser, Richard Rorty, and others have all contributed in the late twentieth century to the questioning of essentialism and the shift to rhetoric and the reader away from the authority of philosophy, religion, and the author as purveyors of truth.[5] Yet in the theory and practice of literature, there is not an enduring consensus about stable and unstable meaning and the connection of rhetoric or philosophy with literature. To speak of theory, as Antoine Compagnon reminds us, is to assume it theorizes a practice or *praxis*.[6] Reading or the interpretation of texts combines with literary history, whose contextual nature grows out of philology or *Wissenschaft*. Theory brings together the text of criticism and the context of history, while, as Compagnon says, it questions both the definition of literature and history.[7] Like Compagnon, who identifies theory as *protervus* (the protestant) or the gadfly, I too identify myself as an *eiron*, who with skepticism, irony, and doubt questions all discourse—literature, theory, and history—and the questioner himself or herself, including me.[8] A good distinction that Compagnon makes is that between theory of literature and literary theory, the one in France a branch of general and Comparative Literature that examines the conditions of literature, literary criticism, and literary history, and the other a linguistic analysis and critique of ideology, including the theory of literature. The theory of literature is a kind of metacriticism or criticism of criticism.[9] Style, history, and value, along with literature, author, world, and reader, make up literature, criticism, theory, and history, and each has an emphasis that affects how a person looks at the three main concerns of my book as reflected in its title.[10] Like Compagnon and Pierre Bourdieu, I wish to avoid "false dilemmas" on positions surrounding art and literature, but assume that literature is an important subject to discuss and that the very debate and opening up of discussion will enrich our understanding of it and its relation to theory and literature.[11] My book, not unlike those of Compagnon and Bourdieu, announces its own limits, showing its own ethics of perplexity because of the difficulty in coming to one view of literature, theory, and history that is sufficient. Comparison does put things into perspective and even admits relativity. No comparison is absolute, nor is any sense of relativism. As people look for truth, the limits of their rhetoric and the irony of their blindness or situation qualify the arrival or the certain end.

Openness helps to put our endeavors in focus. Comparative Literature and history keep one literary position from asserting more than its due as part of a more comparative or expansive context in time and space. The rhetorical relation between speaker and audience, reader and writer, in various fields and periods opens up the possibility of thinking about literature, theory, and history across time and cultures, however fraught it is with difficulty. The texts and contexts of the New World in the wake of Columbus's landfall in the western Atlantic are an important case that involves trauma and changes the shape of "discovery" and knowledge as the Europeans considered them. As New Historicism, feminism, and deconstruction also provide new ways to consider text and context, they warrant consideration. Poetry and poetics are also keys to the discussion of literature that need to be considered in terms of theorists and poets. The question of stereotyping is something that touches on many fields of representation and analysis, and it certainly has occupied theory and theories of otherness in particular. Poetry and history are also related closely, as Aristotle knew, and philosophy or theory can mediate their relation. The role of Bartolomé de Las Casas in the comparative context of the textual archive of the New World, particularly with the role of translation, is another example of how theory and practice (here especially in the classroom), text and context work. Moreover, the image of the title page plays a part. The global frameworks of Comparative Literature and World Literature as well as the importance of translation round off the examples I call on in *Literature, Theory, History*. This volume is exploratory and heuristic, so that it tries to open up discussions and evidence to the reader for him or her to consider these three related fields in close proximity.

Other Considerations

Interpretation has long been controversial going back to Plato's attack on Homer and has, as Patricia Waugh has suggested, stretched back to antiquity between rationalism and literary culture, humanism and Scholasticism

in the Renaissance, and humanism and science in the nineteenth century
as between T. H. Huxley and Matthew Arnold and in the twentieth century in the debate of two cultures, between C. P. Snow's science and F.
R. Leavis's moral aesthetics.[12] David Lodge sees in the work of Gerald
Edelman, a neurobiologist, who views art as the most extraordinary thing
about conscious human beings, a prospect that the two cultures of science and humanism will converge and collaborate.[13] Controversies can be
resolved and the door can always remain open to change and innovation
while making use of past frameworks and interpretations. In advocating
for the importance of literature and for a comparative and global aspect
at different times, I am doing so not simply because literature begets literature but because it is also connected with other fields and times in the
world. At this time, it would be unadvisable to turn our backs on science.
If anything, it needs a watchful eye. The science of criticism was at its peak
in the twentieth century in the work of Roman Jakobson and Northrop
Frye, when genre theory, semiotics, and structuralism were ascendant.
This kind of criticism or theory could also cause discomfort among creative writers who wished to celebrate the individuality and creativity of
their literary works.

My method is not to advocate for one theorist or theory, but to discuss
a number that have been important since the 1960s. In this regard, Bertolt
Brecht seems to have struck on something when on Thursday, September 9,
1920, he wrote in his diary:

A man with one theory is lost. He needs several of them, four, lots! He
should stuff them in his pockets like newspapers, hot from the press
always, you can live well surrounded by them, there are comfortable
lodgings to be found between the theories. If you are to get on you need
to know that there are a lot of theories; a tree too has several, but only
masters one of them, for a while.[14]

Between a discussion of Frank having red hair and allusions to H. Haase's
"imposing bottom," other less-than-flattering comments about women, and
the possibility of writing an operetta, Brecht emphasizes theories as tools
that someone needs to know if he or she wants to get on. Often the ironic
comment about the tree gets left out of this quotation, which usually seems
to trail off earlier.[15] Ignorance of theory is not an option. The writer understands the need for theory and seems to think that a person needs theory
even if the tone is apparently playful and perhaps a touch ironic and almost
jocular.

Often details or subordinate clauses or fragments in archives reconfigure any hasty generalizations we can make about culture. Literature, theory, and history are not simple tales or arguments, linear or unchanging. This is true of Brecht, who, in Finland on August 24, 1940, records in his diary, that when skimming Wordsworth, he "came on '*she was a phantom delight*' and was moved by this now remote work to reflect how varied the function of art is, and how dangerous it is to lay down the law."[16] Although Brecht often emphasizes the social effect of literature over its formal properties and prefers antimimetic techniques over Aristotelian mimesis, his views are intricate and are not given to a simple dogma. Another of his observations that day seems to prefigure the debate surrounding Northrop Frye's *Anatomy of Criticism* (1957), when Brecht remarks: "Art *is* an autonomous sphere, though by no means an autarchic one."[17] Art and literature are in and of themselves but also have relations to the world and to other fields of culture. Brecht's complexity is also apparent in his last observation in the entry in his diary for that same day: "Writing poetry must be viewed as a human activity, a social function of a wholly contradictory and alterable kind, conditioned by history and in turn conditioning it. It is the difference between 'mirroring' and 'holding up a mirror.'"[18] This last comment goes against the grain of Aristotle's view in *Poetics* and Hamlet's instructions to the players. In this one brief entry Brecht moves from the varied function of poetry and thus art, through the autonomy of poetry or art, to poetry and history performing a mutual conditioning of each other. And that is just the bare bones of the entry. In a sense Brecht's entry is a kind of synecdoche for the relation between poetry and history through theory. Critique connects theory and criticism.

Kunstkritik, as Walter Benjamin calls criticism of literature, music, art, and so on, bears an interesting position between philosophy and art.[19] Benjamin explores the tension among philosophy, critique, and art and observes:

> What critique basically seeks to prove about a work of art is the virtual possibility of the formulation of its contents as a philosophical problem, and what makes it call a halt—in awe, as it were, of the work of art itself, but equally in awe of philosophy—is the actual formulation of the problem.[20]

This formulation of content as a problem calls itself up short. Critique finds itself caught between the virtual nature of possibility and actuality, a kind of unrealized realization. Temporality becomes a key for literature, theory, and history, and Benjamin has something suggestive to say about world and time:

> In the revelation of the divine, the world—the theater of history—is subjected to a great process of decomposition, while time—the life of him who represents it—is subjected to a great process of fulfillment. The end of the world: the destruction and liberation of a (dramatic) representation. Redemption of history from the one who represents it. But perhaps in this sense the profoundest antithesis to "world" is not "time" but "the world to come."[21]

In this tension between divine and human, decomposition and fulfillment, temporality and eternity, apocalypse and redemption, Benjamin uses images of theater and drama. History and the promise of beyond history produce death and fulfillment. Benjamin's view is like the prefiguration-fulfillment model that Hayden White finds in different forms in the work of both Northrop Frye and Harold Bloom.[22] Criticism, theory, and philosophy often involve secular displacements of commentary, scholarship, and doctrine in theology. They are their own forms of secular scriptures or making human the divine, translating the other world in the world. The context of this world is the historical.

History has its own theory in historiography. In my own view, many or pluralist ways of representing and seeing in literature and theory also apply to history, so W. J. T. Mitchell's advocacy of dialectical pluralism and cross-pollination in literary theory would work together with Hayden White's view that pluralism be extended to history itself.[23] White explains this variety of perspectives in historical theory and practice as well as in critical practice in literary studies: "The referent of the term *history* is as indeterminable, is as much a matter of principled contestation, as the term *literature* (or for that matter 'philosophy' or 'science') itself."[24] White also discusses textualism, which is part of postmodernism, in which history is a web of figures and tropes, an artifact that consumes itself. He also notes that in postmodernism there is an erasure between literature and history because historical writing is a narrative, a kind of discourse, like literature, so that there is little difference between representing historical and imagined events. This kind of history is at odds with *Wissenschaft*, when from the nineteenth century, the state funded professional historians to study the past of the nation to legitimate it and its unity and purity. The agent and method of history, its narration, connected history to literature even, as White reminds us, when history in this period placed itself between theology and metaphysics on the one hand and the emergent human sciences like sociology, political economy, anthropology, and psychology on the other in their search for "realism" and "facts."[25] In a perceptive way, White outlines some of the intricate affinities and discontinuities among literature, theory, and history. A pluralism or many-sided inquiry or method would have to be open to transitional and humanist ways of writing about the world and history and about the fictions of culture produced in that world.

So when I argue for literature and for comparing literatures and getting to know the literatures of the world, I could do the same for comparing histories and the various world histories. Literature and history shift in their practices and theories over time and so move as the world moves, so their relative relation shifts over time. What I am not arguing for is a fixed literature, theory, or history, but only maintain that these subjects are significant and should be examined even as they shift. This history of culture is no easy matter. David Lodge says that the proliferation of literature and criticism occurred with the printing press and, similarly, as White has noted, amateurs, genealogists, antiquarians, and others, and not professionals, wrote history on the whole.[26]

From these considerations of literature, theory, and history, I would like to outline the movement of the book. Rather than be exhaustive, the chapters are designed to raise some issues in these fields and make connections between them. This introduction provides a context that suggests the limits and the possibilities of the subjects and my own approach to them. In selecting and ordering the topics as I have, I am calling attention to their importance without taking away from what might have been. There are many significant aspects of the three main areas of this monograph that could have been discussed with advantage. The following chapters are meant to open up debate and to engage others and not to be any kind of laying down the law, which, with Brecht, I think ill-advised and even suspect. The book is supposed to be, in whole and in its parts, heuristic.

Structure

The structure of the book begins and ends with views of comparative approaches to literature, theory, and history. In chapter 1, I shall discuss changes in Comparative Literature and the value of the field. The study itself will examine shifts in literary studies in the crucial time from the mid-1960s while emphasizing the value of literature and its interpretation. Since then, there have been many debates about Comparative Literature and many crises identified and many futures predicted for it, including no future. In chapter 1, I analyze aspects of the discussion of Comparative Literature in recent decades and set out one possible proposal as one among many for the discipline, that is, the importance of literature in literary studies and the comparative branch of the field.

In chapter 2, I argue that comparison is necessary to find the contours of a subject. While admitting that studying national traditions, histories, and literatures is necessary and desirable, I find no contradiction in a wider context in which culture and literature are considered comparatively. Each approach leads to new insights, which is so vital in a quest for recognition, something fraught with great difficulty. Even taking two familiar texts and placing them in a new context allows for new understanding. One example of comparison is the literature and narratives of European exploration and expansion from about 1415 to 1945. To get to the root of European identity, one should look to the routes of European exploration and the contact with other cultures.[27] These diverse paths involve varied, displaced, and discontinuous comparisons. A moment of recognition involves the culmination of a movement from ignorance to knowledge or self-knowledge, and it is fragile because it can be an instant of misrecognition. It is sometimes hard to distinguish between knowledge and ignorance.

Communication across time, I argue in chapter 3, allows for writing and reading that endures beyond the time in which the text was written. To communicate is hard in the present let alone considering changes over times and across cultures, but unless futility reigns, some meaning has to be produced between writer and reader, in what I call the drama of meaning. This process is interactive and is therefore basically rhetorical. This rhetoric takes into account difference in the present between writer and reader even as they share the text and humanity generally, but it also assumes historical change to be a significant element of reading and writing. The theatrical model of the text stresses the rhetorical relation between speaker and audience, writer and reader. It involves oral and written aspects and, ultimately, traces. Moreover, I maintain that culture connects images and words with the human place in nature and that this exchange involves communication and miscommunication, recognition and misrecognition. I also assume that even hindsight is fallible in discerning which is which because signs and signification, being many-sided, are prone to error and approximation. In this semantic theater, the present embodies and acts out past and future, so that mutability partly enacts nostalgia and possibility. This embodied temporal continuum also involves the desire for stability and actuality. This drama is both fulfilled and unfulfilled. To address these questions, I discuss briefly literature, systems, law and theater, nature and law, the idea of masters, the paradox of the stereotype, and life after theory by concentrating on a few texts. Moreover, I place them in context with the assumption that close attention to the texture of theoretical texts is as vital as to those of literature.

In making this point, I range over texts whose subjects are ancient or modern and even contemporary.

In chapter 4, I discuss the shock of "discovery" and trauma at first contact and in the wake of Columbus. The encounter between Native and European is a test case for otherness and how authority tries to impose itself. I provide a comparative discussion of western Europeans and how they came to terms with the otherness of Natives in the New World. Moreover, I explore how that encounter called into question the authority of the Europeans as authors and shook their worldview. This representation of the Natives and the New World had implications for how Europeans viewed themselves, their nation, and Europe. Columbus, Caminha, Las Casas, Vitoria, Montaigne, Léry, Ralegh, Aphra Behn, and others raise issues of their own authority in terms of being eyewitnesses to encounters with Natives and slaves. Making familiar the strange and strange the familiar occurs in these texts. Representations of customs, women, and cannibals recall Herodotus, Pliny, Tacitus, and other antecedents. Although Tzvetan Todorov, Michel de Certeau, and other theorists have discussed otherness in the context of New World travel accounts, I do so from a more overtly comparative point of view and widen the discussion beyond Hernán Cortés and Michel de Montaigne. More particularly, I concern myself with questions of being there, the rhetorical contract between writer and reader, and the typology of the Old and New World. These elements relate to the truth and the lies that the authors and readers of travel accounts must negotiate. Many aspects of truth, fiction, religion, ethnology, law, philosophy, politics, and gender are at play in these texts. In this rich textuality and intertextuality an interdisciplinarity occurs.

History, philosophy, and poetry, as I note in chapter 5, were closely related in Aristotle and they can be examined together today. Even in the reassessment of Plato and Aristotle, new kinds of historical and textual studies from the 1960s brought together scholars, students, and readers from different fields. In this chapter, I like to discuss New Historicism and deconstruction in the context of feminism as new negotiations of the connection between word and world. New Historicism came of age in the early 1980s and attempted to decenter or reorient canonical texts. Feminism and deconstruction provided other ways and other insights to thinking about literature and, more specifically, about reading and interpretation. Barbara Johnson's "feminist difference" brings these "schools" together, and her work on gender and difference is important in the context of new ways to look at the old question of texts and the texts themselves. So these textual and contextual methods bring history and literature together, sometimes through philosophy and other disciplines.

In chapter 6, I note that many kinds of texts coexist and are part of the world of the discourse of literature. Here, I examine poetry and poetics in terms of theorists and poets from Aristotle through Philip Sidney and Shakespeare to W. B. Yeats. Furthermore, I assume that as individuals, cultures, societies, and polities, we make stories, theories, and arguments and, in turn, interpret these. This assumption leads me to define culture as a kind of lived interpretation in which people and peoples are involved in an interpretation of interpretation. Where fact ends and interpretation begins is the key question in this context. In the 1960s and beyond, New Criticism and traditional historicism yielded some ground and then a great deal of it to new schools. In the English-speaking world at least, philosophical modes of theory—such as deconstruction—came to the fore. These were related to New Criticism through an interest in the way language works and textual analysis. A further shift in literary studies occurred (as it often does from generation to generation) to more historical, contextual, and content methods like New Historicism, cultural materialism, feminism, and a new and displaced kind of Marxism and psychoanalysis. The text came to be a site of disunity and contention and not some attempt at unity—meaning, genre, character, language, and structure all became contentious issues. These central elements in literature and culture persist. Poetics and poetic worlds are ways of talking about form and content, text and context. I consider poetry, interpretation, and the theory of poetry to be keys to language, literature, representation, and antimimetic modes of seeing, framing, and interpreting. Moreover, I see poetry to be a synecdoche and sometimes a metonymy for literature and all the genres. As poetry is closely related to philosophy in Plato and to history and philosophy in Aristotle, word and world are inseparable in Western poetics, so that while the connection between text and context may take on new shapes, it is hardly new.

I begin and end chapter 7 with a brief examination of Terry Eagleton's *After Theory*. The question becomes one of whether we are posttheory and whether that is even possible. Perhaps there is an ebb and flow in theory as in many other things. This chapter also raises the matter of translation itself. The translator becomes in some regards a new author, mediates, and is involved in loss and gain. There is some discourse in the French tradition that does not quite translate into English. The theory of Roland Barthes, Jacques Derrida, Michel Foucault, Julia Kristeva, and Helène Cixous, for instance, loses something in translation. Yet, their discourse generally is a gain for the English-speaking world, enriching language and culture. Questions of subjectivity, ideology, or the stereotype, in the work of Shoshana Felman and Daniel Castillo Durante in French are also an enrichment of English through translation. This cultural transmission and exchange enriches each national culture in the inevitability of exchange in a world given to communication, trade, and travel.

Epic, as I say in chapter 8, explores the relation between poetry and history. Homer represented love and war, the clash between cultures before Aristotle discussed history, poetry, and philosophy. This chapter concentrates on some important work on epic and warfare and extends that interest to combat, especially between Europe and Asia, in early modern Europe and about the New World. The epic and the history play are genres that reshape history: romance explores the legendary. Historical writing involves a quest for what happened while historical poetry explores what might have happened. The insights of metahistory and New Historicism are suggestive, but the temptation of textualism and constructivism can be taken too far. There is a nature and a past, and while we interpret them in all too human ways, they also have an existence outside the present human mind.

History, like literature, also bears some relation to the world. Such a connection occurs in chapter 9 in two ways—in the specific context of the early decades of the Spaniards in the New World and in how we teach texts from the sixteenth and seventeenth centuries in classrooms. I discuss teaching Bartolomé de Las Casas, who was a landowner then a Dominican in the New World who came to edit Christopher Columbus, in a comparative framework. In this context, I consider notions of translation, intertextuality, and the colonial archive. Writers and translators in France and England contended with the example of Spain in the colonization of the New World. Moreover, the identities of France and England had to assimilate figures like Columbus and Las Casas into their textual and political archive. I balance the French and English emulation of Spain with their use of what came to be known as the Black Legend of Spain. Las Casas is a vital part of the comparative studies of the Americas and is related to others like Columbus, Jacques Cartier, and John Smith, who also came into contact with indigenous peoples. French and English identities became deeply tied to translations of Spanish texts about the New World. This is a kind of comparative history I discuss in chapter 2.

In the tenth and final chapter, I turn to Goethe's *Weltliteratur* and return to Comparative Literature, which I examined in chapter 1. The chapter explores a key time in that field—the late 1980s—and discusses the changes and trends in the subject. I argue that there is something collective or collaborative about Comparative Literature or World Literature partly because of their vastness and the improbability of one person becoming expert in all languages, literatures, and cultures. The late 1980s was a time that was particularly important in the acceleration of globalization and a critical time in Comparative Literature. Translation, "Third World" literature, and the interaction of Eastern and Western literatures are subjects I pursue in this chapter. Here, I maintain that comparing different contexts in literature, culture, and history allows for a dialogue among disciplines and that the separation between text and context is often artificial. Each discipline or even genre within literature provides another way of writing and reading. Words help to interpret the world.

Transitions

As the last chapter begins with Goethe as a way into World Literature and Comparative Literature, I would like to compare an early allusion to him in Brecht's diaries with a late one, partly to show how fluid and changeable authors and comparisons are in this world. On Tuesday, August 24, 1920, Brecht remarks:

> I don't think I could ever have so thoroughly developed a philosophy as Goethe or Hebbel, who must have had memories like tram-conductors where their own ideas were concerned. I'm continually forgetting my opinions, can't ever make up my mind to learn them off by heart.[28]

Whereas the young Brecht differentiates himself from Goethe, the older Brecht identifies himself or his work with him. In the entry in his diary of September 10, 1949, Brecht calls Goethe "modernistic" and in the entry of November 9, 1949, he includes Faust as the only repertoire piece in German theater besides opera and Shakespeare and considers only *Threepenny Opera* and *Caucasian Chalk Circle* among his plays to have that character.[29] And so all of us change and are full of intricacies and contradictions. Literature, theory, and history involve humans writing and reading, and it should be no surprise that they are thus asymmetrical, varied, and changeable.

In chapter 1, I turn to the future of Comparative Literature, which has been an important but fragile discipline in much of the English-speaking world. In a time of increased globalization, it would seem logical that World Literature and Comparative Literature would flourish, but sometimes in eras of great change, people, institutions, and states retrench. They act against their own best interests. The matter of the future is now something for those who consider religion and utopian aspects of politics or projections in demography, medicine, and economics, but, until the professionalization or "disciplinization" of history in the nineteenth century, as Hayden White points out, historians also considered the future part of history.[30] It is only with the institutionalization of literature and history as the study of the culture of nations did the science of the discipline shrink the topic to the past and to one nation. National literatures and national histories were born and served the purposes of the state. Comparing histories and literatures could be embarrassing. Although nationalism may have less of a hold on the West than it did in the virulent phases in the nineteenth and twentieth centuries (especially in the first half of the twentieth), there are still some political purposes that the state favors, and this can be seen in funding from governments, councils, and the universities themselves. Medicine and engineering take precedence over humanities in many places, and the research university sometimes seems to elide or occlude investigation in the humanities, fine arts, and social sciences. This is the way of the world, and this book is a testimony to some possible worlds of the future, the relation between past and present, and the ever-changing configurations of the production and interpretation of literary, theoretical, and historical texts.

To Comparative Literature as Humpty Dumpty, I now turn. Humpty faces one way, and it is not certain whether he faces the past or the future as he sits on a wall, not simply of a nursery rhyme but perhaps of the Berlin Wall or the Iron Curtain. Perhaps he finds himself looking backward and forward with Brecht in Berlin in the late 1940s and early 1950s. Perhaps Humpty cannot decide why, in the last year Brecht wrote his diary—1955—the International Comparative Literature Association, which T. S. Eliot helped to found, held its first congress. Perhaps Humpty, like Goethe, Brecht, and Eliot, despite all their differences, understood that the modern world (perhaps even all worlds of culture) is comparative, worldly, and global. As Humpty, like Sir John Falstaff, outlived his author and these authors, he can look beyond the deaths of Goethe in 1832, of Brecht in 1956, and of Eliot in 1965, to see, at least putatively, where literature, criticism, and the world might be moving.

CHAPTER 1

Comparative Literature

In the context of globalization and multiculturalism, neither of which is new but which have intensified and diversified in the past half century or so, it is perhaps strange that Comparative Literature and even World Literature are in crisis or under pressure. In the English-speaking world this may have to do with the so-called triumph of English. Until the 1960s, one can argue that the elite in England were educated in Greek, Latin, and French in the schools and that English came late at the end of empire. Arguably, English started its rise within England with the Reformation. But until the rise of British power in the eighteenth century and its consolidation in the nineteenth century, and the rise of the United States from the end of the nineteenth century, English yielded to French as a diplomatic language; Spain and France had more power in the politics of Europe until the end of the War of the Spanish Succession, although this diminished after the end of the Seven Years' War and dwindled even further with the defeat of Napoleon.

Still, even in Europe, England (then Britain) was challenged by Germany and Russia after this. There was in a sense a balance of power. Asia had the largest economies until the mid-eighteenth century, and even in the early nineteenth century, China and India had a great deal of economic influence. English and the English-speaking world, although influential, were not the only strong forces culturally, politically, and economically. The rise and intensification of nationalism in Europe and the decline of classical education made for a connection between vernacular language and the centralized state. The suppression of Cornish and Breton are cases in point as England and France extended their cultural and political dominion with a form of internal colonization. This movement also occurred with the expansion of Europe and the extension of empire. A comparative perspective could lessen the claims of national greatness in culture and politics. Any comparative study can provide a context that clarifies, but sometimes qualifies, the claims of national ideologies. Perhaps the very threat that globalization and multiculturalism pose to some who uphold traditional nations and cultures tied to an apparent ethnic identity and shared mother tongue allows for a reaction against seemingly centrifugal forces. At a time when the study of diverse languages and cultures in the world, which Comparative Literature encourages, is vital, people can bury their heads and try to return to what is construed to be a more coherent or simpler time. It is also possible to say that Comparative Literature was Eurocentric and is a vestige, but this field has changed with the times, involving comparisons with languages across the world, including indigenous languages like those of Natives in the Americas. It is also the case that departments of English and other national literatures have become more flexible and include much to do with theory and with the study of culture that Comparative Literature and cultural studies have entailed. Moreover, interdisciplinary studies also make comparisons and bring together literature with culture, music, law, the visual arts, and other fields. The one thing that Comparative Literature has insisted on in most places is the inclusion of two or more languages in comparisons. Translation and the translation of study and of culture are connected inextricably. Chaucer, Shakespeare, and Milton—the foundations of English as a field of inquiry—seem to have been at home in at least two languages. French, Latin, and Greek would have been part of schooling and training. Milton was Cromwell's Latin secretary. Even in the creation of English literature in the Middle Ages and the Renaissance, there was translation and the comparison of languages, literatures, and cultures. It was hard to ignore Italy, Latin, and Italian. Chaucer cribbed from Boccaccio, Shakespeare took from Ovid, and Milton went on a grand tour.

In practice, then, national literatures tend to be comparative even if in recent times this has sometimes been forgotten. All sorts of fields are necessary for fields of vision. To see more, national literatures and Comparative Literature are both helpful. World Literature, even if it often relies on translation more than Comparative Literature, makes a contribution. All these tools are necessary.

Here, I shall provide a reminder that literature needs to be studied and compared no matter how important context and culture are. Schools and universities should not give up the study of literature in literature departments, even if it is studied elsewhere as there is overlap in the arts and sciences. Mathematics can be used in biology. Sociologists can study the role of literature in society. Interdisciplinary work or teams can be productive and can do significant work that would probably not be done otherwise.

However, no one would expect departments of physics to give up the study of physics, and the same should be true of literature in departments of literature. Fields and departments change as they must to innovate and stay vital, but to shift the whole focus of departments of literature away from literature is not productive. If departments wish to combine literature, film, and media or literature and cultural studies, then that is an interesting alternative to an equally plausible model of separate departments of the humanities, or interdisciplinary studies, film, media, or cultural studies. To efface literatures and their comparison would lead, in my view at least, to an impoverishment. Sometimes with budgets being cut in real terms in the humanities, from the late 1960s or early 1970s, there is a shrinking of departments or a merger of different programs and fields. Sometimes as administrations more given to medicine, engineering, and business put pressure on economies, there is a competition for resources and a yoking of many fields under a rubric. Small programs like Comparative Literature come under pressure. Ideoversity and a plethora of disciplines are reduced, and calls are made to make virtue of necessity.

Futures

Predicting the future is a hazardous occupation. The prolepsis or projection of utopian or dystopian scenes for the study of Comparative Literature is not something I wish to emphasize here. Instead, I would like to discuss shifts in the discipline and its value. Whatever the changes in literary studies, it is important to stress the value of literature and its interpretation.

There have been many discussions of the crisis of Comparative Literature over time and many futures predicted for it. Some have said it has no future. After mapping out some of the recent debate on Comparative Literature, I will set out a modest proposal, as one among many possible worlds for our discipline. Comparative Literature has its origins at least as early as the nineteenth century in Europe and North America. As Armando Gnisci has noted about Comparative Literature, "Since its origin, . . . it has always been defined as a discipline in crisis."[1] Gnisci sees Comparative Literature as "a truly global discipline" and looks to translation as a key factor in this mode of education and dialogue.[2] This interest in Comparative Literature, even as it has come under some fire in parts of Europe and North America—often squeezed by departments of literature in the "langues nationales" or national languages—is spreading rapidly in Asia and Latin America. For instance, in Brazil, as Sandra Nitrini has observed, from about 1950, Comparative Literature has been part of the curriculum. The publication of Tania Franco Carvalhal's *Literatura Comparada*, in 1986, helped to spur interest, and the

Brazilian Association of Comparative Literature was formed.[3] Despite this growing interest in Comparative Literature in Brazil, it would be a mistake to ignore older and more complex beginnings. As Nitrini says, "Comparative Literature has existed in Brazil for a long time: in reality, since the time when we started to think about the formation of Brazilian literature and on the creation of a project of national literature."[4] The mobility and resilience of Comparative Literature are reasons for optimism. Comparative Literature changes and adapts, and in a world on the move, this is a positive attribute. Walter Moser has called Comparative Literature "a nomadic discipline."[5] He asserts that comparatists may be able to take advantage of their situation: "The precariousness of the status of their discipline can turn itself into an advantage."[6] This context suggests that Comparative Literature is both in a state of precarious advantage and advantageous precariousness. The international status and growth of Comparative Literature is encouraging even if there are some locally discouraging predicaments.

The Death of Literature

So who is proclaiming the death of literature and Comparative Literature? Two well-known examples during the 1990s were Alvin Kernan's *The Death of Literature* (1990) and Susan Bassnett's *Comparative Literature: A Critical Introduction* (1993).[7] Gayatri Spivak gave the Wellek Library Lectures in May 2000 at the University of California at Irvine, which were published as a volume in 2003 entitled *Death of a Discipline*. In the acknowledgments, Spivak writes provocatively: "I hope the book will be read as the last gasp of a dying discipline."[8] It comes as no surprise that Spivak continues to call for "a new comparative literature."[9] She sees Comparative Literature as something in need of renovation "in response to the rising tide of multiculturalism and cultural studies."[10] Spivak, like Edward Said, has a point that the movement of people does affect institutions like Comparative Literature and the university.[11] I too agree with Spivak's sense that Comparative Literature can "include the open-ended possibility of studying all literatures, with linguistic rigor and historical savvy."[12] Spivak also admits that the best of traditional Comparative Literature was "the skill of reading closely in the original."[13] She also proposes that close attention to language as in area studies would reveal the hybridity of all languages in the Northern and Southern hemispheres. Spivak thinks that cultural studies is given to a kind of personal and presentist vantage that does not include rigor in language study.[14] Her strategy will, in Spivak's view, lead to an act of imagination that involves othering, a kind of translation.[15] Teaching reading is, for me as much as for Spivak, the central part of what we do as teachers of Comparative Literature.[16] To this, I would add that reading is the center of our research and interpretation. Spivak's utopian urge in her reimagining of Comparative Literature is based on working together and friendship and trying to imagine how to see through the eyes of others.[17]

Another aspect of Spivak's desire to revivify Comparative Literature is how she champions literature as something that "escapes the system"[18] and that "contains the element of surprising the historical."[19] She also stresses literature as a means of achieving difference in collectivity.[20] Further, Spivak encourages "careful reading" as a way of seeing difference with respect for texts from the so-called Third World, to find in them themes of tradition and modernity, individualism and collectivity.[21] This is Spivak's new Comparative Literature. Spivak answers Marx's privileging of city over the country by saying that he could not see the future spectralization of the rural, and perhaps with her own pastoral yearning and nostalgia, she offers precapitalist cultures as an imagined world to counterbalance the "global capital triumphant."[22] The reading of the textual becomes a way, according to Spivak, to be "responsible, responsive, answerable."[23] While I have selected what I find most appealing and suggestive in Spivak's brief volume, I am interested here in providing a wider context, that is, in including other voices on the topic of Comparative Literature and in setting out a few short suggestions myself.

As with the death of the novel and the author, the demise of Comparative Literature is premature or a turn of phrase, a kind of important half-truth. Literature and Comparative Literature are changing: reading in an age of electronic media, as Marshall McLuhan and Roland Barthes saw during the 1950s and 1960s, does change.[24] So have writing and knowing, but this change is not so radical that there are no continuities with the past. Revolutions are never clean breaks. In this age of business and applied science, the uselessness of literature is an affront. In fact, Plato found the illusion of knowledge in Homer a challenge to be challenged. Philosophy was—in his possible world of the *Republic*—to displace Homer's poetry in Athenian education. For the Platonic Socrates, poets were to sing hymns in praise of the *Republic* or they would suffer exile.[25] Even during the Renaissance, Philip Sidney had to find a moral compass for poetry. He reversed Plato's new hierarchy that moved from the universal of philosophy to the particulars of history, with poetry wedged between them. For Sidney, poetry was more universal than philosophy because it moved people to moral action.[26] The marginalizing of poetry is not new: in a world given to useful arts, it will continue to be under pressure. Percy Bysshe Shelley's unacknowledged legislators of the world are unacknowledged.[27] Literature, as I shall later argue, is no longer at the center of education in the schools and especially in colleges and universities. It is, however, important, even if its utility is not always readily apparent. If sometimes programs and departments of Comparative Literature are on the ropes, they are hanging in there. Poetry, literature, and their study have survived Plato's attacks and all those who have followed in his wake. Plato was a great poetic philosopher, so that then, as now, the hardest blows come from those who speak the language of poetry and turn it against poetry. Poetry is the core of literature, and I use it as a synecdoche for literature and the literary.

Some Approaches

A suggestive approach to Comparative Literature is one that Douwe Fokkema outlines. He draws on Karl Popper's view that a field of study is limited to a cluster of questions and tentative solutions and argues that "disciplines are not distinguished by the object they study but by the questions they ask."[28] For Fokkema, the literary and literariness are ways of reading—the intentions, semiotics, and effects of literary texts—because others read and interpret literary texts but for different purposes—political, theological, sociological, and so on.[29] The aesthetic dimension, as Fokkema reminds us, can be readily overlooked in discussions of the changes to Comparative Literature. That is not an evasion I will consciously make here. Although sociologists, psychologists and philosophers, art historians, and others can discuss the aesthetic, literary scholars bring their own perspective to this area and can contribute, as Fokkema suggests, to interdisciplinary work in this quadrant of value. How the object of study is studied is a dance or interplay that defines the discipline.

In 1958, as Linda Hutcheon reminds us, René Wellek wrote an essay, "The Crisis in Comparative Literature," in which he focused on the subject and method of the discipline.[30] Like Spivak, Hutcheon finds strength in the role of otherness in Comparative Literature.[31] Hutcheon also sees frustration and attraction in Comparative Literature because of the "continual self-criticism" and inability "to fix its self-definition."[32] Debate has surrounded Comparative Literature for so long. The Levin report to the American Comparative Literature Association (ACLA) in 1965, the Greene report in 1975, the Bernheimer report in 1993, and the Saussy report (draft in 2003) have all expressed the double movement of frustration and attraction and of definition and criticism that Hutcheon suggests.[33]

Rather than go over the ground of the Bernheimer report, which has invoked many responses since its appearance in 1993, including Spivak's lecture and book, I will move on to some of the most recent views as expressed in the Saussy draft report.[34] Haun Saussy begins in a most optimistic mode:

"Comparative Literature has, in a sense, won its battles. It has never been better received in the American university. The premises and protocols characteristic of our discipline are now the daily currency of coursework, publishing, hiring, and coffee-shop discussion."[35] After setting out the rigorous requirements in graduate programs of Comparative Literature in the United States and the influence of its practitioners on other disciplines like English and history, Saussy notes the lack of institutional power of, and the investment of resources in, Comparative Literature: "The omniscience of Comparative Literature ideas does not by any means betoken a large and powerful university department in that discipline; in fact, it might be used as an argument against the necessity of founding one. Comparative literature programs in most universities are thinly-funded patchworks of committee representation, cross-listed courses, fractional job lines and volunteer service."[36] Saussy suggests that we encourage students with training in law, history, architecture, or other disciplines to learn two languages and literatures well instead of three languages and literatures, and he suggests that Comparative Literature take advantage of the gaps in the university, and that it should knock on the doors of the disciplines that have borrowed from Comparative Literature.[37]

The untranslatability of literature, especially of poetry, at once defines the literary and calls Comparative Literature into question. This has been a persistent theme in literary studies and a constant challenge to Comparative Literature. In *Petit Manuel d'inesthéthique* (1998), Alain Badiou embodies the contradiction. On the one hand, he makes the subject of his book a comparison between Labîd ben Rabi'a and Mallarmé, the one a nomad before Islam writing in classical Arabic and the other a poet of the salon in the bourgeois realm of France of the Second Empire. On the other hand, Badiou begins this comparison with the assertion—*"Je ne crois pas beaucoup à la littérature comparée"* or "I do not believe much in Comparative Literature."[38] This lack of belief is not absolute as Badiou inserts the "beaucoup" or "much" as a qualifier, to indicate that he does not believe much in Comparative Literature. But he believes enough to write a book on Comparative Literature and to perform a tour de force in which he takes disparate authors in the wide gap of time in languages from radically different cultures and finds a common or universal truth in them. As Emily Apter has said in her discussion of Badiou's book, "It would seem that the greater the arc of radical dissimilitude and incomparability, the truer the proof of poetic universalism."[39] Apter, who is examining universal poetics and postcolonial comparison, explores, as Saussy did, the untranslatability of translating literature. Perhaps, as Said and Spivak seemed to hope and as Apter argues, possibilities of comparisons beyond imperialism are available, and this renewed Comparative Literature can be open to cultures across the world in a transformative way.[40]

The controversy over dissenting and contradictory voices was so great in the ACLA's report in the 1980s that, according to Bernheimer in his report, as Djelal Kadir says in his essay, "Comparative Literature in An Age of Terrorism," the chair of the committee "was so dissatisfied with the document that he exercised a pocket veto and never submitted it."[41] Kadir teases out the tensions and contradictions in "état présent" or the present state of Comparative Literature:

> One would be hard-pressed to find a comparatist who would argue against the supersession of monolingualism, presentism, and narcissism. The difficulty in the historical moment of 2004 is to differentiate between multilingualism and forked tongues, historical scope and self-serving historicism, non-narcissistic self-effacement and self-critique as cloak of invisibility.[42]

Kadir sees language as a central part of the debate. And the specter of translation and its relation to reading never goes away in these debates on Comparative Literature.[43] As Walter Benjamin asserts, "All translation is only a somewhat provisional way of coming to terms with the foreignness of language."[44] Steven Ungar's contribution to the Saussy report provides thoughts on translation. Like William H. Gass, Ungar sees the importance of close reading. For Ungar, "Close reading will continue to be grounded in efforts to understand linguistic specificity as well as how broader factors of difference bear on linguistic choices made by the writer."[45] Difference and otherness, as Derrida and Spivak have asserted, are central to translation: literature in translation and World Literature in translation, as outlined in David Damrosch's *What Is World Literature?* (2003), make the debate on translation even more crucial because in many places such a World Literature will be translated or edited in Europe and North America.[46]

The canon of translation might well continue the colonial narrative in the realm of culture. In his contribution to the Saussy report, Damrosch opens with a declaration: "World literature has exploded in scope during the past decade. No shift in modern comparative study has been greater than the accelerating attention to literatures beyond masterworks by the great men of the European great powers."[47] While this might be a slight hyperbole and is expressed in the context of the United States academy, the changes have been rapid. In his discussion of anthologies and who is written about and who is not, at least relatively speaking, Damrosch hopes for a way forward that would include "lines of connection across the conflicted boundaries of nations and of cultures, and new lines of comparison across the persisting divisions between the hypercanon and the counter-canon of world literature."[48]

There are other potential problems of exclusion and erasure in Comparative Literature. Two such examples are early modern or Renaissance studies and feminism. In his essay on Comparative Literature and early modern studies, which is part of the Saussy report, Christopher Braider answers Damrosch's observation, in his presidential address at the ACLA meetings in 2003, that studies before 1800 have been pushed to the margins, and that most colleagues concentrate on work produced since the turn of the nineteenth century.[49] Braider appeals to early modern studies as a way to fuse formalism and historicism. For instance, a painting of Lucretia, like all images from a differing past, tells us that we have to understand and criticize ourselves, our language, and our framework before trying to recover the past, something that Michael Baxandall discussed in *Patterns of Intention: On the Historical Explanation of Pictures* (1985).[50] If early modern studies has experienced a displacement or erasure, feminism has been appropriated and assimilated. In her contribution to the draft Saussy report, "What's Happened to Feminism?" Gail Finney suggests, "If we don't encounter the word 'feminism' as much as we used to, I would suggest that this is not because the ideology has vanished but rather because it has proliferated and been assimilated by other theoretical approaches."[51] I would argue that Braider might follow a similar line of argument in saying that New Historicism in the United States and cultural materialism in the United Kingdom migrated from Renaissance or early modern studies to, and were assimilated by, other periods and disciplines. Finney says that in the United States, English, language departments, and Comparative Literature have become feminized in practice. For instance, the three executive officers of the ACLA in the year of writing—2005—were women as were six of the ten advisory board members, and the University of California has a maternity leave that stops the tenure clock for women.[52] Perhaps then, as Finney suggests, the very success of feminism has led to less mention of it and to metafeminism. Metafeminist practice occurs in Lynne Pearce's *The Rhetorics of Feminism: Readings in Contemporary Cultural Theory and the Popular Press* (2004).[53] Pearce gives a rhetorical and stylistic analysis of contemporary feminist journalism and theory.[54] Feminism has not disappeared from Comparative Literature but has been an agent of transformation that has apparently erased or changed its previous surface.

Fedwa Malti-Douglas recalls in her contribution to the draft version of the Saussy report, "Beyond Comparison Shopping: This Is Not Your Father's Comp. Lit.," how at Cornell, Pennsylvania, and the University of

California, Los Angeles (UCLA), she was taught by male professors only, and that female professors in 1977, when she had her first tenure-track job, were an oddity at the University of Virginia. She gives a lyrical call for a new Comparative Literature, although one different from that which Spivak calls for:

> Comparative Literature for me must be a world without limits, assuming that one can navigate several languages. It is almost a domain of fantasy in which high art can be analyzed alongside the cinema which can be analyzed along the comic strip which can be analyzed alongside a verbal world. It is like a wonderful kaleidoscope that allows comparatists a multifaceted view into the world that we intellectually inhabit. Certainly, many a nay-sayer will not be quite ready yet to take the plunge into these rapids, carrying on his or her shoulder the aging body of the old Comparative Literature. So be it. It is precisely because it is not our father's Comparative Literature that we can infuse fresh life into the field.[55]

This image of a portage and a crossing of the rapids might stir those of us who grew up or live in the land of the voyageurs and coureurs de bois, whether crossing the rapids at Lachine or the dozens of portages on the way to the land of the Ouendat or Hurons from Québec to Sainte-Marie on La Mer Douce, now less sweetly called Georgian Bay. The image is also epic, like the great hero carrying his father on his back, but here the hero is also a heroine. It is, as Finney and Malti-Douglas remind us, important not to forget the social changes in the university and in Comparative Literature. One of them has been that the interests of women and people of diverse backgrounds and languages are better served.

Nonetheless, in the responses to the draft of the Saussy report, which will probably find their way into the published version, there is not always a sense that all that should be included in Comparative Literature is. Caryl Emerson advocates for close attention to Central and Eastern Europe as they "have been through every abomination," and their "outsideness to all things" means that "we could begin learning from them."[56] Marián Gálik and Richard Teleky addressed some of these issues in Central and Eastern Europe in an issue of the *Canadian Review of Comparative Literature/Revue Canadienne de Littérature Comparée* in 1996.[57]

Katie Trumpener's response begins with a history of the discipline that includes Franco Moretti's view, in "Conjectures of World Literature," that Comparative Literature was an "intellectual enterprise, fundamentally limited to Western Europe, and mostly revolving around the river Rhine (German philologists working on French literature). Not much more."[58] Like Saussy, Trumpener thinks that Johann Gottfried Herder's comparative analysis allowed for the relations among Eastern, Central, and Western European powers that included "the problems of empire, political domination, and forced bilingualism raised by that geography."[59] Trumpener ends with the study of World Literature, something much more than Moretti's Rhine and perhaps an outgrowth of Herder's comparative analysis. How do Comparative Literature and World Literature relate? Trumpener says that most teachers of World Literature would admit that "our own limitations of training make us largely unable to model such culturally alternative modes of reading, however much we might theorize their existence or try to reconstruct them in and from the texts under discussion."[60] The practical problems of teaching face professors and students of Comparative Literature. Trumpener sets out the pragmatic pitfalls: "In some respects, World Literature remains a daunting, perhaps impossible project. But if not us, who? And if not now, when?"[61] This practical approach reminds me of what Harry Levin used to say and write, "Let us begin to compare literatures," because if we wait for the perfect union of literary sensibility and skill in languages, then we will never get started.

Richard Rorty's response, "Looking Back at 'Literary Theory,'" observes that, in retrospect, literary theory was a fashion in literature departments in the United States and that, as a philosopher, it would now be harder, as he did, to move from being a professor of philosophy to a professor of the humanities to a professor of Comparative Literature while teaching straight philosophy and by writing much the same philosophical works he would have written in a department of philosophy. In literature departments, the philosophical period of Derrida has moved to the historical and cultural world of Michel Foucault. While being grateful for his opportunities, Rorty does not think that students of literature have to read philosophy or any other disciplines or be multilingual. In short, he asserts that "good criticism is a matter of bouncing some of the books you have read off the rest of the books you have read."[62] Rorty has some refreshing ideas about disciplines, interdisciplinarity, and Comparative Literature. He says that "Derrida and Foucault are brilliantly original thinkers who can easily survive misuse, just as Marx and Freud are."[63] Looking into the future, Rorty says, "Literary theory will be seen to be optional for the practice of literary criticism as legal theory is for the practice of law."[64] Rorty also has some advice for philosophers and comparatists who worry about their fields: "Both comparative literature and philosophy departments should be places in which students receive plenty of suggestions about what sorts of books they might like to read, and are then left free to follow their noses. Members of these departments should not worry about the nature of their discipline, not about what makes it distinctive."[65] What should these professors of Comparative Literature and philosophy concern themselves with? According to Rorty, "They should just worry about finding intellectually curious students to admit to graduate study, and about how to help such students satisfy their curiosity."[66] This is the curiosity-driven research and teaching that I personally favor, and while I emphasize the literary more than Rorty does, perhaps because of the marginalization of literature in the university in state or public universities in English-speaking North America, I can, as someone trained in intellectual and cultural history, also see that literariness can be stressed too much. Rorty doubts "Haun Saussy's suggestion that literariness is central to the discipline of comparative literature."[67] Rorty's skepticism is interesting, provocative, and productive:

> I doubt that anything can ever be identified as central to an academic discipline, any more than anything can ever be identified as the "core" of a human self. A self, Daniel Dennett has said, is best thought of as a center of narrative gravity. Like selves, academic disciplines have histories, but no essences. They constantly up-date their self-image by rewriting their own histories. So-called "crises" move the apparently peripheral to the center, and the apparently central to outer darkness.[68]

For Rorty, then, the center of gravity in Comparative Literature and other disciplines outside of science, in which facts make corrections, shifts according to curiosity, interest, and the need for change. Disciplines should not wear themselves out with a kind of scholastic repetition. Comparative Literature, Rorty implies, is no different from history or philosophy in changing identities and updating their histories to accommodate these alterations and shifts. Rorty actually finds disciplines and interdisciplinarity dubious because there can be as much difference between analytic philosophy and nonanalytic philosophy as there is between philosophy and Comparative Literature. In Rorty's view, a discipline is already interdisciplinary if a person can read in radically different parts of it.[69] Finally, according to Rorty, "No healthy humanistic discipline ever looks the same for more than a generation or two."[70] Change, therefore, is to be expected and embraced. A crisis in Comparative Literature is a sign of one paradigm shift in a series of many shifts. We teach and write ourselves into obsolescence.

A Strand

Although what follows is just one strand that I could present and that does largely grow out of the European tradition, I am aware of and embrace multilateral comparisons between disparate languages, cultures, and disciplines, or a word I prefer for the scope of play, reach, and horizon—fields. So while I do not discuss the need for East-West dialogue as scholars who have published in our journal, *Canadian Review of Comparative Literature/ Revue Canadienne de Littérature Comparée,* like Wang Ning from China, I am doing so for this case as something that the limitations of one occasion impose on the writer.[71] Beyond a few examples from Brazil, France, Francophone Canada, and elsewhere, I have largely used the Anglophone context in North America as an example of the crisis, as it has been expressed in the past couple of years, as a means for us to discuss further. Modernization or change is a matter of constant reinvention.

Modern literary studies grew out of the study of rhetoric, philology, and classics. The literary in English-speaking America, for instance, is under threat. In Canada, the Social Sciences and Humanities Research Council (SSHRC) and many of the research universities that depend on it largely for funding in the humanities and social sciences have come to emphasize computers, databases, and group endeavors so much that individual work based on close reading of literary texts can seem to be less valued. Research in the humanities and in Comparative Literature appears to be headed in the direction of bringing in money, partly as a means of making up budget shortfalls. Collaboration and bringing in funds mime this model in social sciences, which imitates that in science.

As someone who has taken courses in Roman law and political philosophy, and who has studied intellectual and cultural history as much as literature and literary theory, I have great respect for many fields. In school, I enjoyed the study of mathematics and physics. To argue for the value of literature is not to advocate against any other field. The significance of literature has long been evident to me, but I think that, in the universities, literary studies are receiving less support than they once did. Perhaps this has been a slow decline since the Renaissance in conjunction with the rise of science, or at least since the study of classics and literature declined in the last century as the chief training for leaders in government. The Sputnik crisis and the Cold War were even more intensely driven by science and technology than the arms race between Britain and Germany in the years leading up to the First World War. The scientific and Industrial Revolutions are central facts in modernization and, despite their excesses and abuses, it would be a kind of intense pastoralism and nostalgia that would wish away all the changes that the advent of modernity has wrought. To value literature is not to be a Luddite.[72]

We need all the imagination we can get. We require diverse tools to understand language, symbols, and the world. Mathematics and literature are key means in coming to terms with the world. These constructs of language are in and of the world but are not the world: they are possible worlds. Through analogy and contrast, comparisons define the two parts being brought together. The same is true of disciplines. By comparing literature with history—although they share rhetoric, analysis, and narrative— interpreters see that these fields show their differences. As Aristotle knew, history has to follow events as they happened, whereas poetry can invent them and reorder them.[73] Literature, then, can be compared with visual arts and film and other disciplines like history, anthropology, psychology, and philosophy, and profit from that comparison. This comparative method can sharpen definition.

Literature shares much with other discourses, but it is not those discourses. To chase what is strange from literature, to flatten out its own symbolic, to make it something else the world admires or needs most for utility—politics, economics, sociology, or business—is to turn against the literary in hopes that its value as a commodity or utilitarian object might salvage it and the jobs of those of us who write and profess literature. Literature must sell or be sold out. Literary criticism and theory dwindle in the marketplace.

But this need not be the case. If we reduce human life to being bought and sold, then we are nothing but breathing commodities. Yes, we and the literature we write, read, and interpret are products of a society with economic and political tendencies and laws, but that does not mean that literature can be reduced to them, that the text can be identified with the context. Given utilitarian tendencies in a range of governments and businesses, it is tempting for those who make policy in a global marketplace or competitive world (choose the metaphor most used) to flatten out literature and the humanities or to caricature them as a quixotic approach to the world, productivity, and the future. Literature and literary studies may be part of the arts, education, culture, and government, but they are not simply a financial, cultural, or educational instrument made for edification and profit. Neither completely useful nor entirely useless, literature is a possible world, an imaginary place, with intricate relations to the actual world, past, present, and future. Moreover, the study of literature has many dimensions, and comparing the literatures makes the literary all the more complex.

Literary study can include literary history and readings that involve a recognition of social, political, cultural, and economic forces in the production of the text and its meaning, but I think that close reading or interpretation of literary texts should be at the heart of literary and comparative literary studies. When discussing various fields and other arts in relation to literature, careful attention to literature is crucial. Otherwise, literature is subordinated. Literature need not be raised above other disciplines, but as those trained in literature, we should not diminish or marginalize it.

Even as we interpret various signs—in art, film, law, and culture generally—we are literary scholars trained in literary practice and theory, and that can involve writing and reading literature. We need a point of departure. Our training and the way we train our students point to literature. What skills do we have? We are students and professors of literature, so that anything we examine comes from our ability to read texts.

Part of that history of reading and training comes from the tropes and schemes of rhetoric. Although rhetoric in the West began as a means of advocating in the courts in the Greek colonies in Sicily, it soon came to be associated with oratory and drew on literary examples as a means of educating young men in Athens. The work of Quintilian and Cicero helped to spread the study of rhetoric to Rome. With the *translatio studii* or translation of study, the study of rhetoric was disseminated through Europe and—with empire in the fifteenth century—beyond the ancient boundaries of the Greek and Roman empires. Education in the European empires involved rhetoric.

The commentary on Homer, Virgil, and other poets is another stream in the growth of literary studies. The medieval and Renaissance commentaries on classical texts, for instance, can reveal a few lines of text with masses of commentary. Modern variorum editions of Shakespeare continue this tradition. This commentary can include explication and allegory. In this interpretation, the reading can move into the text, looking into the tropes and schemes and their relation to intrinsic signification, and away from the text by extrapolating an allegorical relation to the world or a structure of ideas other than those apparently present in the text or the literal signification. The pull between language and the world has been there in reading and interpretation from the beginning.

Biblical exegesis, translation, and hermeneutics, as well as philology, also underpin literary studies in European vernacular languages. Exegesis, like the commentary on the classics, contained the tension between literal and allegorical readings. It began early and was also displaced into secular texts, such as literary works. Translations, whether Jerome's Latin Bible or Erasmus's Greek New Testament, also involved a translation of culture and readings as well as of language. Hermeneutics and biblical studies continued and became intense in nineteenth-century Germany. The text of the Bible was demystified and in many ways dissolved in terms of authorship and history, so that there was a further displacement of the sacred into the secular. Philological studies also concentrated on language, which provided a historical context for language, so that language and the world also read each other. The tension between internal and external remained then.

The construction and destruction of the text, long before Heidegger's essay in 1927 ("Destruktion"), were in play. Even before we got into the twentieth century, it was no surprise to find pressure in and on literature and its study. Textual integrity and disintegration occur simultaneously. Writing, editing, and reading texts are attempts to find identity and meaning as well as problems with them. The exile from knowledge, the asymptotic realm of making and interpretation, is one of the main concerns of literature and literary studies. Literature is the making and unmaking of ground, a representation of the world that asserts and calls itself into question.

To say that literature needs to be the center of what we do as literary scholars and that we need it in intraliterary comparisons and in comparative methodology involving other arts and disciplines does not mean that Western and European literatures need be the sole or main focus of Comparative Literature.

Close understanding and interpretation of aesthetic texts and images differ from culture to culture, but they are found in the Middle East, South and East Asia, and elsewhere. By comparing literary texts and contexts, as well as literature in relation to other arts and disciplines, a clearer sense of each text, tradition, and innovation emerges. Such a Comparative Literature, which is happening now, should become more intense and exciting in the near future.

The Literary

What I am advocating is perhaps obvious. While some literary disciplines are not as interested in literature, Comparative Literature can concentrate all the more on the literary. As the pressure of expensive commercial scientific periodicals is helping to squeeze the humanities and monograph budget in libraries, the very lifeblood of scholarship in Comparative Literature, we need to inform funding agencies and university administrations about the importance of our fields and the necessity to fund them well and to back journals, university presses, libraries, and young scholars in areas of the humanities like Comparative Literature. In a shrinking globe in which trade, health, and peace depend on international cooperation, a multicultural, international, and open field like Comparative Literature can help to create more cultural understanding. Paying close attention to literary texts, probably the hardest works to translate in any language, scholars in Comparative Literature not only define one text or culture through a comparison with another, but also show an appreciation of the most complex verbal, textual artifacts in that culture. There is no skating over these difficulties, and they can be a point of departure for the study of related cultural materials and the context in which they are produced.

So what I am proposing is not an either/or proposition, but a both/and proposal in which close reading or attentive interpretation is a ground in which to discuss context and other cultural affinities. The dramatic tension between the centripetal and centrifugal forces within a literary text and the enriching theater of comparisons with other literary texts and other arts or fields create so many amazing vistas that there is too much life in Comparative Literature to proclaim or accept the proclamation of its death.

One of the comparisons I would like to explore in the next chapter is the relation between Comparative Literature and comparative narratives of European exploration. Here is an instance of cultural contact, and emphatic difference and otherness. The narratives of travel are best understood in a comparative context, so that claims based on ethnicity or nation are qualified and put into perspective. Rather than being moribund or dead, comparison is an agent of irony, perspectivism, and balance, something very much needed in a global world as we try to move forward. Often it is easy to banish these tools, ideas, and perspectives we need most in times of change and crisis because we can reach for the familiar and the past of our childhoods or the imagined past of our imagined communities, consciously or not, to avoid or take a stand against mutability. Comparison is more necessary now than ever for our cultural well-being and for the survival and vitality of cultures worldwide no matter how tempting it is to recede into the pastoral or the paradisal wholeness of the distant past and the far-off future. The eternal now is as much an option in religion as is paradise lost and regained. In the displaced myth and religion of secular scriptures or literature, the present is something we must face with the knowledge of the past, and tentative attempts to predict or seek an understanding of the future of the conditional might be of futurity. Literature and its texts/works and contexts can and should be compared for a better comprehension in a shifting world. This comparison is vital and not dead or dying—comparing is active and innovative. Narratives of encounter have left traces that enliven our life and times. The rhetoric of expansion is part of our expanding discourse over time and is active even when we do not think we see activity. The next chapter will explore these grounds of comparison.

CHAPTER 2

Comparing Empires

To speak of the death of a discipline or a genre is really to describe what is vital in it and what is not, to imagine a world with it and without it. The novel is supposed to have died, and Nietzsche's "God is dead" is a controversy, a spur to thought about how the role of religion has changed in the world and whether belief is possible. The official institutions of religion and literature do not subsume all that is religious and literary. Literature and the method of comparison used in literary studies and in many other fields from science to the humanities are unlikely to cease to exist. How literature is configured in the schools and universities is another matter, as there are continuities and also discontinuities in the history of rhetoric and translation in the curriculum at all levels and in the role of literary works in the education of the young. In this chapter, as in the last, I hope to show the importance of comparing texts in a literary context. Culture needs comparison, among other things, to thrive.

Without comparison it is difficult to find the contours of a subject. Although studying national traditions, histories, and literatures in and of themselves is necessary and productive, it is also important to consider culture and literature comparatively. This approach leads to new insights and recognitions. Even placing two familiar texts in a different context allows for new understanding. That is what I have tried over the years with literature and narratives of European exploration, which were part of European expansion from about 1415 to 1945. To get to the root of European identity, one should examine the routes of European exploration as well as the contact with other cultures.[1] The openness and diversity of these paths lead to intricate comparisons that take into account displacements and discontinuities.

Recognition, which is so often connected with misrecognition, is a moment that involves a movement from ignorance to knowledge or self-knowledge. It can represent a whole range of experience, from the tragic through the absurd to the comic, bringing relief, clarity, loss, terror, ridicule, suspicion, shock, and many other effects.[2] Whereas Aristotle has anagnorisis refer to a knowledge of a tragic situation, Bertolt Brecht does not foreground the term and wants the audience to gain knowledge of its situation through historical difference. Brecht highlights estrangement, discovery, or revelation in the characters, and the audience plays a central role in the drama and its contiguous genres.[3] Often we do not see things clearly at first and have to work in a process of correction that occurs over time. Sometimes, an insight or intuition means that we see something and then have to go back and check it, and find evidence to come up with an interpretation or explanation.

In English, the words "discovery" and "recognition" as viewing or uncovering and knowledge or acknowledging as true, respectively, seem to have grown in the sixteenth and seventeenth centuries, which are times of expansion and of the growth of natural philosophy.[4] Even before these words took root in English, travel narratives represent the "discovery" or recognition of otherness. Herodotus through Columbus to Acosta and Montaigne show this uncovering of difference.[5] This recognition can include an encounter with so-called barbarians or savages that might be an account of strangeness and wonder that mixes mythology and ethnology, the representational and the romantic or fantastic, and may lead to self-knowledge and a sense of identity. These accounts may well efface and displace a recognition of difference.

Classical examples underwrite the later European investment in coming to terms with travel and otherness. Herodotus is where a good deal of this starts in Western culture. He makes a momentary appearance in José de Acosta's history and Michel de Montaigne's essay on cannibals.[6] Here, natural history is combined with an incipient ethnology. Herodotus distinguishes between hearsay and eyewitness report, and he says he will record what he will, but it is not his business to believe what he sets down.[7] What is important here as a background to later travel texts is that Herodotus made exploration and discovery of the world a central part of his historiography. Herodotus's recognition leads to readers: they will find scenes without vast generalizations, as a reflection of human encounters and different cultures.[8]

Cannibals or man-eaters are one marker of difference and of taboos in European culture. They become a staple from classical times onward. In *Persian Wars* Herodotus mentions cannibals.[9] Here is a pattern that will later recur in Columbus's writings. Herodotus writes about the nation of the flesh-eaters, the inhabitants of which resemble their neighbors but are different as they are a threat: "They are nomads, and their dress is Scythian; but the language which they speak is peculiar to themselves. Unlike any other nation in these parts, they are cannibals."[10] The Scythians become a type for Natives in the Americas, whose barbarity is made a central theme of European representations of the New World. Herodotus records Scythian customs in war in striking ways that become persistent forms of alterity: "The Scythian soldier drinks the blood of the first man he overthrows in battle."[11] After giving a detailed account of the Scythian custom of taking scalps as war trophies, Herodotus notes: "The Scyth is proud of these scalps, and hangs them from his bridle-rein."[12] The persistence of cultural tropes from Herodotus onward, even in new contexts, is remarkable. Cannibals, cruelty, and Amazons are elements in Herodotus that persist. The representation, the re-cognition, of the New World is not as new as might at first seem. A comparative study of different periods and cultures within Europe and between the Europeans and other places suggests both similarity and difference, which sharpens our understanding of texts and contexts, of literature and history, which share the ground of culture.

Anxieties with European culture in classical times and later are about what seems unnatural or taboo or foreign to the writers. Cannibals threaten the social and cultural taboos of not eating one's neighbor or enemy in war, perhaps something from an earlier time in European culture, and, as the Wars of Religion in France came to show, not something completely unheard of when peace and order broke down. Another anxiety is of independent women who do not need men and fight their own battles literally. The manslayers (Amazons) are a persistent cause of anxiety. Using another source, Herodotus reports on the danger of these fierce women. He says that when the Greeks fought the manslayers or Oiorpata, as the Scythians called them, they captured the Amazons and put them on three ships, but these women warriors rose up against the crews and massacred them. If that were not enough, afterward they plundered Scythian territory.[13] A surprising event happens that challenges boundaries of gender, custom, and culture. A moment of recognition occurs when after a battle between Scyths and Amazons, the Scythians find bodies of the slain, "whereby they discovered the truth."[14] The truth they discovered is that their foes were women. Perhaps a little surprising to a modern reader is the reason that the Scythians would not fight women knowingly. The Scyths sent young men to them, "on account of their strong desire to obtain children from so notable a race."[15] Love, not war, is made in order to make more effective warriors to make war. The Amazons scatter in ones and twos, and soon a Scythian attacks a lone Amazon: "She did not resist but let him have his way."[16] Through sign language, these two begin the trend of setting up friends for similar "trysts" until the Scythians "had intercourse with the other Amazons."[17] The Scythians marry those Amazons with whom they first had intercourse and the two nations join. Strangely enough, in a kind of admiration for the Amazons, Herodotus says that the men were unable to understand the Amazons' language but these former manslayers were quite able to comprehend the Scythian language. The Amazons have the upper hand. The marriage and exile occur on the terms that the Amazons dictate. Even if there was original violence in war, and in that first sexual attack, the women prevail. For the reader wishing for easy stereotypes, there are always twists, surprises, and complications. Recognition and misrecognition, discovery and recovery, are always intertwined. In this new "nation," the Amazons continue to hunt, fight, and cross-dress, sometimes alone, and sometimes in the company of their husbands.[18] An uncovering leads to a kind of recognition, which engenders the crossing of boundaries and the exploration of the taboo and difference. The use of signs is something Columbus will also come to emphasize in his initial encounter with Native peoples in the western Atlantic. The friction between speech and signs is part of the story. With signs, they cross the boundary into a shared language, although this is Herodotus's interpretation of an interpretative narrative. Herodotus begins his report of the Scythian account of the Amazons as "a marvel," another rhetorical strategy that Columbus takes up. Although the wonders of the world are to be recognized, they are not readily understood. The surprises and misrecognitions in this and other accounts suggest the care that observation needs and the difficulties of teaching even a provisional interpretation, truth, and recognition.

Recognition and misrecognition are difficult to distinguish. During the fifteenth century, the Portuguese use the legal fiction of *terra nullius* to dispossess Africans. The Portuguese and other Europeans used the same strategy in the New World. They argued that the peoples there are nomadic and do not really occupy a civil society. The logic was that the Europeans could possess their lands because these people do not really occupy them. And so European practices of land use became the measure of ownership and the right for exploitation. The Europeans had trouble recognizing the Natives and even more difficulty recognizing their rights. In Africa as in the Americas, the Natives came to be construed and misconstrued.

Columbus's recognition/misrecognition of the Natives and the New World occurs in this comparative context. Columbus's *Journal* and "Letter" appeared after much textual and cultural mediation.[19] Columbus's "Letter" is preserved in the edited form and the extent of editing cannot be determined.[20] For instance, Las Casas's précis of the *Journal* is not complete and it is difficult to know how vital the omissions are.[21] Text and context are intricate and contradictory, and therefore the reader needs to be aware of first appearances. Columbus brought the myths of Pliny's natural history with him in much the same way as the descriptions of exotic peoples were brought in Herodotus's history. It seems that Columbus would have liked the new lands to be Marco Polo's Cathay, but he also discovered that America was neither Africa nor Asia. The rhetoric of classical travel and historical writing was used as a means of promoting the new-found lands at court back home in Europe. However, it was also a barrier to understanding the Natives and the lands in the western Atlantic.

The famous opening of what is said to be the "Letter of Columbus" proclaims: "And there I found very many islands filled with people innumerable, and of them all I have taken possession of their highnesses, by proclamation made and with the royal standard unfurled, and no opposition was offered to me."[22] There is no original of this letter, which has been reconstructed from four Spanish versions as well as three Italian versions and one Latin version. The report of first contact between Columbus and the Indians is contained in a lost document. This situation is not unusual in the early modern period. The "Letter of Columbus" recorded his great expectations. Columbus, as this text has it, wanted to discover evidence of a great civilization to convince his sovereigns of the importance of his voyage and investment: "I sent two men inland to learn if there were a king or great cities. . . . I understood sufficiently from other Indians, whom I had already taken, that this land was nothing but an island."[23] For Columbus, many Indians were in his possession, but they were not yet marvelous enough for his ambitions. The lands became marvelous ("maravilla"), and he proclaims, "Española is a marvel."[24]

Columbus's motivation is difficult to interpret, but an abundant land filled with timid people suggests ready settlement, conversion, and material exploitation.[25] In the "Letter of Columbus," there are contradictions. After having said how timid the Natives were, Columbus admitted that he had taken some of them by force: "And as soon as I arrived in the Indies, in the first Island which I found, I took by force some of them, in order that they might learn and give me information of that which there is in those parts, and so it was that they soon understood us, and we them, either by speech or signs, and they have been very serviceable."[26] Why did he need force when the Natives were timid and inclined to Christianity? Columbus's anxiety became explicit about leaving a few men behind among the timid Natives.[27] Columbus also admitted that he had not come across any "human monstrosities, as many expected."[28] Nonetheless, Columbus proceeded to report at length about danger in paradise. This was a kind of menace that he had heard about but not witnessed, a human monstrosity. He writes about the coming together of cannibals and Amazons, those that eat men and those who can do without them: "These are those who have intercourse with the women of 'Matinino,'" an island without men, in which these females, engaging "in no feminine occupation," employ bows and arrows made of cane and armor composed of copper plates.[29] So there are monstrous humans that threaten the boundaries of gender roles, men with hair like women, and women who fight like men. In Columbus's annotations to *Imago Mundi*, he shows an awareness of stories of human monstrosities, and his notes to *Historia Rerum Ubique Gesterum* demonstrate his acquaintance with stories of lands wholly inhabited by women.[30] These Native women were fated to be the tribe known as "Amazons" in this narrative.

There could be a violence in this act of apparent recognition and possession or misrecognition and dispossession. Like Bartolomé de Las Casas, I do not think that Columbus's forcible possession of the Natives as interpreters was justifiable. It may well have marked the beginning of the Spanish mistreatment of the Indians. Columbus took several Natives with him on the voyage home, and only seven survived the voyage. One of these survivors acted as an interpreter on the second voyage. As we do not have the Natives' account, we can wonder whether they went on Columbus's ship of their own accord or whether they were forced to. We do not have their recognitions and their interpretations to compare. The image of the Native in Columbus's portrayal is of two kinds, the devout Christian and the idolatrous slave. It may well be, as I have argued elsewhere, that the Natives did not have a choice in the image that the Europeans make for them, and that this image materially came to affect their lives beyond recognition. What is expectation and what is the difference between misrecognition and recognition? Who gets to speak and listen then and now?

So what did Columbus hope to see and what did he see? He had expected to find Asia and great wealth. Instead, his encounter with the Natives without vast and opulent cities came as a surprise to him. He had labored for years to convince a monarch that his way to Asia was the most effective route. His hopes, desires, and fears were refracted in his texts. Like us, Columbus and other Spaniards brought expectations with them in interpreting the world and making discoveries. That helped them to judge the Natives before the actual encounter. Nevertheless, the world before them offered resistance and alternatives to their reading, even if the peoples who were there did not have a chance to leave much behind about their version of events.

In the wake of Columbus, who did and did not recognize the New World, the Spanish, French, and English recognized Natives. Columbus makes the Natives part of the land he would possess and he demonizes those Natives who oppose his claim of the land for Spain.[31] Columbus praises the good Native for being like a pure blank slate ready for conversion.[32] Later, Las Casas would defend the Natives as being full of reason and as those who should be free and not enslaved. Recognizing the Natives involved a contradiction.

In this period of colonization of the New World, the French followed this pattern of ambivalence. Trade and mutual suspicion are ways in which Jacques Cartier in the 1530s and Jean de Léry in the 1550s represented the Natives. Cartier says that the Natives he met in Canada displayed "a marvellously great pleasure" in the iron wares and other products.[33] When Cartier and his men set up a cross to take possession of the land, the chief seems to object.[34] The French refused to recognize the Natives' right to the land. This account implies that the Natives become a barrier to the exploitation of the land. Jean de Léry's first view of Natives in Brazil occurs in the ambience of an already-established mutual suspicion. The Margaia and the French experience enmity but dissimulate. When the Margaia assemble near the French ship, Léry's countrymen are wary and "stayed beyond an arrow's reach from land so as to avoid the danger of being seized and *boucané*—that is roasted."[35] The allusion to cannibalism yields to matters of trade. Léry calls attention to the novelty of his "first" sighting of Natives.[36] He says he will postpone this first moment of close inspection.

Nevertheless, the texts and the men who wrote them are often ambivalent if not sometimes critical toward France and Europe. Recognitions, while sharing certain properties, are different. These travel texts confound easy generalizations about European "discoveries" of themselves and others. Léry later sums up the difficulty of representing Brazil and its inhabitants, as if true recognition were something rare even after a year of close observations: "But their gestures and expressions are so completely different from ours, that it is difficult, I confess, to represent them well by writing or by pictures. To have the pleasure of it, then, you will have to go see and visit them in their own country."[37] He involves the reader in this difficulty. In closing the chapter on the bodily description of the Brazilians, Léry defends the women among them as not arousing wantonness through their nakedness. He says that the trifling clothing of French women causes more ills than the "crude nakedness" of the Brazilians.[38] Comparisons created a typology between the Old World and the New World and sometimes allowed the

European author to criticize his own culture and to praise that of the Native. Michel de Montaigne's "On Cannibals" (1580) suggests that when comparing American Natives and Europeans, the usual stereotype of barbarism is not so easy to sustain. He turns the tables on Europe: "We are justified therefore in calling these people barbarians by reference to the laws of reason, but not in comparison with ourselves, who surpass them in every kind of barbarity."[39] Who is recognizing whom? The Natives become a means to turn a critical gaze back on Europe.

Classical antecedents and intertextual instances in early modern Europe complicate the comparison of texts of exploration. Recognitions are refracted in various directions and ways. Like the French, the English could not escape Spanish textual influence when viewing the New World. Cabot had sailed to Newfoundland in 1497, but no journal or log is extant. Walter Ralegh is especially pertinent in a discussion of comparative texts of European expansion. He desires gold and God as much as Columbus, but he said that England takes a higher road than Spain. Although desiring the land of Guiana, like a woman to be raped, he does so on behalf of Elizabeth I, the virgin queen. Ralegh's *The Discoverie of the Large, Rich, and Bewtiful Empyre of Gviana* (1596) includes in the Epistle Dedicatorie a goal, "*that mighty, rich, and beawtifull Empire of* Guiana, and . . . *that great and Golden City, which the Spanyards call* El Dorado, *and the naturalls* Manoa."[40] Ralegh takes his cue from Spanish legends as Columbus had from Marco Polo. In Ralegh's view, the Natives await their true Lord while others may throw off Spanish domination: Spain is so rich and has so many cities, it will not miss this small area of America.[41] Ralegh's *The Discoverie of Gviana* develops the need to observe the Spanish model of colonization while using its own methods to subvert it. This rivalry continues throughout Ralegh's book. The myth that Ralegh is trying to propagate, especially by way of flattering Elizabeth, is that he put her reputation before the sacking of towns and the hoarding of gold because this strategy will support the desire of the Natives of Guiana for England to liberate them from Spanish cruelty. If Elizabeth acts and takes Guiana and beyond, she will gain reputation and, as part of her secular cult of the Virgin Queen, she will be the virginal queen over the Amazons, who will help her invade other empires.[42] A key moment of recognition is that the Natives will yield gold in the glory of God and Christ through Elizabeth. The ghosts of Herodotus, Columbus, and Léry call forth cannibals and Amazons, so that old tropes die hard. Despite their differences, in this period, French and English Protestants use similar representations of new lands and peoples to those employed by Spanish Catholics.

José de Acosta, a Spanish Jesuit, is a case in point. In 1596, the same year Ralegh's work on Guiana appeared, Acosta's *De procuranda* was published in Cologne. Acosta understood the distinctions and the pitfalls of recognitions blind to cultural difference. In the preface to this work, Acosta notes that the nations of America "are very varied and diverse and very different from one another as much in climate, environment and dress as in intelligence and customs . . . It is a vulgar error to assume that the Indians are a single field or city, and because they are all called by the same name to ascribe to them a single nature and mind."[43] Acosta's recognition of cultural differences serves as a warning to latter-day readers who wish to find simplifications in texts of European expansion and so-called discovery.[44] The "shock of discovery" that the Europeans experienced in sighting the New World and its inhabitants helped to contribute to a movement from tradition and ancient texts as intellectual authorities to experience and observation by themselves. That being said, it is a mistake to underestimate the power of classical and biblical traditions that persist in European thought. At one point, Acosta describes how on the way to the New World he reached the equator and did not burn up in the Torrid Zone. This experience made him laugh at Aristotle's *Meterology* and philosophy.[45] This is almost like a recognition scene. The comparison of ancients and moderns, Old World and New World, European and Native, and the differences within these complicates our understanding of one culture or literature.

In my various books on comparing and contrasting empires from *Representing the New World: The English and French Uses of the Example of Spain* (2001) to *Empires and Colonies* (2008), as well as in my earlier work in the area, I have used a comparative method in relation to context and text, history and literature.[46] In *Empires and Colonies* I begin by exploring possible ways to look at the expansion of Europe, which is the context for the texts I have been discussing. I argue that most administrators of empire and their peoples know that empires do not last. Comparisons help to show this pattern. Recognition is difficult. A typology or a double image of past and present haunts great powers in trying to guess their fate. The translation of empire is a myth of continuity between empires as a means of making an empire without end, but there is also a fear of chaos resulting from the fall of an empire. The end of Rome provides such an image.

Empires can make people, even those at their center, uncomfortable and ambivalent about them. Empires are limited ironically in time because they rise and fall or have a beginning, middle, and end, even if they project power and endurance. In the typology of time among past, present, and future, in the theme of history concerning empires and colonies, historian and reader are also aware that change will make Rome, or any empire claiming that the sun will never set on it, less than eternal.

Empires and Colonies provides an exploration of the expansion of the seaborne empires of western Europe from the fifteenth century, and how that process of expansion affected the world, including its successor, the United States. While providing particular attention to Europe, the book is careful to highlight the ambivalence and contradiction of that expansion. This work recognizes that while a study of the expansion of Europe is an important part of world history, it is not a history of the world per se. Its focus on culture is a means of asserting that areas and peoples that lack great economic power at any given time also deserve attention. The alternative voices of slaves, indigenous peoples, and critics of empire and colonization are a vital aspect of the book, which is meant to appeal not only to students of imperial history, but also to anyone interested in the makings of the modern world.

By necessity, this book has Europe as its primary focus, because it explores the expansion of western Europe, its influence, and its overseas colonies from the late fifteenth century to the end of the twentieth century, but that does not mean that my argument need be celebratory, teleological, or triumphant. In other words, a volume about the development of Europe in the modern world need not be "Eurocentric" in what has come to be a derogatory sense.

The expansion of Europe could also begin much earlier, for instance, with the Norse settling of Iceland and Greenland, which ended in the fifteenth century. That way there would be a continuity between the Vikings and the Portuguese and Spanish voyages to Africa, India, and the New World.[47] It is also possible to view the expansion of Europe in terms of ecological and epidemiological damage or imperialism, beginning with the plagues. Some of them, like the Black Death, originated from China when Mongols, who controlled a vast empire in Eurasia (which fell in about 1350), spread the bubonic plague (spread by the fleas on rats) from China into Europe, devastating populations from the East to the West, from 1331 to 1350 and beyond. By the end of the fourteenth century, the population of China and Europe, both connected through the Mongol empire, fell by about a third. The effects of weather and disease on food production, labor, and the economy impacted political, social, and cultural practices and situations in Eurasia and elsewhere. It is possible to see that this death count created a labor shortage in places like Europe that drove up wages and made these states look for gold and silver and for slaves to replace the dead. That seems to have caused an exploration of the New World, where Native populations died in vast numbers from diseases that Asians and Europeans had been exposed to over a long time, and this shortage of labor for exploitation led to the seeking of African slaves.[48] Such a narrative would see that a division between Asia and Europe is really artificial, and would suggest that a global society and economy included Africa, America, and elsewhere in a biological and cultural regime.

Another possible narrative would be based on ideologies, such as religion, class (caste), gender, or race. Ethnographical or racial theories go back in the West at least to Herodotus, but there were plenty of theories or observations on climate, color, barbarity, and race in the Middle Ages. Aristotle had commented on race and climate and had created a theory of natural slavery.[49] Isodore of Seville in the seventh century and Roger Bacon in the thirteenth century connected climate with race and color, and speculation and myth about these matters persisted thereafter.[50] To qualify or have a context for matters of representation and race, it would be important to see other views from different regions of the world, such as those from China and Japan. *The Illustrated Scroll of Tributary Peoples* in the sixth century (CE) shows figures from East Asia through Central Asia to Persia (Iran).[51] In 1825, the first of the *New Theses* in Japan provided another ethnographical angle, categorizing Western barbarians as the thighs, legs, and feet of the universe while saying that the inhabitants of America are stupid and occupy the rear of the world, and, in the sixth new thesis, calling Christianity a base religion used to deceive stupid commoners.[52] In a comparative study of cultures and empires and colonies, it is vital to provide other contexts that serve as a reminder of the obvious, that other peoples besides Europeans had strong texts, images, and actions that related to expansion, empire, and relations with other cultures, some colonized or tributary. The tensions among the Europeans and those they encountered during their expansion were multifold and had a context, that is, past as precedent to a future that soon becomes the past. The narrative or thesis this book sets out is one among many possible worlds, as Leibniz might have framed it.[53]

Even if from one point of view, nothing was or is inevitable, what has happened has happened. Thus, if the inexorability of the expansion of the western European empires is possibly a tool of triumphalism or mythology as much as something related to historiography, to get too deeply into the what-ifs of history might well, if taken too far, serve to deflect attention from what happened and what occurred during the expansion of these empires into the world beyond Europe. Alternative histories are a form of speculation, a philosophical view of human time not too different from fiction, more particularly historical fictions in the novel, drama, and poetry. In *Poetics*, Aristotle had considered history to be that which represents what happened and poetry what might have happened, so that while the historian could not rearrange events for effect, the poet could.[54] So comparative history and literature inform my work on empire and colonies. Text and context are inextricable, while comparison helps to keep observations about single nations and periods more balanced. In attempting to find recognition, the comparative method needs recognition.

Travel narratives and accounts of empire occupy a ground between literature and culture. These texts have fictional and nonfictional, theoretical and historical aspects that are not always easy to separate. Although this relation among literature, theory, and history has many dimensions, in the following chapter I would like to concentrate on paradigms, system, antisystem, law, contracts, theater, and tradition before returning, at its end, to the question of comparison. As literature and culture are vast fields, what follows is a brief analysis of specific theorists, critics, and historians who consider these questions and represents something meant to be suggestive and not exhaustive.

CHAPTER 3

Literature and Culture

If the last two chapters discussed comparisons of literature and empire respectively, there are other ways of comparing fiction and actuality. Between literature and the world lies mythology. Myth veers toward story and literature on the one hand and ideology or argument on the other. The poet and critic (theorist) are both writers and may be the same person. Fictions have their structures or arguments, and nonfiction tells stories. There is some overlap between them. To think about something involves subject and object in a dance, and the writing of literature, theory, and practical criticism involves the creation of possible worlds, the meeting of reason and imagination. There is biography in autobiography and vice versa.

Without some communication across time, there would be little point in writing and reading. That being said, to ignore historical change would be to miss an important aspect of reading and writing. The rhetorical relation between speaker and audience, writer and reader, plays a central role in the world of culture that connects images and words with the human place in nature. This exchange involves communication and miscommunication, recognition and misrecognition, and, except perhaps in hindsight, it is unclear which is which. Signs and signification are many-sided and prone to error and approximation. Mutability and possibility contend with the desire for stability and actuality. Potential is powerful but can be unfulfilled.

Here, I shall include a brief discussion of literature, systems, law and theater, nature and law, as well as the idea of masters. In doing so, I shall concentrate on a few texts and place them into context, and will keep with my assumption that theoretical texts can be discussed in criticism and theory in a similar fashion to how we discuss the "fictional" texts of literature. Prose of thought has long been a part of literary studies, and here I mix an interest in intellectual and cultural history with literary and cultural studies. In doing so, I range over texts that concern themselves with the Renaissance or early modern period and with other times, including our contemporary world.

A Very Brief Meditation on a Life in Literature: Error, Multitude, and Possibility

Meditation and autobiography involve a reading back to origins, as someone in the middle or end of their career reconceives his or her childhood or apprenticeship in terms of a later mastery or accomplishment.[1] Three-year-olds formulate arguments for the existence of God or ask why death exists in the world, and this kind of life-changing experience later leads to a study of Aquinas or Milton, or, if the writer has studied such authors, a recasting of lines written in early childhood or youth in terms of later literary, scientific, political, or whatever terms. Memory becomes a blend of anticipation and reconciliation: sometimes self-aggrandizement or justification nudge aside the uncomprehending mind of the most precocious child. The child becomes the father to the man or the mother to the woman.

Critical readers, who might be much more critical of others than themselves, put up their guard. The official life, however apparently casual, crowds out the more chaotic life lived. The rage for shape, order, and narrative leaves the parings of experience aside. No self-portrait avoids, consciously or not, this dilemma. Critical distance disappears as we represent ourselves, whether through a veil of litotes or through a shower of hyperbole. Aristotle's middle way gets lost in the garden of the forked tongues. In literature especially, most of us are too mortal to avoid the pose of the ironic soul, wandering the earth in exile, displacement, or bafflement, or the hero of epic or tragedy, where the landscape is outsized and the quest deep, tangled, and long.

Possibly, the writer's life, whether he or she writes fiction or nonfiction, is already another part of criticism or literature, and it should not be taken for a representation of events as others might remember or construe them. Perhaps each life is an inner life, interesting for the mythical and psychological truths it can tell in the decay of time and lying. Beautiful fictions have their place even if not in Plato's republic. The seduction of a good phrase or story is strong if not sturdy. Kick a stone and read a poem.

Except for students facing examinations, it is a puzzle as to why anyone reads literary criticism or commentary. The literary priest or critic—priests do not fare well in Homer—tells his flock what this work might mean for his generation or what that line might signify for his or her reading group.

The critic is a cultural mediator or go-between, translating work into the classroom, living room, or street. Go-betweens are interpreters who suffer from both sides: writers might think of them as dry would-be authors while readers may wonder why they have to be subject to the mechanism of a new secular semantic theology.

Critics can be dogmatic officers of the court. This stereotype of the critic is in so many ways unfair even if it has persisted for some time, but there is some truth in it. Are critics administrators or guides to taste or bean counters masquerading as anarchists and revolutionaries? There are many kinds of critics or theorists, but for some writers, like Shakespeare and Joyce, criticism is not an activity they want to pursue. Some readers, sensible ones or not, for instance, readers of Blake, are not interested in the official systematic reading of this eccentric, nonconformist, but often-beautiful poet. Blake famously created a system not to be imprisoned in someone else's. So there seems to be an uneasy relation between system and antisystem, creativity and critique.

Systems and Antisystems

In literature and culture, paradigms are crucial, and an interplay occurs in system and antisystem. The systemic and field approaches to literature reflect the shift over the past generation to literary theories that take into account the history, context, and function of literature. Literature as an institution, as Harry Levin once observed, was a method that literary studies needed to investigate.[2] Some of the key systematic views of literature are the polysystems theory of Itamar Even-Zohar, the field theory of Pierre Bourdieu, and the systems theories of Niklas Luhmann and Siegfried J. Schmidt.[3] A central question that Henrik Van Gorp enunciates is the relation between system and environment: he also expresses a significant hope for an underlying common ground between the different theories of literature as a system or field.

Rather than duplicate the observations of Hendrik Van Gorp, I would like to present a few thoughts about the significance of systemic approaches to literature in English-speaking countries where this kind of methodology, while having important adherents, has not exerted the same influence as in Israel, Belgium, France, the Netherlands, French-speaking Canada, and Germany. In the English-speaking countries, beginning in the 1930s, a shift occurred in literary studies from intellectual history to New Criticism and the great tradition of F. R. Leavis, from a contextual approach to a textual method. The dominance of hermeneutics, although it was still one methodology among many in literary studies, continued even after

Jacques Derrida's visit to the United States during the mid-1960s. Instead of teasing out the organic unity of the work, as New Criticism did—among other things (hermeneutics or close reading is also a historical act)—the deconstruction of Paul de Man and Derrida uncovered the disunity of the text. Meaning was contingent but textual. In English-speaking countries feminism, cultural studies, New Historicism, and cultural materialism in theorists like Elaine Showalter, Stuart Hall, Raymond Williams, Stephen Greenblatt, Jonathan Dollimore, and others put pressure on the text and reminded hermeneutic acolytes of contextual power. Intellectual historians and "old historians" in the English-speaking world may have been a little outraged by these new theories, but some of them were secretly pleased at the return to history. During the 1970s, Marx, Louis Althusser, Antonio Gramsci, and Pierre Macherey were especially influential in Britain: Terry Eagleton, Catherine Belsey, and others "translated" these continental influences anew in a British context. Systematic approaches to genre, like Northrop Frye's *Anatomy of Criticism* (1957), were superseded by the deconstructive untying of genre theory in the 1970s by Derrida, de Man, and a younger generation of deconstructionists, like Barbara Johnson. Jonathan Culler and Christopher Norris chronicled this shift from structuralism to poststructuralism, although Frye was neither but had affinities with the structuralists, New Critics, biblical hermeneuts, and so on.

The move to deconstruction and postmodernism, as well as the deterministic, fragmentary, aphoristic, almost pre-Socratic probes into the media by Marshall McLuhan, created an environment in Britain, the United States, and English-speaking Canada that was hostile to systems as analogues of the political, economic, and military machines that made for Vietnam and for the repression of civil rights and student demonstrations. A kind of romantic people's history, or the study of the everyday life of the common people or skepticism about power underlay the new modes of the academic study of literature. Any move to history, like New Historicism or cultural materialism, reflected an unmasking of an establishment machinery, a dogmatic network of enforced meaning. Systems were perceived as power grids of the dominant group. Any effective study of systems should skeptically seek to know how they operate but not, as Jean-François Lyotard might suggest, set up new systems in their place. Instead of seeing this skepticism about systems as a problem, I think of it as an opportunity. In explaining their systems to the English-speaking world in particular, theorists of systemic and field approaches to literature need to address this skepticism while recognizing a residue of textual fetishism or hermeneutic remembrance in literary criticism and theory in English. In fact, deconstruction, postmodernism, and many of the theories I have mentioned share with the systemic and field approaches to literature in this issue, although from different points of view, an unmasking or critique of the ideology of the machinery of producing and receiving literature. Symbolic capital, cultural recognition, or reputation is made in society and is not simply something based on genius. A systemic/ field view of literature is not necessarily a totalizing system or an acceptance of the social, economic, and ideological powers behind literature.

The neglect of the sociology of literature has not been complete in English. Although few, literary theorists writing in English on the history or ideology of the aesthetic have discussed Pierre Bourdieu; for instance, Polity Press in Cambridge produced translations of his work in 1988 and 1996. Some work—for example, by Polity Press and a special issue edited by Van Gorp and his colleagues—helps to meet the challenge of making theories of literature as a system or field better understood in English.[4] The work that Van Gorp and his collaborators have produced should find readers who not only consider hermeneutics to be important but also recognize that texts without contexts are as incomplete as contexts without texts. Systemic and field approaches are not univocal and monolithic and often question a romantic essence to literature. In short, from various points of view, it is possible that skeptics of system and field and these theorists of systems are at least talking about many of the same things. As someone who has crossed boundaries, most often between literature and history, for many years and has written on difference in culture, pluralism, possible worlds, and colonialism and postcolonialism, I welcome the work of Hendrik Van Gorp and others who take us beyond the focus in English and can help to shake up our paradigms. In recent years, Hans Bertens has seen over the past three decades an increasing rapprochement of theory and interpretation, seeing the continued importance of New Criticism, as reading for meaning, and of structuralism, as reading for form, in understanding subsequent literary theories that vary from the systematic to those that question systems.[5]

What is important is to remember William Blake's dilemma. If we are ruled by another's system, we have no intellectual or spiritual freedom; but if we all create disparate systems, how do these private mythologies speak one to the other? The texture of each poem is different, but poems are part of poetry. Each poem we read is an element of our repertoire as readers. The codes of expectations or genres affect how we write and read. There is a tradition even as we might attempt to break with it. The classical and the Romantic vie in the recovery and the rediscovery of the past in a framework of rules and in proportion, and the rebellious individual spirit that recognizes our individuality balks against this very apparatus. The scientific method and the artist as Romantic outcast or rebel come into collision. Literature is a science and an art, an experience and an institution.

One thing sure is that translation and the translation of study has always enriched languages, literatures, and cultures, so that in English we need to learn about systematic views of literature from outside the English-speaking world written in English and in other languages. English itself was a mixture of languages just as England was a confluence of peoples. In the late sixteenth century and early seventeenth century, Richard Hakluyt the Younger showed, as did his successor Samuel Purchas, that translation and borrowing from other cultures was the only way to gather collections of travel, encounter and geographical narratives as the only means to launch what was to become first the English Empire and then the British Empire. With globalization and decolonization, and the rather surprising rise of English from a small island off the coast of Eurasia, it is even more important that the myriad of peoples who speak English as a mother tongue learn to speak other languages and embrace those who speak English as a second or even as a fifth language. The elite in England have in some ways only begun to use English as the primary language to study in the schools from the 1960s (Norman French, and Latin and Greek were the languages before then) or perhaps in the wake of the Second World War.

Moreover, it is only with the rise of literary studies in English and other vernaculars in Europe that the more general category of writing (for instance, philosophy, law, poetry, and history) became more specialized in the universities. For example, poetry shares language with theater and law. Past and present also have a dialogue, or at least the present feels compelled to interpret the past, which interpreted its past, and to project into the future. The performativity of language occurs in law and theater, which tell us something about culture and literature. One of the crucial moments for theater in England and Europe occurred during the Renaissance, and an examination of the relation between law and theater in a key collection should tell us something about literature and culture more generally and in ways that touch on our present concerns. Language and literature, and theater, all involve performance in theory and practice, how we think we see or frame something and how it is in the moment on the ground. Rhetoric, which is the relation between speaker and audience, writer and reader, as a way of moving, swaying, and persuading, connects story and argument, poetry and rhetoric, sometimes to the point where they are so intertwined, it is difficult to separate them.

Law and Theater

An ambivalent attitude to the law and to theater has prevailed since antiquity. The Platonic Socrates explored the fraught relation between law and justice and between the poet and the republic. How could human laws be a just representation and embody wisdom and knowledge? Theatrical and legal representation posed problems for the philosopher, who loved truth, and not the seductive ways of forensic argument or illusory role-playing.

Like Plato, Isocrates and Aristophanes commented on theater. Aristophanes attacked theater and philosophy in his Old Comedy satire, taking Socrates to task in *The Clouds* and taking a run at Euripides in *The Archanians* and *Peace*. In *The Frogs*, Aristophanes set up a debate between Aeschylus and Euripides, the one defending the poet as a teacher of morals and the other saying that the poet represents reality. Plato takes up this question in Book 10 of the *Republic* in the quarrel between philosophy and poetry. Plays have a specific power: "Dramatic poetry has a most formidable power of corrupting even men of high character, with a few exception[s]."[6] Such performance moves people in the audience to give themselves up to sympathy for actions that in life would be scorned, so that feeling overwhelms reason. Passion, language, and role-playing can, in drama or in law, obscure reality and the path to truth, knowledge, and wisdom. Although being more favorable to poetry and drama than Plato is, Aristotle still places philosophy above poetry, which is above history, because of its universal nature. In the Renaissance, however, Philip Sidney placed poetry over philosophy. And so the ancient world and its revision framed the debate of law and theater in the Renaissance.

This is one of the contexts for my discussion here, which will focus on *Solon and Thespis* (2007), a volume that Dennis Kezar has edited, because it involves implicit and explicit comparisons and raises issues about law and literature.[7] The Renaissance or early modern period has implications beyond itself and can speak to issues about past and present, theater and world that occupy us even in the present. The collection explores the relation between law and drama in the plays of Shakespeare, Jonson, Marston, and others. The title of the book comes from a meeting between Solon, an Athenian lawmaker, and Thespis, a Greek poet and actor, over the issue of whether lies in a play lead to falsehood in society. Role-playing and the relation between art and life are central in this debate. Why is the law real and drama a fiction? Why the friction between law and drama in early modern England when they shared spaces and rhetoric and both interpreted the social and the imaginary? Both involve fictions, so why are legal fictions of any more worth than dramatic ones?

The three parts of Kezar's collection help approach some of these problems. In the first part, "Jonson and the Tribe of Law," Matthew Greenfield notes that the War of the Poets shows the tension between Roman law (Jonson) and common law (Dekker's use of a jury). Dekker trusted juries and the audience while Jonson did not. Paul Cantor argues that the seeming artlessness in the form of *Bartholomew Fair* actually allows it to develop characters and content. The tension between law and spontaneity in this representation of the marketplace is one important manifestation of the relation between law and theater. According to Frances Teague, setting *Volpone* in Venice rather than in London freed it from topicality, especially of the recent investigation and prosecution of those involved in the Gunpowder Plot. The law could be errant and asinine, badly conceived and full of perjury, and the consideration of the relations among law and lawlessness, nation and providence, is something that Teague draws out in comparisons between the Gunpowder Plot and the plot of *Volpone*.

The second part, "Legal Rhetoric and Theatrical Pressure," begins with Heather Dubrow's discussion of land law in Shakespeare's *King Lear* and in his culture. Arguing for more notice of workaday law, such as land law, and in particular rules surrounding property disputes, Dubrow seeks to interpret the lawless world of this great play, invoking tensions over property as illuminations of anxieties over housing and being dislodged, as well as fears of trespass, which occur when Gloucester is driven from his house. Ernest B. Gilman discusses the law in *The Tempest*, especially in the buried story, or excluded trial, of Sycorax. This submerged world of Sycorax is something that Prospero and the audience need to consider in the birth of colonialism. Dennis Kezar, who also contributes a useful introduction to this collection, avers that in *The Witch of Edmonton*, Thomas Dekker, John Ford, and William Rowley produced challenges to representing witches in the Renaissance. This work plays on its own text, a drama that possesses its audience's desire as if it were a material possession.

In "Law Staged and Theory Troubled," the third part, Debora Shuger examines texts, lies, and censorship. She sees censorship as seeking to check falsehood rather than uncomfortable truths for those in power. While not defending censorship, Shuger raises questions about the purveyance of falsehood and fear in oppositional writing in Tudor and Stuart England. Karen J. Cunningham brings together the Inns of Court and *Gorbuduc* and tries to draw attention away from court to mooting and to the Inns. Sackville, Norton, and the Inns of Court represent struggle in fictions in order to anticipate and prevent foreign reign. The law and the theater secure the nation in the imagination. Luke Wilson analyzes corruption in seventeenth-century England and focuses on Chapman's *Tragedy of Chabot* and the case against Bacon for bribery. This play explores the connection between corruption in public office and the bond between king and subject founded in generosity and dependence.

Literature and Culture • 53

In the epilogue, Deak Nabers offers ideas about legal theory, for instance, how Lear and Gloucester raise the issue of natural law at 4.6.148–56. In summing up, Nabers points out, as the collection does, that the law is the center of the world and central to its disappearance, which is a little like theater. Law and drama represent the world in a fiction of the world that claims truth. They have integrity and question it. This tension is one of the reasons that the work of Kezar and his colleagues is suggestive. But law connects with comedy as much as it does with the theater, and this is something Renaissance scholars have observed and something that serves out exploration of the relation between literature and culture. Shakespeare is a central cultural figure in English and now in the globalized world of English and beyond. Shakespeare is global and local, English and not. He works with comedy but he is also an innovator of genre and combining genres worthy of Polonius, the counselor and one-time actor in *Hamlet*.

The relation between law and comedy is an old one. The law can be comic because it is an ass, but it is also a part of the structure of New Comedy, whose legacy has been so enduring since Plautus, Terence, and others first made plots in which the younger generation expressed a spirit of love that had to circumvent the law of the older generation often embodied in the *senex*, or old man. Law in a general sense was a means of social control for one generation over the next as well as the way by which the ruling class exercised power over their subordinates. The parental block is often a trial for the lovers. The challenge to the old order leads to chaos and the establishment of a new order. And the older generation, especially in Shakespeare's romantic comedy, becomes educated into this new order by the very children they sought to teach and control. The spirit of youth schools the law of the elders. Comedy becomes, then, a means to teach the limits of that law.

If law relates to theater, it is also connected with nature. Shakespeare is crucial in this shift in legal comparisons. In pursuing the connection between the legal and the natural, I wish to focus briefly on A. G. Harmon's *Eternal Bonds, True Contract: Law and Nature in Shakespeare's Problem Plays* (2004). What makes Harmon's study particularly interesting is that it combines an examination of law and nature with that of the problem play, that is, one involving a social study and the other a formal problematic.[8] Harmon's argument, or at the very least his title, depends on what plays are considered under this category. The usual triad is *Troilus and Cressida*, *All's Well That Ends Well*, and *Measure for Measure*, although some critics consider *Hamlet*, *Anthony and Cleopatra*, and *Timon of Athens* to be problem plays. There are other plays that critics have thus classified. (I once argued for *Henry V*.)[9] Harmon includes *The Merchant of Venice*, which stretches the genre and the time period to about five years earlier than the usual first play of this "genre," so that he should probably elaborate a justification for this inclusion. Whatever one thinks about this addition, it allows for a discussion of trials and justice that it would not otherwise permit. As in any scholarship in Shakespeare, the ground is well-tilled, and this creates quite a challenge for any scholar. In addition, whether one considers *Merchant* a problem play or not, discussions of law in it are important.[10]

Harmon works in the area of law and literature. He admirably brings to bear his legal training and legal history—as well as the philosophical underpinnings in Aquinas—amid the dangers of change in both the ecclesiastical and secular laws. Moreover, Harmon discusses contracts in *Measure*, and sees in it evidence of what is a proper marriage contract in Shakespeare. Harmon points to Isabella's distinction between crimes attempted and those fulfilled. What probably confuses this issue is the nature of theology (Christ's words about lust and intentions), politics (who has the power and authority?), and drama (what involves the redemption of this "comedy"?). The notion of the mock contract in *Troilus* that Harmon offers is suggestive. He argues that in this play, which he views as parodic, there is a perversion of nature through the connection between sex and war. The disruption of order is something the satire in the play represents. Different orientations to nature, according to Harmon, connect the plays under study. For instance, in *Measure*, the agents of nature restore order by correcting those who cheat nature, whereas in *Troilus* this does not occur. In *Merchant* friendship and commercial bonds are part of these doubling orientations to nature. In this connection Harmon reminds us of the importance of Aristotle, as elaborated by Aquinas then Richard Hooker, and brings in material, efficient, formal, and final causes as a gloss on the commercial enterprise and contract. How effective the law is in this play depends on the quality of mercy, that is, the nature of charity and faith, and therefore, I would add, religion and love affect the legal and dramatic representations of the bond.

The self-conscious nature of debate is a key element in the problem plays. *All's Well* is no exception. Harmon calls attention to the metaphysics in this play and how it is a summing up of the three plays he has discussed because it shares qualities with each. It is designed as a play to fulfill its contract. *Merchant* and *All's Well* share similar imagery between the bond and the marriage contract. Harmon sees in the bed-trick a fusion of the ends of a contract and of marriage: Helena gets the ring to beget a child. Deficiencies in contracts in these four plays need to be rectified to restore social integrity. This has a comic aspect to it: the structural imperatives of comedy demand this kind of new order. In aiming the discussion beyond these plays, Harmon draws his argument together clearly, discussing *Cymbeline*, *The*

Winter's Tale, Twelfth Night, King Lear, and *The Tempest,* which he refers to as "his most metaphysical poem."[11] Harmon also concentrates on the marriage contract as an ordering principle, which was as true for Elizabethan and Jacobean law and religion as it was for Renaissance comedy. The marriage at the end of comedy is generative socially and dramatically. Harmon's book leads up to the epiphany that Shakespearean characters have at their wisest and most patient moments: a fulfillment in "contentment in a genuine existence."[12] The law in these plays helps to find quotidian resolutions to the imperfect and problematic worlds of these dramas—except for *Troilus and Cressida*—that allow for generative paths to better times. The exception of *Troilus* creates its own implications for a double bind to the double name of nature that Harmon discusses in his exploration of eternal bonds and true contracts. This book, a useful contribution to Shakespearean studies and to law and literature, is clear, able, and generative despite the problems it faces and embodies. Comedy also helps to bring together this discussion of Kezar and Harmon, who both use the law to anchor their comparisons, the one to theater and the other to nature. Shakespeare is central to these comparative pursuits. The writer can be the teacher and teach lessons to who come after. This is how the double focus of past and present becomes a matter of perspective in teaching and research.

Teaching, Learning, Scholarship

Here, and in the chapter on Las Casas, I want to emphasize what is sometimes written out of humanities, though not education, that is, discussions of teaching in literary studies, theory, and history. It is as if to prove the scientific model of research in the humanities, scholars have to focus on their laboratory, the archive, and the library, and leave the classroom. There are, of course, exceptions, as in Northrop Frye's *The Educated Imagination* (1963). More recently, George Steiner has contributed to the debate on education in the humanities. Steiner begins the book that grew out of his Charles Eliot Norton Lectures in 2001–02, *Lessons of the Masters,* by exploring unexamined assumptions about the nature of professing or teaching.[13]

The drama between master and disciple can be one of mutual destruction or one of reciprocal trust and love in which an intense dialogue creates friendship while both parties learn. The origins of teaching yield some evocative instances. The example of the Sophists and of Socrates embodies some of the tensions in teaching and learning and also the uneasy connection among the ancient Greeks between the oral and the written. It was at this time that systematic teaching, grammatical and hermeneutical analysis, and textual citation arose as the foundations of future education. Socrates's connection to those he inspired is something Steiner thinks is lacking in scholarship on Plato, and the reactions to Socrates that Plato dramatizes range from hatred to admiration. A gap occurs between Plato and the Socrates he represents: "For Socrates, true teaching is by example."[14]

Through writing, Plato and Paul of Tarsus, the two paradigmatic teachers in Western culture, assured their masters' reputations. Plato knew Socrates but seems to have been absent at the death of Socrates, whereas Paul never saw Jesus. In this transformation of the oral into the written, these two great disciples are faithful to and yet betray their masters; Neoplatonism and Christianity would become great influences in Europe. In his own considerations of the relation between master and disciple, Saint Augustine understood the tensions between the enticements of rhetoric and the intentions of teaching. Are Shakespeare and Montaigne dramatizing their own authority (perhaps embodying or evading avant la lettre Walter Jackson Bate's burden of the past or Harold Bloom's anxiety of influence) by not dwelling so much on the agony and friendship between master and disciple?

Steiner discusses Dante's taking leave or relegation of Virgil by way of elaborating on the ambivalence of masters and disciples. This is a rich explication that draws out the many sides to Dante's language and motivation. The motives of eloquence, as of teaching and learning, are multiplicitous and intricate. No wonder Saint Augustine considered the seduction of rhetoric in the intentions of teaching and learning; an eroticism informs teaching, particularly in teaching music, writing, and the arts. From the infinite specificity of Flaubert's tutorship of Maupassant to creative writing courses on Anglo-American campuses, there is in the relation of master and apprentice both potency and potential scrutiny, epiphany and eroticism, a mysterious mixture, a little like Dante and Brunetto.

The *magnificus* is another dimension of Steiner's exploration of teaching and learning, master and disciple. The exploration of knowledge is something that Christopher Marlowe achieved through a fine education in Latin and Greek and theological controversy. His representation of Doctor Faustus is a key to the pursuit of mysteries and natural phenomena. The Faust legend and tradition in literature is an example of this European quest from Marlowe's German source through Goethe's version to Valéry's and beyond. Other masters and disciples—Tycho Brahe and Johannes Kepler, Edmund Husserl and Martin Heidegger, Heiddegger and Hannah Arendt—amplify and complicate the master-disciple relation. Heiddegger, who supported the Nazis, was the assistant and the teacher of two prominent Jewish thinkers, and he seems to have fallen in love with his student and to have shared with her an interest in Saint Augustine and his concept of love. Considering the events after 1925–26, this relation between Heiddeger and Arendt was a very different version, as Steiner suggests, love between Abelard and Héloïse.

Steiner also explores the notion of the mastery of thought, discussing Nietzsche, Stefan George, and others in that context. Henry James and Henry Adams complicate the irreverence Americans have for this European notion of clerisy, intellectuals, and masters. For Steiner, "A Master is the jealous lover of what might be."[15] The American and Canadian mind, whether Allan Bloom's or Anne Carson's, has not closed to the Greek exemplars. Memory and identity are markers of masters and disciples in their quest for knowledge. In the ruins of Europe in 1919, Max Weber had seen the powerlessness of the scholar and the university before the disaster of war and how the old professor might become an academic bureaucrat in the rubble. Steiner is, however, hopeful that in this age of technology and science, of democracy and media, teachers will still awaken "an ache for understanding" and a love that dreams beyond itself.[16]

Steiner shows that the pursuit of knowledge and understanding through teaching has a strong comparative element. He ranges from classical antiquity through the Renaissance to the present, discussing philosophers, writers, and scientists. His writing, like Frye's and the best of those concerned with the humanities (even those who would not want to be called humanists), is an embodiment of teaching. Books are the most enduring teachers.

More Comparisons

Another literary critic or theorist whose comparisons teach is Eva Kushner. My discussion here is based on her book *The Living Prism* (2001), a selection of lectures, papers, and previously published essays about Comparative Literature, a pressing topic especially in Canada, where it has been squeezed between the monoliths of English and French Studies.[17] Paradoxically, in a country with two official languages, no matter how multicultural and multilingual its inhabitants, the investment in the literature and language departments of the two primary founding European cultures presents Comparative Literature with a double challenge rather than the usual resistance it meets in many countries that have one official language. Being interdisciplinary and moving between cultures and languages has made life exciting and difficult for Comparative Literature. Eva Kushner—long active, influential, and productive nationally and internationally in this cross-disciplinary field—is well placed to set out problems and offer ways ahead for those interested in literature and culture in Canada and elsewhere. This collection is a retrospective that also looks forward.

I am sympathetic to Comparative Literature and to Kushner's journey as a scholar because they are mediators that cross boundaries: she began in Protestant theology and moved through philosophy and French literature, first of the twentieth century and then of the sixteenth—"widely separate disciplines, guarded by specialists who would view any border trespassing with suspicion"—before arriving at comparative literary studies.[18] Kushner disavows any allegiance to a particular school of thought and to any discipline in the humanities, but maintains that she was drawn to "their common relationship to the understanding of the human person." She moves in the borderlands between the modern and the postmodern.

The Living Prism is divided into five parts, the first being "Legacies and Renewals." Here, Kushner asks about the possibility of universals, of seeking knowledge or truth through particulars, and suggests that universals in the global village are already at work in various literatures. She sees the comparative method as fostering the postmodern, by which she means "generously pluralistic and respectful of others."[19] How valid Comparative Literature will be depends "on our ability to serve all cultures in ways that will ensure and enhance their membership in the world system of literatures."[20] Systems are for exposition, not something of "universal validity."[21] Kushner sees the human at the center of literary and cultural studies, so that they complement each other. As Canada is a diverse but sparsely populated country and as its education is a jurisdiction of the provinces and as "Canada's multicultural character, Canadian comparativists are well prepared to handle fragmentation of perspectives in the global village."[22] Kushner also represents a brief and useful history of the institution of Comparative Literature in Canada; calls attention to the important subfield of Comparative Canadian Literature, which Université de Sherbrooke focused on in one of its programs; and insists on the significance of separating the political and cultural grounds of comparing literature in French and English in Canada and of placing these literatures in a North American context in addition to examining their European origins. She has a specific interest in universals and argues for the need for demonstration and authentification in "emerging truths."[23]

In "Changing Perspectives in Literary History," part 2, Kushner covers an array of topics. For instance, she sees a dialectic between the synchronic and diachronic in the history of the humanities. In her meditation on time, which involves a discussion of the relation between history and poetry, Kushner quotes from one of my favorite passages in R. G. Collingwood, which includes the striking phrase "the historian must reenact the past in his own mind."[24] "Malleability" is key to Kushner's literary historiography.[25]

She envisions a "dialogue" or creative interplay between literature and other disciplines and not a reduction of one discipline into the other.[26] The relations among history, metaphor, fictionality, hermeneutics, and difference allow for a dialogue between the historical and the imaginative. This consideration of history and subjectivity continues in part 3 but focuses on the early modern, particularly on its distance from the present, the presence and absence of self and subject. Dialogue and paradox are significant in the emergence of self and selves in this period. Part of these apt "meanderings of the search for truth," the world of Renaissance dialogue, may be a paradox of subjectivity—for which Kushner holds up Erasmus as a model.[27] She extends her explorations of subjectivity to otherness in Petrarch and to the lot of the child during the Renaissance. Part 4 is devoted to Northrop Frye, who instituted "cultural communication as a domain of research," and discusses universals and communication, particularly in the form of intercultural dialogue, and the historicity of literature, or "the stories of stories."[28] For Kushner, Frye's social responsibility maintains "a dialectical tension between symbolical vision and concrete reality."[29] Part 5, "Comparative Imaginings," includes a discussion of the liberating effects of fiction on the imagination of children, the common ground of myth and literature in a proposed course on modern drama, the paradox of permanence and transformation in the use of Greek myths in modern plays, and the image of China in the poetry of the French poet Victor Segalen. Kushner's comparisons show the reach and the benefits of such a method.

In theory and practice Eva Kushner provides a wide-ranging and open view of Comparative Literature in Canada and beyond. She uses the words "dialogue" and "paradox" in different and suggestive contexts. Kushner invites the reader to explore the possible worlds of literature and to compare them, to communicate across time and culture. This is an important and worthy invitation. Literature and culture are closely connected and are vital for understanding the fraught and intricate relation between word and world.

Transitions

Within the subject of literature and culture, system and antisystem, law and theater, nature and law, teacher and student, word and world are among the pairs that this chapter has discussed. They are alternatives as well as opposites. They bind as they are binary. They divide and dwell together.

These are topics with great implications within and beyond themselves. Another vital comparison is of I/Thou, self and other. Distinction defines identity, as many like Martin Buber, Tzvetan Todorov, and Kushner herself have noted.[30] From Wladimir Krysinski's discussion of fiction, we might extrapolate the other of society and vice versa, so that the fiction of the world is also the world of fiction, as one is the other to the other.[31] Author and reader are also other to each other. It is to the question of otherness and authority—which gestures to past and present, history and fiction—to which I now turn.

CHAPTER 4

Otherness and Authority

Comparing literatures and cultures provides perspectives on a person's own language, culture, and nation. It allows for a deeper knowledge of self and social context, so it is as self-regarding as it is altruistic. All of us are other to ourselves, so that our personal pasts and the past of our language, culture, and nation, with all their changes and shifting configurations, tell us about ourselves. They also discipline or ironize, some might say relativize, ourselves and, paradoxically, put us all into relief and keep us from narcissism or solipsism. The classical past, the expansion of Europe, the Reformation, and the various revolutions and evolutions since then help us to read our present without being presentist. The Viking expansion, which also included the Norman Conquest of 1066, is a great force in Europe and the New World (Iceland, Greenland, and Newfoundland). Moreover, the quest for a trading route to Asia by sea, which included the expansion of Portugal into Africa, then Brazil and India, as well as Columbus's westward enterprise, was as crucial an event as there was in the history of globalization. Ultimately, the move from the biological order to the industrial one, based on fossil fuels, like coal, oil, and gas, revolutionized the world and transformed the face of the earth even more than the agricultural revolution 10,000 years before. This is one way to explain why I speak about earlier periods in my discussions of literature, theory, and history and, more particularly, about otherness and authority here.

Points of comparison are never far off from my discussion, and the past, even our past, is a foreign country. Perhaps it is more accurate to say, the past is our country from which time has exiled us or from which we try to reassemble the disparate and fading and chipped fragments as we and the past move further apart. How much authority the author actually has, or the reader that at one time seemed to be displacing him or her, is another matter. In the rhetorical contract of meaning, speaker and audience, writer and reader, meet in a moving and fluid middle ground and enact and reenact a drama of meaning. This semantic shift means that communication and understanding can occur across languages, cultures, and times, but that it is fraught with difficulty and requires all that feeling, thinking, imagining, and being can muster. All this pleasure of the text requires hard work, but the work becomes pleasure. The beauty of the text is what makes it endure, so its seductive qualities enable the truth that it is lured from and makes it endure. The aesthetic and ethical aspects of the text in the mutual act of making and performing through hearing or reading are both part of the seriousness and the play of the work. When the text collapses into either play or seriousness alone, then it loses its balance, and solemnity or frivolity can choke it. Texts are often mixtures with centripetal and centrifugal forces, and I like to refer to what I call the messiness of the text.

In what follows I wish to come back to the moment of shock, discovery (in the classical Aristotelian sense of uncovering), and trauma, which was the Columbian and post-Columbian moment when the Natives of the New World found their lands invaded by unexpected and ultimately unwelcome newcomers. The Europeans may have first been welcomed in many instances, but they abused that welcome. The New World and indeed the world would never be the same. Here is a stark test case for otherness, and how authority tries to impose itself and breaks down or breaks down the other, and reduces the other to bare survival or nothingness. Obliteration makes it hard to salvage otherness as a necessity or a utopian wish or even as a nostalgia for the time before a trauma has occurred.

Comparisons among cultures open up new perspectives. Here, I shall present a comparative discussion of western Europeans and how they came to terms with the otherness of Natives in the New World, and how that called into question their own authority as authors and indeed their worldview. This representation of the Natives is a recurrent theme. Often this representation and "translation" involved an overcoming of or coming to terms with other "barbarous" cultures as well as an inheritance from a previous empire or a rival. Figures like Columbus, Caminha, Las Casas, Montaigne, Léry, Ralegh, Behn, and others call attention to the question of being an eyewitness to encounters with Natives and slaves, or as those who represent the strangeness of the Americas. Making familiar the strange and the strange familiar happen simultaneously in some works. Customs, women, and cannibals all recall Herodotus, Pliny, and other antecedents. Theorists, like Tzvetan Todorov and Michel de Certeau, have examined otherness in the context of New World travel accounts, but I shall attempt to do so from a more overtly comparative point of view. Moreover, I shall try to widen the discussion beyond their interests in Cortés and Montaigne. Notions of being there, of the rhetorical relation between writer and reader, and the typology of the Old and New World will be among my concerns over the truth and lies that the authors and readers of travel accounts must negotiate. This might be an ethnology of reading or a use of ethnology to see the otherness within, or the dramatic tension between self and other that writers and readers then and now experience. First, I wish to provide some context for otherness.

Background

Otherness is something we can come to recognize in ourselves.[1] We are sometimes alienated from ourselves in the sense that we are conscious of our estrangement from nature or the precariousness of life and the untold certainty of death. Even if we were to stay in the same place and not go far, we would see the cycle of life and death and understand our being apart from, while being a part of, nature.

If a person were to live in a circumscribed space and was to observe nature, he or she would see birth, growth, and death, and witness peace and violence, especially in the countryside. Nature is a book that yields many points of view and can give evidence for many ideas about life. The same would be true about observing people alone and in groups. None of this is surprising, but it is worth remembering that otherness is not in and of itself exotic or distant but constitutes an aspect of ourselves.

When a child learns to read, he or she encounters in print a reenactment in a different mode of the acquisition of language. Infants encounter the world without being able to articulate words for the first months of their lives. They hear sounds and then imitate and apply them to the world about them. In time they build sentences, paragraphs, and narratives in speech and writing. They come to learn that words represent and refract the world symbolically but are not the world.

In a sense language attempts to integrate us into the world through description and understanding, but it also reminds us of our alienation from the world. If our thoughts and being were one and the same with the world, we would not need language. Language is, then, not only a tool to understand the world, but also a means of expressing the estrangement that human consciousness feels from the natural environment. In learning to read, if a child had only two books, and assuming this was a child who grew up with a Western education some time in the past five hundred years, then he or she might read the Bible and a book of Greek and Roman myths. Let us assume this volume to be Ovid's *Metamorphoses*.

In these two books, the child, who might have more basic redactions of those works until a certain age, could find the fall of Adam and Eve, who came to eat of the fruit of the knowledge of good and evil, and of the various transformations in life and death of figures among the Greek and Roman mortals who play out a drama of transformation. These changes in the Bible and Ovid show that life is not stable, secure, and unified, but, rather, unstable, insecure, and divided. But in the Bible and Ovid there are transformations that try to mend this Judeo-Christian and pagan sense of alienation. In Ovid, transformations occur that save the mortal from a situation or death and may even take a human and make him or her an animal or plant that can escape a dilemma or threat in the human world. The stories of Philomela and Adonis are such instances.

In the Bible, the tragic Fall in the Garden of Eden reveals an alienation from nature in which sin and the shame of the human body as something estranged in nature are discovered. Yet the Bible is a divine comedy, even if it also contains many human falls and tragedies in the *de casibus* sense. The shape of the Bible is both typological and comic. The typology is, for example, between the Garden of Eden and the New Jerusalem that heaven promises. Jesus of Nazareth is the new Adam. The cross of the crucifixion is a new version of a tree of sin and death, like the tree whose fruit so tempted Adam and Eve. But the killing of Christ on a cruciform, a human-made shape like a tree and derived from a tree, is a sin that brings death in order to free humans from lasting shame and death in the natural world because God enables Christ's redemption of that sin and death.

The human Fall from grace in the garden is a kind of othering of the person from the person. Because of this division of the self from the self, what we might call the divided self, estrangement is part of the personality, at least as it is constructed in Western culture and in Christianity in particular. A sense of shame and guilt, for better or worse, enters into a child's view of the world. Quite possibly, adults inculcate this remorse, consciously or not, into their children.

The reenactment of the Fall is puberty or adolescence, which intensifies any milder or more latent sexual feelings a child might have. This sexual awakening, if it may be called that, is like Eve and Adam discovering the awkwardness of their bodies as they are revealed through their disobedience toward God in the garden. The body comes to mean shame, which is a very difficult thing in the face of the overwhelming urge of sexual desire. How can this body, so alienated from nature, want to seek another body to reproduce another body, which will be born not only into innocence but also into original sin? It is the death of the body of Christ as a human sacrifice, as the son of Man, but also in the development of theology, as the son of God, that the fallen human body is redeemed. The Fall began with the choice of Eve and Adam in a solitary, and then social, act of disobedience and rebellion against the unalienated garden into which God had planted them.

The Fall becomes a matter of knowledge (epistemology) and being (ontology) and has a moral dimension (good and evil). The betrayal and killing of Christ is also an instance of humans betraying humans and, in their later tellings and theology, a human turning against God. By crucifying the son of God and the son of Man, Pilate, a representative of the political power of the Roman empire, allows for the violence of division among people. This is an evil deed that comes from human sin. The death, paradoxically, is a redemption and purification that enables God through Christ to allow a sacrifice to redeem humankind. Typologically, God asks Abraham to sacrifice Isaac, and here He sacrifices his own son. The Second Coming of Christ at the Last Judgment means an atonement, an unothering, of those who will be saved. The damned, of course, go on in the hell of alienation for eternity, but those who achieve salvation become part of a divine comedy as they overcome the otherness and self-division of fallenness and sin.

But there is a pagan side to Western culture. And the child struggles with the pleasures of the body and desires that adults will, and certainly in the doctrine of Christian religion, try to downgrade, discipline, or even demonize. Sex becomes a form of negative otherness. It is something, especially outside the institution of marriage, that is seen as a shame, sin, and aberration. But for the pagan, especially for pagan gods like Zeus, who is described as taking the form of a swan when raping Leda, the violence and the pleasures of sex and sexual conquest are seen in another light. In the pagan world, and this is how in "Leda and the Swan" W. B. Yeats represents the "feathered glory" of Zeus's act. Rape is a prerogative of the god of gods, but Tarquin's rape of Lucretia [Lucrece], even if he is a king, means banishment and the end of the Roman monarchy in favor of the republic.

In shame, Lucrece kills herself, and Brutus, more than her husband Collatine, at least in Shakespeare's *Rape of Lucrece*, avenges this heinous act. The reader of Shakespeare's poem is, however, not only introduced to the moral lesson and indignation of the rape but also experiences the rhetoric of seduction that Shakespeare uses in representing the temptation and lust of Tarquin. In fact, Tarquin knows that his lust for Lucrece is wrong but cannot help himself. She feels tainted and violated and becomes a sacrifice for Rome. Why she has to die is a matter of ideology and depends on views of rape and sex that make women feel alienated from themselves through no fault of theirs. And so the young reader, like the adult reader, sees that we can become others to ourselves, divided from what we are, are said to be, or hope to be in many different ways.

In Ovid as well as in the Bible, knowledge is sexual almost from the start. The gods seduce mortal women, and Eve gives in to the urge to eat the fruit. Temptation is everywhere, and the structures of narrative, theology, and society are set up in such a way as to lecture children and adults about their shortcomings, their fall from the world and themselves. Innocence and experience allow for an ambivalence of pleasure and displeasure. Uncovering the body is, like discovery generally, a movement from ignorance to knowledge. Columbus's uncovering of the New World is often expressed in terms of clothed European bodies and naked Native bodies. There, desire and innocence are mixed together.

How much is recognition and how much is misrecognition is always difficult to say. So much depends on points of view. The child is in, but fallen from, nature. Culture teaches him or her to revel in the body and to feel shame for having a body and certainly one that has sexual urges. The pagan and Christian selves are divided. In many cultures, there may be equivalents in different refractions and configurations. Here, I shall concentrate on ethnographic otherness, something more to do with travel to other places and peoples. It is good to remember that this hypothetical person who barely traveled and read only two books was already a stranger to himself or herself. Now to be a stranger in a strange land intensifies the question of otherness. It is to such a brief discussion that I now turn.

Being There and the Eyewitness

I have made much of childhood, and it is possible to say that what constitutes a child has changed a good deal over time. In the nineteenth century, Victor Hugo said: "Christopher Columbus only discovered America. I discovered the child."[2] This was part of the Romantic invention of innocence in childhood that is also found in William Wordsworth and that William Blake explores in relation to what follows in *Songs of Innocence and Experience*. But here we begin with marvels and eyewitness reports of adults in strange places set out by Herodotus.

The strangeness of the experience of other countries is something that Herodotus reports in his *Histories*. He is very much what we might call an ethnographer, discussing the customs of others. In one case, he highlights the breaking of usual gender roles among the Greeks in one group of women. In Book 4, his description of the Amazons is one that stresses difference and alterity:

> It is reported of the Sauromatae, that when the Greeks fought with the Amazons, whom the Scythians call Oior-pata or "man-slayers," as it may be rendered, *Oior* being Scythic for "man," and *pata* for "to slay"—It is reported, I say, that the Greeks after gaining the battle of the Thermodon, put to sea, taking with them on board three of their vessels all the Amazons whom they had made prisoners; and that these women upon the voyage rose up against the crews, and massacred them to a man.[3]

Here are women who can overcome men in an overwhelming and ruthless fashion, something that Herodotus explains with their name—manslayers. Although they do not know how to sail and drift after the Greek men are dead, they take control when they arrive in Scythia: "The first herd of horses which they fell in with they seized, and mounting upon their backs, fell to plundering the Scythian territory."[4] Having massacred, the Amazons plunder. The strangeness of all this Herodotus emphasizes: "The Scyths could not tell what to make of the attack upon them—the dress, the language, the nation itself, were alike unknown whence the enemy had come even, was a marvel."[5] The marvelous and the wondrous are part of facing the unknown. The Scyths make assumptions about the Amazons and act accordingly: "Imagining, however, that they were all men of about the same age, they went out against them, and fought a battle."[6] What happens is a surprise to them, so that they come to see their own misrecognition.

What they found on the battlefield was something quite different from what they expected. Herodotus reveals this with understatement and discretion: "Some of the bodies of the slain fell into their hands, whereby they discovered the truth."[7] Their reaction might be conventional in one sense, that these men, having discovered that their adversaries were women, considered the question in terms of kindness to the opposite sex and not a recoiling in horror or shock or a desire to dominate them through physical or sexual violence. "Hereupon they deliberated, and made a resolve to kill no more of them, but to send against them a detachment of their youngest men, as near as they could guess equal to the women in number, with orders to encamp in their neighbourhood, and do as they saw them do."[8] The strategy is one of balance and traction, but there is also another twist that avoids confrontation: "When the Amazons advanced against them, they were to retire, and avoid a fight—when they halted, the young men were to approach and pitch their camp near the camp of the enemy."[9] There is almost a comic element to the men fleeing and then coming near again so they can get used to each other. Herodotus makes the strategy of the mating ritual explicit: "All this they did on account of their strong desire to obtain children from so notable a race."[10] Ultimately, the Scyths pay the greatest compliment to these women, so strange to them, at least in the economy of sex and reproducing the group or nation. Their very difference from other women makes them "notable."

This initial strangeness leads to a rapprochement. As the Amazons realize the youths meant them no harm, they find that the camps approached nearer each day. This allows them to make the discovery that "both parties led the same life, neither having anything but their arms and horses, so that they were forced to support themselves by hunting and pillage."[11] In otherness comes sameness or at least difference in similarity.

Well before Columbus said that he and his men communicated with the Natives by speech or signs, Herodotus relates the two. Scyths and Amazons have to negotiate in a situation of strangeness: "At last an incident brought two of them together—the man easily gained the good graces of the woman, who bade him by signs (for they did not understand each other's language) to bring a friend the next day to the spot where they had met—promising on her part to bring with her another woman."[12] Sign language is a part of the encounter with radical difference early on. There is a sense of shared communication and of trust in it: "He did so, and the woman kept her word. When the rest of the youths heard what had taken place, they also sought and gained the favour of the other Amazons."[13] She is as good as her unspoken pledge, and this became an example for the meeting and mating of the Scyths and Amazons.

From this difference a new culture arises. They seem to be equals: "The two camps were then joined in one, the Scythians living with the Amazons as their wives."[14] But if anything in this narrative, Herodotus has made the women more unusual and capable. Here is another instance: "And the men were unable to learn the tongue of the women, but the women soon caught up the tongue of the men."[15] Without the women, there could be no full communication. "When they could thus understand one another, the Scyths addressed the Amazons in these words—'We have parents, and properties, let us therefore give up this mode of life, and return to our nation, and live with them. You shall be our wives there no less than here, and we promise you to have no others.'"[16] And so while the men promise to have them as wives alone, they underestimate the otherness of the Amazons when they think they will go home with them and change their way of life. Herodotus highlights the alterity: "But the Amazons said—'We could not live with your women—our customs are quite different from theirs. To draw the bow, to hurl the javelin, to bestride the horse, these are our arts of womanly employments we know nothing.'"[17] The nature of their status as warrior and hunter comes up again. In rejecting the idea of being domesticated in Scythia, they show that the Scythian men will have to come closer to the Amazon culture: "Your women, on the contrary, do none of these things; but stay at home in their wagons, engaged in womanish tasks, and never go out to hunt, or to do anything."[18] These men have to give up on the gender roles with which they have been raised: "We should never agree together. But if you truly wish to keep us as your wives, and would conduct yourselves with strict justice towards us, go you home to your parents, bid them give you your inheritance, and then come back to us, and let us and you live together by ourselves."[19] This new domestic and cultural arrangement is a novel situation without traditional domesticity. The Scythians have to leave behind their notions of gender roles and see things anew. They must accept a new otherness within them and their group.

The women are not finished with their conditions even though the young men complied with their earlier ones. The Amazons tell their young returning husbands: "We are ashamed, and afraid to live in the country where we now are. Not only have we stolen you from your fathers, but we have done great damage to Scythia by our ravages. As you like us for wives, grant the request we make of you. Let us leave this country together, and go and dwell beyond the Tanais."[20] These young men comply to this request as well, so that the Amazons set out how and where they will live. Their home will become a stranger to them.

Crossing the river they find a new land in three days and established this as their new home. Herodotus is presenting a history and a tradition: "The women of the Sauromatae have continued from that day to the present to observe their ancient customs, frequently hunting on horseback with their husbands, sometimes even unaccompanied; in war taking the field; and wearing the very same dress as the men."[21] There is no sense weakening of the otherness of the Amazons. They are not contained or assimilated into a Scythian male world. Instead, they have been warriors who set the terms for their new culture and homeland and continue to avoid conventional gender roles and domesticity. Herodotus does not put this into the past as a myth but as a living tradition to which he turns his ethnographic eye even if he is gathering this from the reports of others.

Being interested in ethnography, Herodotus ends this section on the Amazons with observations about language and customs: "The Sauromatae speak the language of Scythia, but have never talked it correctly, because the Amazons learnt it imperfectly at the first."[22] Even though Herodotus has made the Amazons into better linguists than the male Scythians, they were not speaking their Native language and build that into the language of their new home. It is a little curious that the Scythians themselves could not have corrected this shortcoming because it was originally their language, and one might assume that children would learn their mother tongues from their fathers as well. Herodotus is adept with detail: "Their marriage-law lays it down that no girl shall wed till she has killed a man in battle."[23] This is a strange condition of marriage, and would be in Greek or Scythian society, but makes some sense in the context of a society of women warriors who have been threatened by and have had to fight men. Rather than comment on this or censure the Amazons, Herodotus adds another detail: "Sometimes it happens that a woman dies unmarried at an advanced age, having never been able in her whole lifetime to fulfil the condition."[24] This observation is more factual, and the otherness here is accepted within the logic of Amazon society. They have their husbands, who have listened to them, but they must still kill men in order to marry men. This strangeness rests like a contradiction, but as long as the men listen and agree, as they have in Herodotus's narrative, then all is fine. The men bend and compromise, and in turn they have been linked in a new arrangement with the Amazons. Herodotus does not include any ravings of threatened masculinity or any attacks on women who would not be women. They may be marvelous and strange, but they are also notable. Alterity need not be something terrible to be denounced.

Columbus also comes to terms with others who do not share the same dress and customs and who seem to have a different way of looking at the body and at war. In writing about his first encounters with indigenous peoples, he says: "The people of this island, and of the other islands which I have found and of which I have information, all go naked, men and women, as their mothers bore them, although some women cover a single place with the leaf of a plant or with a net of cotton which they make for the purpose."[25] This is the boldness of being naked and to some extent the modesty of taking some cover. It is as if Eve had realized she were naked after eating of the fruit of the knowledge of good and evil. Columbus switches from nakedness and cover to war: "They have no iron and steel or weapons, nor are they fitted to use them, not because they are not well built men and of handsome stature, but because they are marvellously timorous."[26] Their character is pliable and not fierce, quite unlike the Amazons in Herodotus. According to Columbus, "They have no other arms than weapons made of canes cut in seeding time, to the ends of which they fix a small sharpened stick. And they do not dare to make use of these."[27] Their weapons are not threatening to Columbus, who finds innocence and pliability in them. They are not fierce, which is perhaps prelapsarian, but they also do not pose much of a threat in war if their technology is taken into consideration.

Columbus has his ethnographical side. He tries to express it sometimes as an eyewitness. He writes about the topics of women, monsters, property, race, and climate. In Columbus's account, men, except the king, seem content to be with one woman. He also, perhaps quite conveniently, thinks that the Indians share and do not seem to value property as a private possession. Having expected (as others did) to see monsters, Columbus admits that he has not.[28] But Columbus reports something he has not witnessed: the mating of cannibals and Amazons, those that eat men and those who can do without them: "As I have found no monsters, so that I have had no report of any, except in an island 'Quaris', the second at the coming into the Indies, which is inhabited by a people who are regarded in all the islands as very fierce and who eat human flesh." The danger of these fierce flesh-eaters is combined with the threat of women warriors, which does not seem to have concerned Herodotus as much as it does Columbus: "These are those who have intercourse with the women of 'Matinino', which is the first island met on the way from Spain to the Indies, in which there is not a man."[29] Columbus then does get into a kind of ethnological zone that seems more descriptive and dispassionate, so the registers of language and tones shift within sentences and passages. He continues: "These women engage in no feminine occupation, but use bows and arrows of cane, like those already mentioned, and they arm and protect themselves with plates of copper, of which they have much."[30] Like Herodotus, Columbus tries to make sense of other cultures and genders while establishing the authority of his own text. For Columbus, the echoes of Herodotus, however intended, create a network of textual authority and even tradition that place his text of the shockingly new—this is the New World after all and it got in the way of Asia—within a familiar framework that Herodotus helped to establish with his history and ethnology.

There are other eyewitness accounts that also call attention to textual authority and writing. Pedro Álvares Cabral is another good example. His voyage included a journey to the New World, Africa, and Asia. Brazil was to be a key colony for the Portuguese, who claimed it during Easter week of 1500. Pero Vaz de Caminha, one of the crew of Cabral, recorded the events of the voyage. Caminha represents themes that Columbus had reported in the New World. For instance, he brings up the innocence that made it easy to convert the Natives, the nakedness of the inhabitants, the Native signs that indicate gold and other riches, the will of God, and salvation. Even before Cabral's ships left Brazil for India, Caminha, who held the position of writer for the fleet, wrote a letter to King Manuel. Here, he described the stay in Brazil. Caminha, who seems to have sailed on Cabral's ship, says that he is taking the middle way: "May Your Highness take my ignorance for good intention, and believe that I shall not set down here anything more than I saw and thought, either to beautify or to make it less attractive."[31] He presents himself as a reliable eyewitness, a stance much taken at this time.[32] Another instance of an early explorer is Binot de Paulmier de Gonneville, whose relation of the voyage to Brazil in 1504 is the oldest account in French concerning an eyewitness report of the New World. This narrative wrestles with some of the same issues as Columbus's writing does. For Columbus, in the account of his first voyage, the Natives considered the Spanish to be gods. Gonneville thought that the indigenous people he encountered considered the French to be angels. Like the aboriginals that Bernal Díaz described in his narrative of Hernán Cortés's conquest, those whom Gonneville meets were much taken by the power of writing. Moreover, Jacques Cartier maintained that the Natives thought the French to be gods. Like Gonneville, Cartier planted a cross as a sign of possession. There becomes a ceremonial use of the audience. The French pattern of taking possession, which Gonneville used, involved Natives symbolically or literally as part of the audience during the ceremony of planting the cross. The authority of the text was political as well as ethnographical and was as much for rivals as well as other peoples encountered anew. The French were making claims as a challenge to the Spanish and the Portuguese.[33]

Other important ways of considering otherness is translation, that is, the assimilation of the work of another culture into an other. For instance, Richard Eden used translation to advocate English colonization and then the imperial union of Spain and England.[34] Another instance of considering alterity is the use of eyewitness accounts of the conflict between the French and Spanish in Florida, such as Thomas Hacket's translation of Jean Ribault and Nicolas Le Challeux's narrative. Translations can be used for different political, religious, and ideological purposes. Eden explores the potential alliance of England with Spain. Ribault and Le Challeux are French Protestants whose texts helped to produce the Black Legend of Spain.[35]

The Black Legend and Columbus were two important aspects in creating and questioning authority, antecedents, and origins in texts about the New World. The charges Richard Hakluyt the Younger took from Bartolomé de Las Casas against the Spaniards in the Americas were dire. They included allegations of depopulation and devastation of more than 12 million men, women, and children, over forty years. These accusations were familiar because they appeared in earlier European sources. Among these texts were English and French versions of Las Casas. Hakluyt translated passages from Las Casas's description of Hispaniola, cruelties that included the author's testimony. Las Casas's condemnation also occurred in a marginal heading that stressed his status as an eyewitness to the cruelty: "I haue seene all the aforesaide thinges and others infinite."[36] Hakluyt's section on Las Casas left off with the Spanish attacking the Indians with their dogs and making a pact to kill 100 Natives for every Spaniard they killed. Hakluyt also understood that even in his own Anglican world and with his ties to French Protestants like Philippe Duplessis-Mornay, he needed to be balanced in matters of religion in relation to European and international politics. Thus, Hakluyt supplemented this description of atrocities, by turning to another authority, this time Johannes Matellus Sequanus, a Catholic, who confirms the words of Las Casas, a member of a Catholic religious order.[37]

André Thevet was important among the French for providing early knowledge of the Indies. Like Oviedo, a Spaniard who wrote a key text in the 1520s, Thevet emphasized eyewitness accounts. Often writers after Columbus in various western European languages showed their anxiety over originality. Who was there first became a motivated question for explorers and writers after Columbus. There were many responses to Columbus. For example, his successors praised him and supplemented him. They also claimed to have additional kinds of knowledge and undermined him as the discoverer of the New World. Sometimes they attempted to ignore him.[38] Truth and lies, the lack of reliability, and the claim of authority worked in tension in the texts of Thevet and his predecessors, contemporaries, and successors.

Other Issues and Conclusions

The rhetorical contract between the writer and the reader is sometimes key to the context of these ethnographical texts. Rhetoric was used to persuade others, whether monarchs or courtiers or readers, for or against exploration, expansion, settlement, and empire.[39] Rhetoric, or the art of persuasion, is also the relation between speaker and audience, writer and reader. What this connection is depends on the tension between the authority and the play that the reader has, that is, how much give and take is involved in the textual interplay of production and reception.

It is not as though the audience always approved of expansion or plans to change patterns from the past. A royal council in Spain rejected Columbus's petition. During the period between December 1486 and January 1487, the Columbus commission, composed of *letrados* (mainly university-educated lawyers at court) and *sabios* (men learned in cartography and astronomy), rejected Columbus's arguments for the support of his voyage. Moreover, they passed their findings along to Ferdinand and Isabella, the Spanish sovereigns. The audience was not always receptive to persuasion. The learned and the leaders in Spain, or Europe, did not necessarily embrace expansion and empire and when they did so, they approached the idea with care. Even after the landfall in the western Atlantic, Columbus and the Crown of Spain fought over governance, ownership, and profits in regard to the new lands. The writers of these accounts also show ambivalence in European representations of the lands and peoples of the New World, representing the Natives as fierce and paradisal. Verrazzano is similar to Columbus in this respect. The idealization of the land and its peoples is redolent of paradise. Sometimes the indigenes appear as barbarians. There is a kind of mix of the Ten Lost Tribes of Israel and the riches of Asia. At other times, the New World is an innocent place that helps to judge in a kind of typology the corruption and shortcomings of the Old World. This could take the form of a Christian critique of riches and power. Some church intellectuals used this tradition to draw attention to the absurd and cruel aspects of European expansion into the New World. During December of 1511 in Hispaniola, one of the members of the Dominicans, Antón Montesino, preached two sermons that were critical of the abuses of the Natives in the place where Colombus had first landed. The sermon attacked the governor and the established settlers of the colony as infidels. Montesino enraged the son of Christopher, Diego Columbus, who appealed to the king, who ordered the Castilian provincial of the Dominican order to correct the situation. This actual reaction is different from that of a parallel fictional account of a similar context but written later. Lope de Vega's *El Nuevo Mundo descubierto por Cristóbel Colón* (ca. 1598–1603) represents the Indian king, Dulcanquellín, saying to Columbus's brother, Bartolomé, that a gentle, peaceful Christianity is a kind of advocacy that will convert the Natives.[40] Words, spoken and written, became a ground of contention in interpreting the New World.

Each of the texts of the New World involves the authority of earlier learning, the status of the author or the patron, or the eyewitness. There is in all this a typology of the Old and the New World. In *Utopia* (1516), Thomas More uses Vespucci's voyage as part of the context for Raphael Hythlodaeus's account. One aspect of the fiction of finding Utopia is that Raphael and his friends stayed behind at the fort in Brazil after Vespucci left. Thomas More emphasizes how the generosity of a Native ruler allowed these Europeans to survive and what excellent institutions the aboriginal commonwealths had. More also uses a typology between the Old and the New Worlds to satirize Europe. Gonzalo Fernández de Oviedo's *Natural History of the West Indies* (1526) addresses Charles V. In this work, he also emphasizes the importance of experience and eyewitness accounts and supports his view with an appeal to classical authority. Oviedo advocates an observation of nature rather than of other books. Still, he appeals to the authority of Pliny, who, in his *Natural History*, included firsthand observations and accurate scholarly citations of the sources for the stories that he had read or heard.

In *A Short Account of the Destruction of the Indies* Las Casas speaks of himself as a witness and an eyewitness to the terrible events in the Indies. In the synopsis, he says: "Some years later, he observed that not a few of the people involved in this story had become so anaesthetized to human suffering by their own greed and ambition that they had ceased to be men in any meaningful sense of the term."[41] Jean de Léry's *History of a Voyage to the Land of Brazil* (1580 ed.) presented the Natives in Brazil in such a way as to criticize the French at home. During the Wars of Religion, Brazil became something of a touchstone for Léry. In 1574 Léry had published his account of the siege of Sancerre. He had been there during those horrors. The typology was thus: he was an eyewitness who had lived through hardship in the Old World and the New. In "Des Cannibales" (1580), Montaigne uses Plato's representation of Solon's account of Atlantis to criticize French and European expansion and commerce in the New World. In the exploration of cannibals, Montaigne concentrates on the French and Europeans in relation to the New World. In "Des Coches," Montaigne focuses on the Spanish and asks why the new lands could not have been conquered under the Greeks and Romans. That way the Europeans would have brought the people virtue rather than teach them European avarice and cruelty. Montaigne's motive sometimes aims for a plain and true narrative of the New World. This stance sometimes led him to qualify the use of rhetorical and narrative embellishment. In one instance, he establishes the credentials of someone who worked for him as a witness: "This man who I had, was a simple and plain man, who was in a proper condition to bear true witness, for refined people are more curious and notice more things, but they gloss them, and to add to the value of the interpretation, and to persuade, they cannot prevent themselves from altering the History a little."[42] It is possible that Montaigne mimics the travel literature he discussed. This is the view of Michel de Certeau, who thinks of Montaigne's essay on cannibals as having the same structure as that of a travel account. De Certeau says that this essay includes the "outbound journey," the depiction of "savage society," and the "return voyage."[43] The relation between then and now has many layers of interpretation as writers are readers who are also read and written about. Authors have as their other the readers within them, not to mention those without, so authority has a readerly dimension.

There is, of course, extensive scholarship on these figures and therefore the questions of authority and authorship and the nature of their texts are much debated. Oviedo can serve as an example. Oviedo attracted controversy. Tzvetan Todorov describes him as a historian who is a conquistador and a xenophobe and racist.[44] J. H. Elliott represents Oviedo as someone who thinks Columbus deserves better recognition; who is a natural historian full of wonder who respects Pliny too much; who supports direct personal observation over traditional authority; and who is a skeptic, like Léry, about Amerindian conversion.[45] For Anthony Pagden, Oviedo is an example of a European observer who describes things that looked alike as identical and a natural historian who has a low opinion of the Natives and whom Humboldt calls the Pliny of the New World.[46] There are layers upon layers, then, in relation to author and audience, then and now.[47]

As we have seen, there were controversial figures like Oviedo and Thevet (who was cosmographer to the king of France). Oviedo had lobbied for a similar post in Spain three decades before. Thevet claimed to provide valuable advice and insisted on his unique ability to combine astute observations of the New World with strong scholarship. Whereas Jean de Léry and François de Belleforest ridiculed his scholarship and character, Ronsard and Du Bellay esteemed his work. In so many ways, Spain had led the way in the discussion of the New World. Francisco de Vitoria was a key figure in asking difficult questions of his country's involvement there. For instance he asked what right (ius) his country had in subjecting the barbarians to Spanish rule. He also considered what powers in temporal and civil matters the Spanish monarchy had in regard to the "Indians." He also explored the spiritual and religious matter of what powers the monarchy or the church had or did not have in relation to the "Indians." This self-criticism complicated the notion of the authority of church, sovereign, and state (in this case Spain). Walter Ralegh also shows ambivalent and intricate attitudes in *The Discouerie of the Large, Rich, and Bewtiful Empyre of Guiana* (1596). Here, he tends toward the anti-Spanish and pro-Native position of the literature of the Black Legend. He argues that the Spanish conquest was an illegal act that killed 20 million. Still, his argument is also one of out-conquesting the Spaniards and finding even more gold than they did. In the body of this text, Ralegh developed the need to observe the Spanish example of colonization while using its own methods to subvert it.

More than nine decades later, in 1688, Aphra Behn published a novel, *Oroonoko*, which showed another dark side of colonization. This book exposes the inhumanity of slavery. The work is a defense of a noble African prince who was enslaved, and it is full of ambivalence. The narrator and the characters create an ambivalent narrative landscape. It seems to invite the question of whether the narrator is a character or an expression of Aphra Behn in something approaching a memoir in the form of a novella, romance, or travel narrative. The dedication claims to be a representation of Behn's experience in Surinam. Personal experience and fictional expression mix and are part of a social as well as a literary movement.

Truthfulness, fictions, and outright falsehoods are some of the important things that the authors and readers of travel accounts must negotiate. In *Gulliver's Travels* Jonathan Swift has the king of Brobdingnag call the English vermin. Olaudah Equiano's *The Life of Olaudah Equiano, or Gustavus Vassa, the African* (1789; rpt. 1814), an autobiography, is also critical of Europeans. In the dedication of 1792, Equiano (ca.1745–1797), addressing the House of Lords and the House of Commons, sounds like Gulliver describing the Europeans, and especially the English, as vermin because he remembers with horror the first sight of a European. Even at the conclusion of his narrative, Equiano continues to press for the end of the cruel practice of slavery.

The truth of one culture or empire can be called into question. Narratives of helping others or of superiority can be turned on their heads. The authority of the authors comes under scrutiny in representations of the other in the encounter with new cultures. In western Europe and in the Atlantic world, authors and readers came to question the authority of Europeans at home and away in a typology that complicated textual, cultural, and political life. The awakening of otherness in the child and in sexuality, the otherness from within, can also be intensified in the ethnological urge of texts about other cultures.

Similarly, just because novels were and are being written at a great rate does not mean that these novels are always enhancing and enlivening the novel as a genre, and so production can be deadening. The novel grew out of epic and romance (prose and poetry) and was not even on Aristotle's radar for the pinnacle of genres—tragedy and epic—in his *Poetics*. The rise of the novel with the middle classes and with industrialization and urbanization meant that it had to compete or at least find its place with poetry and the theater. Later, radio, television, the computer, and the Internet modified the place in the literary market for poetry, theater, and the novel. So the novel was always being born and dying, a little like people and everything in nature and culture.

The death of the author and of readers and reading is a cultural anxiety at a time when change is apparent, perhaps even more than that owing to the shift from manuscript to print in the Gutenburg Revolution. So amid this change, I will try to find a way between past and present to preserve the endangered author, not just from the threat of death, but from death itself. Not that one person can perform this task—annihilation is hard to guard against—but since the author is on the ropes and not knocked out, I am just trying to give him or her a breather between the rounds.

From Nietzsche's emphasis on language and his view on the death of God, a different kind of theory and philosophy developed, especially in the 1960s. Rhetoric and skepticism as well as the philosophical doubts about the truth of literature became parts of a deconstructive approach to texts. Combined with a renewed interest in historicism from the 1980s onward, the critical and theoretical landscape changed in English-speaking countries. Part of this change involved deemphasizing the author and decentering the text and trying to have more regard for the reader-context, the dispossessed and the marginal. All this brought more richness to literary studies. Although texts were still important, the unity the New Critics had sought led to a rhetorical untying of the text among deconstructionists or poststructuralists. Moreover, context, intertextuality, and difference helped to reorient interests in literature, theory, and history. In the next chapter, I shall discuss New Historicism and feminist difference as two of the new ways of reading that came of age in the last decades of the twentieth century.

CHAPTER 5

Historicism, Feminism, and the Poetics of Difference

Poetry and the world are connected even as one seems so separate from the other. History, philosophy, and poetry were closely related in Aristotle's mind, and until recent times some writers would write all three, as can be seen in the likes of Voltaire. With the development of academic disciplines, the German PhD with research thesis, and the ever-increasing specialization of labor in the economy and in the university after the Industrial Revolution, fewer writers were involved in or devoted to all three. University students had to choose a department or perhaps two departments, and disciplinary boundaries were guarded. Some of this specialization led to great work that would not have been otherwise done, but this way of knowing and writing could also involve the siloing of thought for writers and readers. One of the interesting aspects of the new kinds of historical and textual studies from the 1960s was that they could bring together scholars, students, and readers from different disciplines. More specifically, I would like to turn to New Historicism and deconstruction in the context of feminism as two of the new ways of negotiating the relation between word and world.

A New History

In the study of literature, philosophy, and history, there are shifting methods and interpretations, and so the history of history, or historiography, also shifts. As in Aristotle's *Poetics* philosophy, poetry and history were given precedence and were closely connected, even as Aristotle made a hierarchy of them in terms of universals and particulars. In the past three decades in literary studies, history, while never going away, has received particular attention and has been elevated as a most, perhaps the most, desirable way to talk about literature. In the United Kingdom, cultural materialism embodied this movement, whereas in the United States it was New Historicism. This was the new history in literary studies. This is what I will emphasize here, although I call attention to *la nouvelle histoire*, or new history, which, as Peter Burke notes, Jacques Le Goff launched in France.[1] This new history among historians, as Burke says, has reacted against political history and is concerned with all human activity; provides an analysis of structures rather than a narrative of events; concerns itself with history from below rather than from above; examines all types of evidence and not simply governmental and archival records; focuses on collective movements in addition to individual actions, trends, as well as events; and admits to subjectivity, prejudices, and cultural relativism while understanding the ideal of objectivity.[2] Thus, in the same period of the 1980s and early 1990s, historians, as well as literary scholars with an interest in history, were taking into account the changes to the study of history. New Historicists were part of this milieu.

New Historicism came of age in the early 1980s. In the turmoil of contemporary theory, shelf life may not equal half-life. New Historicism still makes an important contribution to the study of literature. Rather than speculate at length on the future of this loose confederacy or multivalent movement, I would like to discuss its attractions and accomplishments and mention its occasional shortcomings. A good text to survey New Historicism can be found in the collection of essays that H. Aram Veeser brought together, as it came near the high-water mark of New Historicism. This chapter concentrates on the changes to New Historicism in its first decade or so, on its use of anecdote or narrative and on the techniques it shares with other methodologies, and on its disparities, which may have implications for its future.

Louis Montrose says that although in 1980 Michael McCanles was the first to employ the name "New Historicism," Stephen Greenblatt's use of the term in 1982 gave it currency. New Historicism underwent three great changes in its first decade or so. First, in the United States it became the dominant discourse of studies of the English Renaissance. Second, it extended its range of practitioners to include those interested in feminism, deconstruction, Marxism, and other discourses. Third, it moved outside the Renaissance to other periods just as deconstruction came to range beyond Romanticism. Most scholars and students of the English Renaissance in this period cited Greenblatt more than any other critic. It took a few years for the full import of *Renaissance Self-Fashioning* (1980) to be felt. The paradoxes and subtle qualifications that mark the opening of this book begin and end another work that consolidates Greenblatt's influence, *Shakespearean Negotiations* (1988).[3] Both texts historicize their terms, so that Greenblatt finds that the verb "fashion" comes into its own in the sixteenth century in writers like Spenser and that "energia" derives from the Greek rhetorical tradition that became so influential in the Renaissance.[4] Just as self-fashioning creates anxiety, so too does social circulation. This method, Greenblatt says, moves against an ahistorical and essentialist view that allows for critics to apply a technique to any text regardless of its historical period. Both texts begin their chapters with anecdotes and proceed by analogy between the nonliterary text or social context and the literary text. Greenblatt has helped to create a genre that many others have followed. He furnishes the lead article for this collection. Besides confessing his surprise over the success of the term "New Historicism" and his penchant to do practical work before establishing his theoretical position, in "Towards a Poetics of Culture," Greenblatt engages Marxism and postmodernism in a debate that runs throughout the collection.[5] Greenblatt questions Fredric Jameson's view that capitalism becomes "the agent of repressive differentiation" that shatters our integrated selves and separates us from the public domain and Jean-Francois Lyotard's contrary view that it constitutes "the agent of monological totalization" that makes discursive domains untenable and integrates them into a monolithic discourse.[6] For Greenblatt, both Marxism and postmodernism use history as "an anecdotal ornament," fail to address "the apparently contradictory historical effects of capitalism," and totalize capitalism as a philosophical principle. Greenblatt appeals to historical "evidence," an important but a more complex term that he wants to admit here.[7] In a recuperative dialectical or ironic move, Greenblatt says that American capitalism and its cultural poetics oscillate between Jameson's "differentiation" and Lyotard's "totalization."[8] Greenblatt advocates a study of the mutual relation or movement between social and aesthetic discourses and the construction of an "interpretative model" that accounts for "the unsettling circulation of materials and discourses" within "the hidden places of negotiation and exchange."[9] He does not say whether these hidden spaces dwell in the unconscious or are subliminal, whether they represent a hermeneutic mystery whose meaning literary criticism must coax, whether they constitute intricate manipulations or relations of currencies and negotiations, or whether he means something else. What distinguishes New Historicism from old historicism is, in Greenblatt's view, a methodological self-consciousness that does not assume transparent signs and interpretative procedures.

Feminism, Deconstruction, Marxism

Other discourses are interrogating New Historicism. Feminist, deconstructive, and Marxist views have enriched this debate on historicism in literary studies. These intersections are productive. Jane Marcus's "The Asylums of Anteus" and Judith Newton's "History as Usual?" examine feminist interest in New Historicism.[10] Marcus accuses New Historicism, including its feminist versions, of colorizing history for present consumption.[11] She wishes "to demonstrate that history and literature deserve equal narrative force in a cultural text," to "propose a theory of the feminist fetish, collating and adopting recent work of Naomi Schor on female fetishism and Tom Mitchell on iconography and commodity fetishism to discuss the poster art and political dress of British Suffragettes," to name female fetishism and to say that its failure to survive "wartime iconoclasm" shows a complicity with a "new iconoclasm" in opposition to feminist versions of New Historicism.[12] Newton asserts that most histories of New Historicism have barely alluded to "the mother roots—the women's movement and the feminist theory and scholarship which grew from it."[13] Feminist criticism of male assumptions of objectivity, feminist views of knowledge as politically and historically specific, and feminist analyses of the cultural construction of female identity and the role of ideology in subjugation all have contributed to the "postmodernist" premises of New Historicism.[14] Although in the first chapter of *Shakespearean Negotiations* Greenblatt argues against totalizing the artist and the society, Newton, who does not address Greenblatt in particular, makes a strong case that nonfeminist New Historicists represent the ideologies of the male elite as the typical way to construct culture, and suggests that they amend their method to include the material world of the domestic and the anxiety of women and other oppressed groups.[15]

Gayatri Spivak and Richard Terdiman explore the relation of deconstruction and poststructuralism to New Historicism. Spivak agrees with Derrida that the conflict between New Historicism and deconstruction constitutes a "turf battle" between Berkeley on the one side and the University of California, Los Angeles (UCLA) and Irvine on the other. She says: "Since I see the New Historicism as a sort of academic media hype mounted against deconstruction, I find it hard to position myself in its regard."[16] In discussing the move from the term "Marxism" to "materialism" or "cultural criticism," Spivak finds much fault. She also asserts that "one of the things that one cannot do with Foucault is to turn him into a hermeneut who talks about nothing but the microphysics of power and thus make him an alibi for an alliance politics which takes for its own format the post-modern pragmatics of non-teleological and not necessarily innovative morphogenetics, giving rise to more and more moves."[17] Spivak thinks of "history" as a catachresis, the abuse or misapplication of a metaphor, or the improper use of a word. Her program differs from the New Historicists': "We live in a postcolonial neo-colonialized world. And we should teach our students to find a toe-hold out of which they can become critical so that so-called cultural production—confessions to being a baby-boomer and therefore I'm a new historicist—that stuff is seen as simply a desire to do bio-graphy where actually the historical narrative is catachretical. If you think of the '60s, think of Czechoslovakia, not only Berkeley and France, or that the promises of devaluation didn't come true in some countries in Asia in '67."[18] For Spivak, the politics of history are not the politics of New Historicism: the state of criticism seems pale beside the state of the world. In "Is there Class in this Class?" Terdiman links education with social and political hierarchy and observes that whereas poststructuralism concerns itself with "the constitutive, irreducible play of signifiers," New Historicism concentrates on "their constitutive, irreducible power."[19]

A strong interest also exists in the relation between Marxism and New Historicism. In "Marxism and the New Historicism," Catherine Gallagher grants the value of New Historicism by listing its insights: "That no cultural or critical practice is simply a politics in disguise, that such practices are seldom intrinsically either liberatory or oppressive, that they seldom contain their politics as an essence but rather occupy particular historical situations from which they enter into various exchanges, or negotiations, with practices designated 'political.'"[20] She also tries to explain the opposition to New Historicism: "The search for the new historicism's political essence can be seen as a rejection of these insights. Critics on both the right and left seem offended by this refusal to grant that literature and, by extension, criticism either ideally transcend politics or simply are politics when properly decoded."[21] Contrary to Spivak, Gallagher thinks that the radical American politics of the 1960s was imperative, says that her own experiences with Marxism and deconstruction did not provide the explanatory power that New Historicism did, and tells how the women's movement taught her, and radicals like her, that the more resistance in personal and mundane matters, the more it confirmed the importance of their struggle.[22] Gallagher argues that new historical work has kept New Left assumptions "about the sources, nature, and sites of social conflict and about the issue of representation. Instead of resubscribing, as some Marxist critics have, to a historical metanarrative of class conflict, we have tended to insist that power cannot be equated with economic or state power, that its sites of activity, and hence of resistance, are also in the micro-politics of daily life."[23] In the 1980s as in the 1960s, this radical politics attempts to destabilize history and text, sign systems and things, and representation and the represented. Although Gallagher admits that New Historicists often use methods similar to those of Left formalists like Louis Althusser and Pierre Macherey, especially when they assume an unstable text that is historically stable, they also oppose them by suggesting that ideological contradictions can help maintain oppressive social relations and that the anatagonism between ideology and literature constitutes "a powerful and socially functional mode of constructing subjectivity."[24] In Gallagher's view, the arguments from the Left tend to accuse New Historicists of failing to stress the subversive potential of the text and the critic's function to activate it, so that they are quietists who make others despair in opposition.[25] New Historicism has continued to study the complexity of the modern subject and will be as oppositional as Marxism, even if Marxists do not always think so.[26] How history is presented, either through the narration of events or analysis, is important to those in literature, philosophy, and history discussing the nature of the historical. There are large and small narratives, and in the next section, I will discuss what might be called micro-stories in the use of the anecdotal.

Narrative

Another methodological question involves narrative rather than direct political allegiance: the use of the anecdote in New Historicism. How the story of the anecdote is part of the story of the past is a key consideration in discussing the New Historicists. Joel Fineman's essay "The History of the Anecdote," assumes this method to be paradigmatic in Greenblatt's essay "Fiction and Friction," but defers it to the last.[27] He examines the genre of the anecdote in literary and historical writing.

In discussing Thucydides and Hippocrates, Fineman concludes that the anecdote, the narration of a singular event, is the historeme or the smallest unit of historiographic fact. He wants to know how the anecdote, which refers and is literary, "possesses its peculiar and eventful narrative force."[28] One of the goals of New Historicism, according to Fineman, is "to discover or to disclose some wrinkling and historicizing interruption, a breaking and a realizing interjection, within the encyclopedically enclosed circle of Hegelian historical self-reflection."[29] Rather than casual and accidental, the anecdote, Fineman says, represents the literary and referential, and it affects historically the writing of history. Here is Fineman's thesis: "The anecdote is the literary form that uniquely lets history happen by virtue of the way it introduces an opening into the teleological, and therefore timeless narration of beginning, middle, and end."[30] The anecdote, in Fineman's view, produces the effect of the real and of contingency by representing an event inside and outside the context of "historical successivity." Anecdote opens and destabilizes the context of a larger historical narrative that can be seduced by the opening anecdote.[31] Fineman would like to examine the "operation of the aporetic anecdote on the history of writing," and suggests that this "anecdotal historiography" might be accomplished by discussing texts from Thucydides through the lives of saints and through jest books to the works of New Historicists. Paradoxically, Thucydides is trying to create a teleological and therefore ahistorical history, but, in a culture that is attempting to produce an ahistorical philosophy and literature, he betrays his totalizing intentions for historiography and shows its very contingency.[32]

During the Renaissance, Fineman maintains, a technicist science and history arise, the latter carrying with it the cost of "its unspoken sense of estranged distance from the anecdotal real" when it gives to science "the experience of history, when the force of the anecdote is rewritten as experiment."[33] Fineman characterizes the writing practice of New Historicism as a "Baconian" essay that introduces history, an amplification, and a moralizing conclusion that puts an end to history and, sometimes, another anecdote that tries to keep things open. Like history in the Renaissance, New Historicism promises openness until antihistorical currents threaten it with more closed scientific or ideological historiography.[34] If Fineman's essay examines the tropological and narrative functions of anecdote, it also suggests that what appears to be incidental actually constitutes the very basis of history. The possibility that this thesis deserves consideration should prevent any of us from being dismissive of the methods of New Historicism, and it should encourage us to test Fineman's thesis and read new historical work even more carefully. Although the study of the Renaissance was important to New Historicism, other periods also came within its purview.

Other Periods beyond the Renaissance

Those who might be called New Historicists, even if they would agree with such a category for them, have varied interests in various eras. If, as Fineman thinks, the openness of history in the Renaissance and in the period of New Historicism, and the resistance to that openness, has created an especial affinity between the two historical practices, we can also observe more new historical work in other periods. Marcus, Newton, and others have used this method in discussing twentieth-century works, and some essays in this collection also apply it to nineteenth-century literature. Jon Klancher's essay "English Romanticism and Cultural Production" warns of the risk of "making historical criticism a transhistorical echo of the politics of the present," and suggests that an emerging critique of Romanticism in Britain is attempting to break the bond between the ideologies of the past and the present and to refuse the estrangement of culture and politics that the Romantic writers proposed.[35] Klancher advocates the use of "cultural materialism" to avoid the Romantic opposition of power and culture, individual and society, and the New Historicist identification of them.[36] Cultural materialism, as practiced by Alan Sinfield, Jonathan Dollimore, and others, inquires "into relations of cultural practice and politics that cannot be posed as alternative between 'subversion' and 'containment.'"[37] In "The Sense of the Past," Stephen Bann examines the relation of image, text, and object in forming historical consciousness in nineteenth-century Britain.[38] Bann argues that historians have been unable to understand historical consciousness as it developed at this time because of the myth that nineteenth-century historians liberated history from literature and founded a historical science. He suggests a new understanding, akin to Foucault's, that would include the pursuits of archaeologist, antiquarian, and historian. Jonathan Arac's essay "The Struggle for the Cultural Heritage" discusses the implications for the canon of Christina Stead's response to or "refunctioning" of Charles Dickens and Mark Twain.[39] Arac's refunctioning of Stead examines issues that still obtain in political and cultural debates from "totality" and feminist strategies to an exploration of popular culture and mass media.[40] In "The Nation as Imagined Community," Jean Franco considers whether the term "national allegory" can be applied to Latin American novels that writers produce in places where "nation" represents a contested word or seems like "a vanished body."[41] Using Lizardi's *El Periquillo Sarniento* (1816), Azuela's *Los de abajo* (1816), and Hostos's *Pelerinaje de Boyoan* (1863) as examples of novels that debated the nation, Franco looks at the representation of nationhood in the modern novels of Fuentes, Llosa, Carpentier, Marquez, Bastos, and Julia. She suggests that "going back to the forties and fifties, the novel which, in the nineteenth century, had offered blueprints of national formation more and more became a skeptical reconstruction of past errors."[42] The range of New Historicism and related methods is extending more and more beyond the English Renaissance. Whatever contexts New Historicists discuss, their work can be controversial, which often shows that something lively is going on and that something is at stake.

Controversies

In some ways by being included in volumes on New Historicism, scholars identify themselves at least in part with it. The collection that Aram Vesser has put together demonstrates the range of scholars interested or participating in the multivalent movement of New Historicism.[43] In the "Introduction," Veeser describes New Historicism as transgressing the objectivity, specialization, and blandness of conventional scholarship, which, although perceptive to some extent and an effective polemical strategy, totalizes and generalizes scholarship as if all the predecessors or opponents of New Historicism never explored interdisciplinary boundaries in an attractive style.[44] Many of Veeser's points about the opposition to New Historicism seem correct, such as its threat to turf and method (deconstructionists and Marxists are as self-protective as old historicists and New Critics), but Marxists, philosophers, lawyers, and historiographers are concerned about evidence because of its centrality to discussions of the social, the political, and the cultural. This concern is not simply a "right-wing" revanche, although it can take this form.

Veeser effectively notes the basic assumptions of New Historicism without making it appear formulaic; agrees with its premise that through circulation, negotiation, and exchange, capitalism envelops critic and text; and observes that after his collection, it will be all the more difficult to dismiss this movement. In "Professing the Renaissance," Louis Montrose defends New Historicism from attacks, implicit and explicit, by those like J. Hillis Miller, who regret the return to history in literary studies, and those like Edward Pechter, Allan Bloom, and William Bennett, who oppose what they perceive to be a radical, leftist, or Marxist threat to the canon and traditional scholarly methods.[45] As in any battle, both sides offend and defend.

Both sides discuss the influences on New Historicism. Bacon, Marx, Nietzsche, cultural anthropologists like Clifford Geertz and Victor Turner, feminist works like *Sisterhood Is Powerful* (1960), the Warburg Institute, Michel Foucault, Stephen Orgel, Jacques Derrida, and other influences find their way into explanations of the origins of the movement. In "The Use and Misuse of Giambattista Vico," John Schaeffer looks at Vico's influence.[46] He hopes "to show why Vico's thought is critical to a theory of discourse and also critical of some of the theories which use him" and proposes that Vico's theory is more radical than Foucault's or Hayden White's because it constitutes a rhetorical paradigm that challenges rationalistic, secular, and ironic assumptions from the Enlightenment in current attempts to construct a theory of periodicity.[47] Although Schaeffer may be right in defending Vico's radicality, I cannot agree with him that Vico is pre-ironic because the ironic posture occurs in Plato, Aristotle, Cicero, Quintilian, More, Erasmus, and in others well before the Enlightenment, and it becomes increasingly complicated in post-Enlightenment ironists and ironologists like the Schlegels, Tieck, Solger, Müller, Hegel, and Kierkegaard. Ironic posture is not strictly a phenomenon of the Enlightenment.

In addition to discussing the influence of Marx and alluding to that of Geertz and Nietzsche on Greenblatt and the New Historicists, Frank Lentricchia's "Foucault's Legacy: A New Historicism?" concentrates on what its title suggests.[48] In examining the anecdote that ends *Renaissance Self-Fashioning*, which relies on the analogy or similitude between the Renaissance and now, Lentricchia thinks that as a Foucauldian, Greenblatt implies that we sustain a dream of free self-hood amid our disappointed liberal imagination because we think we know that the structure of power denies freedom everywhere else. New Historicism, Lentricchia says, is a representative story about the contemporary American academic intellectual, who frets about liberalism in the face of a presumed totalitarianism or that sustains totalitarianism as the denial of freedom except in a dream.[49]

Gerald Graff's "Co-optation" also discusses Foucault's influence on New Historicism, especially the later Foucault of *Discipline and Punish* and *The History of Sexuality*.[50] New Historicism calls into question the Romantic opposition of art as spiritual autonomy to the material world as alienation and repression, a questioning that Graff says is long overdue. He also asserts that the idea of the co-optation of power had its beginnings not in Foucault but in Baudelaire, Herbert Marcuse, the counterculture of the 1960s, and other sources.[51] Like Stanley Fish, Graff points to the embarrassment that New Historicists display when confronted with their own success, except that Graff speaks more specifically about "Left New Historicism": "The problem with the co-optation argument as often wielded by the Left is that it tends to cast an attitude of disapproval on success without making clear the conditions under which success might be legitimate."[52] Right New Historicists or neopragmatists like Fish, Steven Knapp, and Walter Benn Michaels are, in Graff's view, Foucauldians without Foucault's politics—they argue that since co-optation occurs in every form of culture, the idea of an oppositional position is silly. Graff cannot agree with their view that it is foolish to make any political judgments about cultural forms.[53] In the work of Fish and Michaels, Graff observes an apparent "conflict between the New Historicist tendency to over-specify the characteristics of discursive systems, in order to produce analyses of interpretive communities and literary works, and the pragmatist tendency . . . to dissociate those systems from specific practical uses."[54] Graff examines the confusion in oppositional criticism and shows his ambivalence over its possible demise.[55] Beyond these concerns, there are anthropological, poststructuralist, and textual aspects to New Historicism that suggest the intricacy and richness of this approach.

Anthropology, Poststructuralism, Textuality

In recent decades, anthropologists have been important to historians and literary scholars. There is a circulation between literary studies and cultural anthropology that manifests itself in suggestive ways. In "The Limits of Local Knowledge," Vincent Pecora analyzes the influence of Clifford Geertz on New Historicism.[56] He aptly observes: "Geertz introduces into cultural anthropology ideas borrowed, ironically from the present vantage, from literary studies—rhetorical analysis, Kenneth Burke's 'representative anecdotes,' the interpretation of cultural events as 'texts' which represent stories a society tells about itself to make sense of its life-world, the continual tacking between part and whole of the hermeneutic circle elaborated by Wilhelm Dilthey and by critics like Leo Spitzer."[57] After criticizing Geertz's work on Indonesia for ignoring the national and international politics of the time, and discussing related problems of methodology in New Historicist texts, Pecora concludes that Geertz's interpretative anthropology, which constitutes a cultural semiotics that resides behind New Historicism, conserves the dominant ethnocentric concerns.[58] Pecora also suggests that New Historicism tends toward a formalism that traps "the critic inside the semiotic systems he or she would wish to explain, even as the definition of such formative systems requires the assumption of a non-semiotic, non-textual outside which is to be shaped."[59] The distinction between inside and outside remains more problematic than New Historicists and other cultural semioticians have admitted. If New Historicists are self-conscious, they need to be more so.

In addition to anthropology, poststructuralism has also interacted with New Historicism. Both are textual. Whereas the poststructural view tends toward the philosophical, New Historicism leans toward history as its name would suggest. Historiography is the theoretical aspect of history, so it, too, is theoretical. There is a philosophy of history as well as one of literature. New Historicism and poststructuralism meet in the realm of interpretation. In "The New Historicism and other Old-Fashioned Topics," Brook Thomas observes the importance of a poststructuralist critique: if New Historicists seem to promise a novel understanding of the past, "poststructuralists, following Nietzsche, can argue that bringing about the new, requires an active forgetting, not remembering. Creation of the new, like representation, inevitably involves an act of repression."[60] Thomas historicizes New Historicism and poststructuralism. He discusses James Harvey Robinson's *The New History* (1912), and how poststructuralism shares much with the new history and the resulting relativism among progressive historians, especially in the latter's assumptions that historians do not scientifically or objectively recover the past but reconstruct it according to a present view.[61] If New Historicists tend to "reoccupy" the narratives of historicism from which they would break, poststructuralists, Thomas says, can practise the totalization they censure. New Historicists are caught in the contradiction that the past must matter for the present but that history cannot represent what the past was: in advocating an enabling tension between poststructuralism and New Historicism, Thomas rests his case on a paradox—"the present has an interest in maintaining a belief in disinterested inquiry into our past."[62]

Other critical inquiries question the place of New Historicism in relation to other historical and literary theories and practices. Elizabeth Fox-Genovese, Hayden White, and Stanley Fish all look at the notion of textuality that so concerns New Historicists. In "Literary Criticism and the Politics of the New Historicism," Fox-Genovese agrees with Fredric Jameson's view in *The Political Unconscious* that we must discuss questions of causation and extratextual "reality" and she asserts: "History cannot simply be reduced—or elevated—to a collection, theory, and practice of reading texts."[63] Unlike Thomas, she finds fault with historicism and criticizes New Historicism for denying that texts are products of and participants in a history that remains a structured set of social, political, and gender relations and that will allow the excluded their reclamation.[64]

Both Hayden White's "New Historicism: A Comment" and Stanley Fish's "Commentary: The Young and the Restless" address some of the issues raised throughout the collection.[65] White asserts that critics of New Historicism also ultimately construe history in textual terms and that they assume historical sequences to be "code-like" rather than "poetic" as New Historicists do.[66] The cultural poetics of New Historicism identifies aspects of historical sequences such as "the episodic, anecdotal, contingent, exotic, abjected, or simply uncanny" that "conduce to the breaking, revision, or weakening of the dominant codes."[67] Like the poetic, these aspects of history challenge both grammar and logic while expressing meaning. Like anyone who turns to history, New Historicists discover no specific historical approach to "history," but find only a philosophy of history, which depends as much on how one construes one's object of study as on one's knowledge of history itself.[68]

Fish aptly observes that these pleasurable essays "are not doing New Historicism, but talking about doing" it.[69] He also points out a recurring theoretical question that will become increasingly important for New Historicism: if you think, with Lynn Hunt, that history cannot be a "'referential ground of knowledge,' . . . 'how can you, without contradictions, make historical assertions?'"[70] The critique becomes subject to its own critique. Fish argues that one can argue for the textuality of history and make specific historical arguments, but that one cannot make those arguments following from the assertion that history is textual.[71] He also says that New Historicism asks us to be unhistorical and detached from the structures of politics and society when this demand is impossible in daily life. The New Historicists can effect professional change and enjoy its benefits but, unless the larger social and political structures change, they cannot be the acknowledged legislators of the world. Fish also asserts that we cannot stand simultaneously in a legal, historical, critical, or literary practice and survey its supports. For historicism to be new, it must assert a new truth and thus oppose, correct, or modify a previous one, but that newness cannot be methodological.[72]

Prophecy usually consists of a temporally extended hypothesis or projection or, in historical writing, of the future projecting a more recent past from a more distant past in order to make itself seem inevitable.[73] To avoid the snares of prophecy, I shall provide a guess: in discussions of New Historicism the methodological anxiety over whether the critic-theorist can be inside and outside his or her theory/practice, and the debate over the power or limitation of textual history will persist. With pleasure and anxiety, New Historicists and their supporters and critics may explore these questions in view of "society" and "politics" while redefining these very terms.

Like the anecdotes that often introduce New Historicist texts, New Historicism constitutes a complex and indirect practice that encourages a plurality of methods and interests, displays the ability to change, and shows the power to endure. In time and for various reasons the works of New Historicists will still be read.[74] Whether the work of New Historicists constitutes more access to reality than those in Veeser's collection might admit, it will become part of the recalcitrant histories in which they participate in their lives and in their texts. In lively and fractious voices the contributors show the vitality of New Historicism and the debate surrounding it. Besides historicism, I would like to discuss feminism and deconstruction to gauge the moment in theory in the 1980s and 1990s when text and context were part of the changes and controversies gripping departments of literature in the universities.

Texts/Contexts

Whereas New Historicism has attempted to decenter or reorient canonical texts, it cannot, like any mode or any school of literary theory or practice, do everything that needs to be done. Feminism and deconstruction bring other ways and other insights to thinking about literature as a field, or for reading and interpreting literary texts. Gender and textual uncertainty reorient the points of view of writers, readers, critics, and theorists. Ways of seeing differ in relation to traditional and received views of word and world, literature and society.

Feminism and deconstruction were new ways to view old texts, a means to see the world anew. Barbara Johnson was able to bring these two methods together in what she called feminist difference. Even though Johnson wrote eloquently on a number of topics and on aspects of difference, her work on gender and difference is what I would like to concentrate on here. Johnson's generation is probably the first in which women started to occupy a large number of leading roles in the humanities. Johnson's writing and her engagement with students and others in her teaching and her public talks exemplified the best of the scholar in the world and what in conversation she called textual lives. The relation between gender and difference was something Johnson discussed in ways that engendered understanding and further discussion.

Feminism has made a big difference this century. In literary studies it has transformed the field, and the way men and women read. Differences in gender have been not simply deconstructive of our ways of seeing and knowing, our perceptual and epistemological frames, but, perhaps, also of our ways of being, our ontological in-the-worldness. Difference itself questions the grammar of "our," and part of this inquiry and disruption has to do with gender. Can female and male be part of a collective possessive possessing a common humanity? Are people, regardless of gender, universal subjects that Aristotle, Plato, and many thinkers in the Enlightenment assumed for different reasons? Part of this exploration in difference relates to other distinctions, such as the theoretical trinity of race, class, and gender.[75] While this threefold difference of difference might seem to some to be the wearisome threesome, not so much because of the content or importance but owing to its repetition as a mantra in the currents of critical theory, race, class, and gender have transformed literary studies and have their basis in distinctions in lived experience.

World and word, text and context, to state the relation chiastically, have a difficult but significant connection. Difference, then, is not about a hermetic play of text alone, but, even in stating the intricacy and ironic regard between word and world, the context is something performed and lived and real. An awareness of the significant role of language and a skepticism about the unseemlessness, sometimes the unseemliness of language, prevents blunders into a transparently representative linguistic realm of an actual world. Our flesh is not a fiction but the words of our flesh are problematic. Language mediates our world but is not the world although it is part of it. Then there is that "our" that slips in and needs to be differentiated.

Feminist Difference

Difference is something Barbara Johnson discusses so articulately in *The Critical Difference* and *A World of Difference* that it is no surprise to find her reorienting the subject in *The Feminist Difference*.[76] What is most suggestive in the reconfiguration is the movement toward questions of poetry and authorial voice. While this poetics of feminist difference examines the now-familiar ground of psychoanalysis, race, and gender, it does so from an innovative cultural perspective. A brief introduction brings together this collection of essays that appeared in various publications from 1988 to 1995.

This introduction raises questions about the state of feminism in the 1990s. Johnson suggests that ambivalence is neither temporary nor unfortunate nor remediable, but "is perhaps the state of holding on to more than one story at a time" and agrees with bell hooks that contradiction is not a bad thing but can lead to change and transformation.[77] *The Feminist Difference*, according to Johnson, derives from simultaneous contradiction and transformation. She asserts that the United States has begun to starve the humanities as women have gained some power. Johnson's collection, then, is a call to look into the conflicts, contradictions, and ambivalences in the institutions of law and literature in the United States. In the vital relation between legal and literary conventions and rules Johnson also returns to the question of identity and social control, and of psychoanalysis for feminism. One of Johnson's principal interests is the nexus of the relations among feminism, psychoanalysis, and race. In the context of Jane Gallop's "transferential relation" to black feminism, Johnson observes: "It is sometimes as though psychoanalysis were being used by white feminists as a way of offering those French men *to* black feminists."[78] There have been, as Johnson says, black feminists, like Hortense Spillers, who have long been engaged with psychoanalysis and literature.

The method of *The Feminist Difference* is comparative: some of the essays juxtapose a text by an African-American with one that is psychoanalytical. Other essays depend on different kinds of pairings. In one comparison Patricia Williams and René Descartes "read" each other. In these comparisons Johnson wishes to maintain "literariness" and "literature," which "is important for feminism because literature can best be kept and opened for examination, where questions can be guarded and not forced into a premature validation of the available paradigms."[79] The utopian cultural work, which is not a predetermined canon, appears to be an unfolding space of freedom and consciousness, waiting for the future to avail itself so as to explore "those impossible contradictions that cannot yet be spoken."[80] What is refreshing here is a comparative method and interdisciplinarity that is not apologetic about literature and the literary, so that "it is the 'literariness' of the texts that resists and displaces the opposition."[81] This openness enables others in different future contexts to read and re-read binaries in ways beyond our present discourse and imagination.

Theory, Fiction, and Law

In her book Johnson shows a marvelous range in discussing feminist difference in connection with theoretical, fictional, and legal texts. Part One includes literary differences such as psychoanalysis, race, and gender. In the first chapter Johnson examines the analogy of female to male as ground is to figure, as well as relations between feminism and psychoanalysis in terms of failed cures in three texts by Nathaniel Hawthorne, Charlotte Perkins Gilman, and Sigmund Freud.[82] Among other matters, Johnson calls attention to the recursive figure of sexual difference—"in which both figure and ground, male and female, are recognizable, complementary forms"—the dream of psychoanalysis.[83] Silence and background in these texts become one of a number of important problematics. In the second chapter Johnson brings together Nella Larsen's novel *Quicksand* (1928), which W. E. B. Du Bois admired, and Heinz Kohut's self-psychology, which Lacanians have seen as an instance of being caught in the fictions of an autonymous self.[84] Here, Johnson is suggestive in asking questions about the relation between oral and written in literature and psychoanalysis, and among the self, narcissism, insight, and social change.

In the third chapter Johnson continues to stress the significant role of African-Americans in difference. She discusses Richard Wright's "Blueprint for Negro Writing" (1937)—in which he called for a collective voice of political and social consciousness rather than a suppliant and individual and bourgeois voice—and analyzes his novel *Native Son* and other texts. For Johnson, Wright envisions the black woman as his audience—the reader his writing must encounter.[85] In chapter 4 Johnson also brings into view the political nature of the aesthetic in politics, private life, and history, and takes the response of African-American critics to Toni Morrison's novels—as familiar, lost, and beloved—as a way into aesthetics. By concentrating on Morrison's *Sula*, Johnson is able to explore the relation between the detachment of aesthetics and the connectedness of rapport. The boundaries between the two become blurred in something oxymoronic. Morrison's novel represents home as familiar and strange, unsettles heterosexual institutions, and provides a representation mirror and recognition for black lesbians, displaced Southerners.[86]

Gender and poetry are the concerns of Part Two. Johnson returns in chapter 5 to Wright's "Blueprint" essay of 1937 in which he characterizes past "Negro writing" as a kind of servile curtsying to white America, or as being produced by poodles who do clever tricks for their masters.[87] Johnson chooses black writing from the 1770s, by Phillis Wheatley, Countee Cullen, and James Weldon Johnson, to examine Wright's claim and to uncover covert and implicit strategies of protest in black poets. Wheatley has had a problematic relation to her white masters and to her black successors, including critics, anthologists, novelists, and poets. English readers seem to have put John and Susannah Wheatley in an uncomfortable place because they asked why Phillis, whose work they helped to see into print, was still a slave. Johnson sees in Wheatley—who achieved freedom through the pressure of these readers—the first of a successful line who were able to manipulate and demystify "the narcissism inherent in white liberalism."[88]

Chapter 5 discusses poetry and gender in Charles Baudelaire, and in Marceline Desbordes-Valmore (1786–1859), someone whose poetry traditional critics and feminists have applauded or condemned often for the wrong reasons. Like Simone de Beauvoir, Johnson points out the false separation/division between the feminine and seriousness.[89] Johnson notes that Baudelaire and others, with misogyny in their minds, praised Desbordes-Valmore, and she suggests that the misunderstanding of this female poet provides an opportunity to take another look at the connections between the construction of gender and poetic convention.[90] In discussing Baudelaire's hysteria, Johnson sees masculinity as replacing sexual difference with self-difference and suggests with evocation: "Rhetoric is the domain of male self-difference reframed as universality."[91] In chapter 7, Johnson speaks about the envy in poetry of what is mute, invoking those who invoke silence, quiet, and muteness like Keats, Mallarmé, and Macleish. Does this muteness envy among canonical male poets, a displacement of the Freudian displacement of penis envy, relate to sexual difference?

Perhaps, as Johnson hypothesizes, the resistance to feminism arises from its substitution of speech for silence in women, thereby running interference with the self-pity that maintains patriarchy and telling "the truth behind the beauty of muteness envy."[92] Feminism reconfigures Keats's beauty and truth. Perhaps, as I would suggest, race and class also retell that tale and intricate that traditional figuration. Johnson has provided a wider context for difference here and in other books and essays.

Part Three examines the author's "voice." Chapter 8 puts on lesbian spectacles without making a spectacle of lesbians. Barbara Johnson examines Morrison's *Sula* and Larsen's *Passing* for their implicit, not explicit, lesbian plot and does so in terms of Barbara Smith's reading of the former and

Deborah McDowell's of the latter. Johnson is frank, courageous, and direct in talking about the political incorrectness of her fantasy life—how violence and power inform the unconscious and how the repetition of the unconscious and the desire for change in the political oppose each other and might change places.[93] To which I would add: desire and fantasy lives challenge and blend with the social and the political in the quest for the real. All of us, as humans, however, cannot always bear too much reality.

In chapter 9 Johnson switches emphasis to the alchemy of style and law. Like Patricia Williams, Johnson explores the connection between hierarchy and the ideology of style: Johnson reads Williams as we read Johnson, with and without difference. Reading and misreading vie just as Johnson tries to read Williams whereas the anonymous reader at Harvard, whose words the law seems to have protected with silence (Williams was not allowed to quote the assessor without his or her permission), misreads her. Johnson explores the controversy over the posthumous article—left unfinished by the murdered law professor, Mary Joe Frug—that was published unfinished, but with sensitivity and some reverence, and the spoof of which was projected at the annual banquet of the *Harvard Law Review*. The role of women in society and as writers enters into the connection between writing and reading besides Frug, Williams, Johnson, and those of us who read Johnson. Williams's *The Alchemy of Race and Rights* opposes Descartes's notion of methodical doubt in his *Meditations* because, according to Johnson, accustoming the mind to an independence from the senses "*underwrites* rather than eliminates prejudices."[94] In chapter 10, Johnson returns to Frug, and responds to her in terms of the postmodern in feminism.

This chapter was one of three responses that the *Harvard Law Review* solicited in reply to Frug's unfinished essay, "A Postmodernist Legal Manifesto." One of the important aspects of Frug's article was her response of being fascinated and terrified by the division of the feminist legal community over the campaign led by Andrea Dworkin and Catharine Mackinnon to enact an ordinance enabling women to have the possibility to recover damages for the harm pornography had done to them. From Frug's reaction to this campaign, Johnson sees that feminists have to face the misogyny in themselves as well as in patriarchy. Even though, for its own purposes, patriarchy has manipulated differences among women, "feminists have to take the risk of confronting and negotiating differences among women if we are ever to transform such differences into positive rather than negative forces in women's lives."[95] Such differences must be faced, and after Frug's terror and fascination, Johnson ends her essay and book with "It is up to us to go on in her place."[96] Does this "us" include Johnson, feminists, and a variety of readers beyond feminists, who have a difference of their own? The "we" and the "us" may be a room of feminists or feminists making room for women of all differences—and some men, despite the misogyny of Baudelaire, the muteness of Keats, and the strategic divisiveness of patriarchy.

Conclusions and Transitions

Barbara Johnson's book has much to say to the multitudinous "we" and "us" and should complicate the notion of "other" and "they." I have only touched on the theoretical and textual insights that she has presented with deftness. Part of the pleasure of reading Barbara Johnson is the way she brings theoretical, legal, and literary texts into a dialogue full of wit and irony, and of seriousness without leaden solemnity. Here, Johnson makes a difference once more in the world of textual lives and the living text of the world, where repetition and change play off and with each other.

Johnson explores questions surrounding authors and texts and does so in terms of the difference of gender. Poetry, race, and law supplement and make intricate the feminist difference. Her distinctive style and analysis brings together poetic worlds and society. What joins New Criticism and deconstruction in the works of de Man and others is the concern with close reading and with texts. Johnson shows a great sensitivity to poetics and rhetoric and takes each word, its tone, and turn and place, as it comes. She reads with care. Moreover, she brings to these texts a different point of view from Derrida or de Man or others in the Yale School. She came to talk about race in African-American texts, about law, and gender. Here was a deconstructionist who brought up and explored the difference it made in being a woman reading texts and making theory.

So text and context, philosophy and history are key to literary theory in the last four decades of the twentieth century. Fiction can mediate word and world. In earlier periods in English, the word "history" signified a story and a story about the past, so that literature and history, present and past seemed to meld. Poetry, which is the traditional core of literature, can represent the historical world, but its fictional nature complicates its historical content. Poetic worlds, the subject of the next chapter, yoke together in oxymoronic fashion fictionality and actuality in some putative place that might be called reality. Poetics and poetic worlds call attention to fictions while also being reminders of their connection to voice, ear, and eye, in the way people make sense of their lives, of the time and space that constitutes their days.

CHAPTER 6

Poetics and Poetic Worlds

Poetry is part of the textual lives Barbara Johnson spoke about, and her careful attention to language is something that has been in literary commentary and the study of poetics and rhetoric in the West since Homer. The poetic worlds the poet makes and the reader enters and the critic and theorist respond to have individual contexts but are also part of a cumulative experience or tradition. A tradition includes change and innovation, so it is not a museum. Johnson and others have helped to open up the canon to others not traditionally part of the tradition. We now have literature in English that includes more the texts of workers, women, African Americans, indigenous peoples, and others who wrote without thinking of themselves as literary. There are diaries, letters, testimonies, memorials, oral accounts, and many other works that are not the tragedies or epics Aristotle prized so highly. This is all to the good.

All sorts of texts can coexist and be part of the world of the discourse of literature. Although in this book and elsewhere I have discussed many different kinds of works by people of different periods and backgrounds, in this chapter, I shall examine poetry and poetics in terms of theorists and poets who are well known, from Aristotle through Philip Sidney and Shakespeare to W. B. Yeats and beyond. They still raise key questions and their elegance still attracts readers. So while I celebrate variety in writing, I also think it important to continue the long-time conversation about these figures.

As individuals, cultures, societies, and polities, we make stories, theories, arguments, and, in turn, interpret those, so that culture is a kind of lived interpretation and people and peoples are engaged in an interpretation of interpretation. A key question over the course of my life has been where fact ends and interpretation begins.[1] During the 1950s and 1960s a shift in criticism and then to theory occurred in Western Europe and North America. Just as critics could proclaim their independence and importance, not being simply helpers and guides through literature, so too they found themselves before the theoretical abyss. This occurred in a remarkably short period after the Second World War to the riots and protests of 1968. In the wake of the 1960s, theory became a central aspect of departments of literature, sometimes with great resistance, in the West. At the same time, in the Anglo-American world at least, philosophical modes of theory—such as deconstruction—which were somewhat related to New Criticism through an interest in rhetoric and close reading found a challenge in more historical and content methods like New Historicism, cultural materialism, feminism, and a new and displaced type of Marxism and psychoanalysis. Context pressured text and content form. It was no longer a disjunction between the unifying reading of New Criticism resisting the untying of the text through deconstruction, but a far more plural configuration than battled over meaning, genre, character, language, and structure.

Those central elements in literature and culture never really go away and are part of the conversation no matter how refracted. This is probably true north and south, east and west. When I speak about poetics and poetic worlds, it is in some ways a means of talking about form and content, textual and contextual realms. Poetry, interpretation, and the theory of poetry are central to language, literature, representation, and antimimetic modes of seeing, framing, and interpreting. Poetry, which is a synecdoche and sometimes a metonymy for literature and all the genres, has rubbed shoulders with philosophy in Plato and history and philosophy in Aristotle, so word and world are inseparable in Western poetics.[2]

Coming to Terms

Poetry and poetics are about hearing and seeing. As a term, "poetry" itself has taken on new meanings in English, so that accounting for semantic shifts is important. From the Renaissance through the Romantics—in Philip Sidney, Shakespeare, and W. B. Yeats—poetry assumes the beauty and the truth that John Keats saw in it. These poets, as well as the critics and theorists who discuss their work and poetry and poetics generally, recreate and transform the poetic tradition in English, drawing on the Greeks and the instruction and delight that Horace made so famous.[3] The *Oxford English Dictionary* (*OED*) gives a definition of "poetry" that embodies this shift from earlier definitions (although Longinus would not necessarily find it all that strange): the embodiment or expression of beauty through imagination, thought, or feeling, usually in metrical language but sometimes in nonmetrical language. Poetry can also sometimes be in prose: those who read Plutarch, Montaigne, Virginia Woolf, or James Joyce know the poetry of thought and expression that biography, essays, history, and philosophy can embody.[4]

Poetry and theory are also connected because theory can be poetic. This is not a surprise as Plato was a poetic philosopher and Aristotle is said to have written dialogues that have been lost. Although Jacques Derrida may have tried to turn Plato on his ear (aural as well as oral culture being looked at anew), he, too, has his poetry.[5] Moreover, Nietzsche, McLuhan, and Roland Barthes used suggestive aphorisms and narrative to express their thoughts: their theory has a poetics and vice versa.[6] Story complicates argument: poetics and theory read each other. Even though a distinction exists between the two, a blurring occurs here and there in ways that might suggest a reconciliation of the two in this age of theory or a false dichotomy or opposition. Hierarchies that would now place theory above poetry involve a move like Plato's subjugation or banishment of the poets in *Republic*. Plato's priority of philosophy helped to produce this attitude toward poetics, but doing the opposite is also limiting. The ranking of poetry, philosophy, and history, no matter how Plato, Aristotle, Sidney, and others have ranked them, is not something that helps, partly because it gets stuck in the valuation of the hierarchy of universals and particulars. Poetry and theory help us to understand the natural and human worlds. Theories can help explain the work of these fields as they do in science. Poetry, theory, and science can all coexist as modes of thought and imagination, and poetry is allowed the additional realm of feeling. A world without poetry, history, and philosophy would be the poorer, and many would say the same about science, theory, and technology. The spiritual and later Romantic notion of poetry is something that contrasts with the utilitarian or instrumental view that if time is money, then why make time for poetry? A poet has a role in an age of theory and technology in which a mechanized or mass-produced making is valued or seen to be good, useful, and productive.

Etymology reminds us that making and seeing are at the heart of the matter. The word "poet" has its origins in Greek: as is often the case, it came to English through intermediary languages on the Continent. It has an interesting history. The poet could be someone who wrote poetry or literature. This maker or practitioner could also be a theorist: Philip Sidney is a good case in point. Even in Elizabethan London, in which one of the great flourishes of literature occurred, Sidney could complain, as the *OED* records, "1581 SIDNEY Apol. Poetrie (Arb.) 71 The cause why it [Poesie] is not esteemed in Englande, is the fault of *Poet-apes, not Poets." England did not, even at this great moment, esteem poetry.[7]

What then would happen when in the last decades of the twentieth century, universities in English-speaking countries generally raised up cultural and literary theory above the practice of literature among its professors and as a form of discourse in the culture in general? Perhaps this was old news and it was always thus. Possibly, the Industrial Revolution (of William Blake's "black Satanic mills") or the technological revolution of McLuhan's global village were just new turns in a long story of poetry as an ornament, kept and fragile in a practical and political world. The craft might have always had to have been crafty to survive and profit. Songs and stories were maintained in a world driven by power and ideologies. On the other hand, some less-official aspects of religion and poetry lost the world for their souls. The spirit of poetry in a material world may well be, at least in many periods, precarious and uncertain, no matter how beautiful and true the expression and craft.

Making Poetic Worlds

Poetry is a making of poetic worlds that critics and theorists see and interpret. Even in etymology, the ancient Greeks saw critics and theorists as those who could see. The Greek *kritikos* meant to be able to discern whereas *theoria* suggested contemplation and *theorein* signified to observe.[8] Two connected ways of seeing led to a shift in literary studies in the 1960s: the critical path and theoretical way. The critic became the theorist. Explaining what a text meant and how the author constructed theme, character, and structure to produce meaning or an effect on the reader were still topics for those who advocated a hermeneutics of suspicion or a skepticism about the possibility of stable meaning in literary and other texts.

Poetry as making and theory as seeing or perceiving are caught up together. Poet and theorist need not be prophet or seer, but they are related through recognition and interpretation. The etymology of "theory" contains within it long-standing tensions. The origins of the English word derived from the Italian, which came from the Latin, which borrowed from the Greek. As the *OED* tells us, in late Latin *theoria* came from Greek, which meant viewing, a looking at, speculation, contemplation, theory, sight. About the turn of the seventeenth century, theory also came into English as a spectacle. Richard Hooker understood in discussing the church that "theory" was a scheme, method, or principles. From the 1630s, the word was used in natural philosophy as ideas or generalizations that account for a body of facts or phenomena, a hypothesis to be tested by experiment or observation, or the general laws or principles of something known or observed. Theory could also mean being oblivious to the facts, hypothetical but unproven. The theory and practice of poetry may be two very different things. This controversy over poetry has been, in this language, long-standing. Ambivalence over theory permeates the English language. English has derogatory words for theory and theorists— perhaps even worse than poetaster or versifier. Ambivalence characterizes historical attitudes from the early eighteenth century to the late twentieth century.[9] The poet, a maker, is the subject to the eye or gaze of the looker/ seer/thinker, but he or she has other perspectives to represent. This view involves a tension between images and words, imagination and thought.

The word "poetry" is not so straightforward in its history and etymology. In English during the fifteenth century, poetry could also mean a treatise or theory or a critical view of poetry. Geoffrey Chaucer used poetry as a general fiction or fable, but also employed "poetry" in its modern English sense.[10] Even though Horace, Galifridus Anglicus, and others have written their arts of poetry—their theories—in verse, poetry is then a kind of special writing different from the prose of contemporary theory. Historically, in English poetry can mean literature and it can also be theory, so that in terms of intellectual history, it makes it hard to separate the terms "poetry," "literature," and "history." Making and story mix with ways of seeing in the swirl of speaking, writing, hearing, and reading.

Poetics and poetic worlds, the made world of the poet and the hearer-reader, are matters of interpretation and recognition. Reading connects writer and reader. Whereas the original senses of the verb "read" meant taking care or charge, it also signified having or exercising control over something. To read could also mean taking or giving counsel. Shedding light on something obscure is basic to various uses of words related to "read" in Germanic languages. Reading is an interpretation of texts, ordinary speech, and everyday works.[11] "Interpreting," which suggests spreading or spreading out (perhaps dissemination), comes from roots that convey the idea of expounding, translating, explaining, and understanding.[12] Reading and interpreting poetry are cultural activities. The root of "culture" points to cultivation. As I have argued more extensively elsewhere, to interpret culture is to read the signs of what is cultivated in various communities with their continuities and discontinuities.[13] The etymology of "recognition" involves a thorough acquaintance with something, investigation, or getting to know once more. Reading poetry or the poetic world it represents is an engagement in and about culture. This reading and even thinking about poetry and poetics are ways of perceiving built around moments of coming back to knowing, thinking, and seeing what texts, speech, and images grow up over time and what they might suggest.

The making of poetry is a form of cultivation and craft. It is important to be aware that culture, interpreting (interpretation), recognition, and reading are all contested and suggestive terms. Poetry is read in a cooperation-contest between poet and reader. There are comic, tragic, and historical aspects of "discovery" for poet, reader, critic, and theorist. A central question becomes one of whether there is a poetics that applies to the different ways of discussing culture. Recognition is a moment that involves an apparent, possible, or actual movement from ignorance to knowledge or self-knowledge. It can represent all kinds of experience from the comic through the absurd to the tragic. A moment of discovery or recognition can bring about many different effects from relief through terror to suspicion. In practice and theory, what is story and what is argument, or do all the makings of poetry merge word, image, myth, and ideology? In other words, the relation between mythology and ideology, story and argument, and the blurring of these terms into story-argument is an important point of departure in poetry, reading, and theory as part of the poetic world, whose possibilities are and are not representative of the actual world. Is everything balanced in the between of story-argument?[14]

Possible and actual worlds interact. Word and world intertwine: the distinction between texts and contexts, as Hayden White has said, has become problematized.[15] Fictional and possible worlds intermingle, so to divide them through definition is more a matter of necessary convenience than determined accuracy. Such distinctions, as in Doreen Maitre's between a possible nonactual world and a possible actual world, defy simple and clear-cut division, and suggest reciprocal interaction between fantasy and actual worlds.[16] Delight and instruction, even in Horace, are not readily divisible, so that the distinction between possible and actual worlds is problematic, especially in theory. Delight, deflection, and escape, as I once noted, are not frivolous activities. Poetry and poetic worlds are not nugatory.

Fiction does not diminish poetry and poetics because no writing can long escape imagination and speculation beyond the here and now, beyond the known facts. Legal fictions permeate our society, and the history of science is full of discredited or revised theorems and laws that we now regard as inaccurate, even as myths and fictions, as failed explanations, or as beautiful plotting. In time history can turn truth into fiction. Today's reality is tomorrow's historical fiction. The world of ideal and matter, mind and body, are inseparable. The aesthetic has its own pragmatics. The apparent uselessness of poetry has its apparent use.

Not everything is actual or actualized, real or realized. Poetry represents beauty and truth in a kind of reciprocity that John Keats represented.[17] Possibility, probability, and necessity become ways of discussing fantasy and verisimilitude. A mixture occurs, and seldom is the fantastic and the verisimilitudinous in a pure state. Poetry provides a space for a wide range of linguistic and representational strategies and effects. Poetic possible worlds are a kind of fictional world.

The putative and possible are aspects of the fictional, of which poetry is a prime genre. Fiction is not necessarily what Plato and those church fathers, who adapted his view, thought, a copy of nature that is more illusory the more it veers from nature.[18] Form and content constitute meaning and are part of recognition and "reading." The poet is speaker and hearer, writer and reader, speaking the truth as he or she professed or telling the noble lie as Plato suggested.[19] The decaying of lying is Oscar Wilde's comic, satiric, and ironic take of the writer's lot in the modern world. In the library of a country house in Nottinghamshire, Wilde's two interlocutors in "The Decay of Lying" (1889), Cyril and Vivian, debate the truth of lying. The attitude of art for art's sake helps to raise the question of self-sustaining aesthetic in the face of morality and the representational world. At the end of the dialogue, Cyril asks Vivian to clarify her new aesthetics. She replies in terms of three doctrines: "Art never expresses anything but itself"; "All bad art comes from returning to Life and Nature, and elevating them into ideals"; and "Life imitates Art far more than Art imitates Life."[20] Vivian also sets out two corollaries: "External Nature also imitates Art" and "Lying, the telling of beautiful untrue things, is the proper aim of Art."[21] The spirit of John Keats and Walter Pater is also in these views. How reliable is the poet or writer is something that has been a preoccupation from Plato to Wilde and beyond.

Faith and reliability become issues in the relation between poetry and poetic worlds. It is also interesting to question, as Thomas Pavel does, the reliability of texts representing worlds faithfully because the assumption of a reliable text is an act of faith.[22] The flux of Shakespeare's texts is a case in point, as he did not have copyright (which began in the first decade of the eighteenth century in England) and did not seem to oversee the printing of his plays and poems. His friends and fellow actors, Henry Condell and John Heminges, to whom he left mourning rings, were those who as editors brought together his collected plays. About half of the plays were unpublished until this First Folio in 1623, which probably followed the collection and publication of Ben Jonson's works in 1616 (the year Shakespeare died), and some of the dramas, such as *Hamlet*, had good quartos and bad quartos. Here is one example of textual instability. Even the attempt to establish a sound and stable text of James Joyce's *Ulysses* in recent decades shows that even in our age of typewriters, electronics, and computers, texts are protean. The poetic poetry and prose of Shakespeare and Joyce are matters of flux both in terms of text and interpretation. How and what are we recognizing? The relation between instability and unreliability is an open question. The light of history is refractory; fiction shares distance and relevance with other activities. Like Pavel the novelist and theorist, I tell fables, use metaphors, and see in the theory of fiction the importance of logic, game theory, linguistics, and science.[23] Poetry and poetics blur like art and the world imitating each other (if we are to believe Wilde), so that we come to understand and be what we see in an ever-changing dance of being, making, perception, interpretation, misinterpretation, misrecognition, and recognition.

Poetry involves narrative, argument, image, and suggestion. Poetics generally has a theoretical and personal or psychological aspect: seeing and perceiving, and making up one's mind about the matter at hand, suggest possibilities in the relation between poet as speaker and writer and the audience (auditors, readers). Jerome Bruner relates actual and possible worlds, theory, and psychology. Take the case of story, for instance. There exist two modes of coming to terms with narrative: one is of bringing to a text argument and theory, and another is of working from the text. This distinction can blur, into what I have called elsewhere, story-argument, where narrative and thesis intertwine.[24] The poet is a maker, one of the key world makers. It is interesting to see Bruner's own variations on world making, a process akin to recognition and interpretation. Reality is not something set but involves an interaction in the semantic process. Reason and imagination are part of a poem's making of a poetic world. Bruner recognizes the elasticity of the real and describes how discourse enlists the imagination. In this context, he speaks of three aspects of the human subjunctive in which discourse, rather than establishing certainties, opens up possibilities, allowing the reader to create his or her own world or virtual text. First, presupposition is the creation of meanings; second, subjectification is the depiction of reality through the protagonist's consciousness; and third, multiple perspective is beholding the world prismatically. The making and interpretation of a poem involve creativity, self-awareness, and multiplicity in seeing. Language, mind, and vision are all connected in Bruner's exploration of possible worlds.[25] While recognizing the importance of literary texts generally and poems specifically, we should realize the significance of the role of other kinds of texts and images. Poems are key types of representation but are part of a larger group of texts and works of art.

Do lyric poems really tell stories or put forward arguments, or are they the illusions of story and argument, are questions not readily answered? Is the movement of a poem like that of an essay or a logical argument? Perhaps even in a lyric, which is not a narrative poem, some form of story-argument comes into play. Mythology and ideology are intertwined in so many kinds of texts, could it be so in that type of text most thought to be beyond plotting and ideology—the lyric? Can lyric poetry resist the temptation and pressures of ideology? Narrative, political, and dramatic poetry certainly cannot escape the tension between mythology and ideology. The history play, as Shakespeare shows, mixes the aesthetic with the political, past stories with present pressures. Shakespeare also transformed sources, such as Plutarch's lives and the chronicles by Hall and Holinshed, into dramatic poetry.[26] Here and in other genres, whether a story-argument is enough is a question for all of us. Writers are readers and readers are writers. For instance, Shakespeare wrote plays, acted in them, and presumably attended and read plays, including his own. Writerly readers may be fictionalizing fictions as much as realizing them. Narratives make history, science, and fiction, so that these human knowledges share something. Conversely, argument occurs in all three. The actual-possible world is an intricate continuum. Poetry sees and hears and is seen and heard. The practice and the theory of poetry involve ways of seeing.

This visionary matter is ongoing. Recognitions and readings do not need to be final, solid, and definitive. They might suggest intuition, insight, knowledge, and wisdom that change with texts and images and with readers and audiences coming back to them. Poetry and its forms, like plays by Shakespeare, are putative and provisional. Subject and object change over time in a dance. Poetry dwells between the poet and the audience in a single poem and in the collectivity of poems.

Story and Argument

Poetry and mythology might be connected through story. The numbers of poetry, music, and mathematics join them—rhythm, symmetry, time, and space belong to poetic, musical, and mathematical forms. Nonetheless, the muse of poetry may share certain aspirations and inspirations with that of music and that of mathematics but can never be identical with them. Being in the words of language used every day to communicate, poetry cannot be as readily abstract or free of content. And content gets in the way of a poetry of mathematics or even, more putatively and controversially, in abstract music (more and more in the past decades, discussions of ideology in music have arisen).[27] Mythology and ideology can seem inseparable in verbal forms, even in some lyric poetry. In other words, the *mythos* or *muthos* of story has a hard time keeping clear of the argument of ideology. Mythos has the root sense from ancient Greek of speech, narrative, fiction, myth, and plot: Aristotle uses the term in *Poetics* (1449b5, 1450a4, 1451a16).[28] Since then, mythos has taken on various meanings. During the eighteenth and nineteenth centuries, mythos and mythoi often appeared in English in discussions of myths or stories in the Bible or classical poetry, such as Homer's. Mythos was used to mean a mythology—a body of interconnected myths or stories, in particular religious, political, or cultural tradition (that is, a personal or collective ideology or set of beliefs)—long before George Orwell and Roland Barthes, in English and French respectively. Political writers from the 1840s onward in the United States were using the word.[29] As Destutt de Tracy in the 1790s conceived of ideology, it was a science or system of ideas, but the world could also mean abstract speculation, idealism, and the way in which ideas are expressed.[30] Thomas Jefferson and John Adams responded to Tracy's coinage.

As with irony and a number of political, literary, or rhetorical terms—as we have just seen with "ideology," "mythos" expanded its sense over time. After the Second World War, Northrop Frye extended to any narrative form Aristotle's use of the word "mythos" with regard to drama, the meaning of a structuring of events in a text, particularly in terms of archetypal themes or patterns.[31] Despite the intricacies in relating myth and ideology, the opposition between the mythological and ideological helps to clarify the relations between form and content. For instance, in the middle ground of dialectics, mythology and ideology clash and contend. As words move in speech or writing, they often do not progress. Language often contains story-argument or argumentative story, both varying mixtures of the rhetorical imperative to move the audience to action in the world and the poetic practice to move in the putative world of fiction.[32] Even lyric poetry, as we shall see, can mix the political and the aesthetic.

How much is shown or suggested and how much is told and explained is hard to discern and harder to divide. The relation between mythology and ideology is a troubled one. Although an aspect of modernist poetics involved a sense that a poetic space free from politics existed, many theories of literature in recent decades have emphasized the political and ideological bent of poetry.[33] A political element abides in poetry, but going over completely to a politics or sociology of poetry would neglect its aesthetic dimension. What distinguishes poetry as poetry, the mythos and music that might be intertwined with politics and history but are not identical to them, constitutes a central concern here. The untranslatable in poetry makes up what we desire poetry to be. We must try to translate that which cannot be translated in poetry in our cultural conversation even within a language and its literature, not to mention between languages and literatures. Poetry, like the archive, throws up unforeseeable questions and a textual messiness that thwarts and modifies theories even as it invites them.

Ideas and myths contend in and between poems and their interpretations. Whereas ideology is the motive to convince, to convert, to control, mythology is the desire to enchant, to evoke, to sing. This coexistence or uneasy existence of mythology and ideology (confused because they are sometimes used as synonyms) extends to sacred texts. Gnomic utterance and riddles also have the same evocative and connotative quality. A parable by Christ is a story that suggests, whereas if the interpretation of that parable is codified and systematized, then it becomes doctrine and dogma. Religion turns to theology. Poetry becomes codified and framed in criticism and theory. Even though systematic knowledge is helpful and might even be necessary, universals also need particulars. A kind of secular hermeneutics, criticism can also become, in its systematic form, a secular theology. The commentary on the Bible, Homer, Virgil, and Dante came to exceed the lines glossed by a multiplier. Comment transformed the sacred and secular scriptures into paraphrase, explanation, and a sea of words beyond the economy and perdurable mystery of the utterance, which so goaded the Platonic Socrates in his evaluation of Homer and the poets.

A need seems to exist to tame poetry or to bring it into a more readily understandable community of readers or a society bent on making the inexplicable explainable. Natural philosophy, then science, had this same movement to interrogate nature. Poetry may well invite explication, but that invitation to interpretation can turn the craft of words, the made poem, into a fetish. The encrustations of interpretation can become an allegory, a metonymy for the poem itself. A theory can be tested against a poem or many poems, but this does not always produce the kind of verifiable results that testing a hypothesis through an experiment involving natural phenomena does in science. In poetry and the humanities, opinion and politics seem more overt than in science, especially in the pure sciences of physics and mathematics. Political criticism can not only seek to be a substitute for poetry but can also try to displace or squash poetics. This rivalry between philosophy and poetry is played out in the tenth book of Plato's *Republic*. If only, Socrates argues in the climax of this great work of his student, poets would sing a hymn to the republic, then they would not need to be exiled.[34] The most poetic of philosophers, who had a penchant for ideological allegory, embodied the mixing of story and argument. Neither poetry nor philosophy is entirely itself. Nor, it seems, is philosophy, so this complicates any quarrel between them. Criticism is also split, for it divided into criticism or hermeneutics and into theory or philosophy. Although the shift in recent years from philosophy to sociology, cultural studies, and politics has allowed for new perspectives, with this turn, theory has also neglected, and in some cases denounced, the formal properties of poetry. To pretend that poetry has no content is perilous, but to reduce poems to their content is also a peril. Philosophy, history, and poetry—or theory, historicism, and the literary— should be able to coexist and, through comparison and interaction, flourish. The mythology I am speculating on is not the return to purity or the fear of the stranger, but rather, that speech and writing that have the power of openness over time, an expression that opens readers and audience to experience and thought. The truth of beauty, no matter how dangerous and seductive, endures and invites readers now and later to return to a poem or to poetry. Buffon's equation of the person and the style, something Alexander Pope and Matthew Arnold also struck on in their own ways, may not be so far from the voice of the poet and the hearing of the audience.[35] The double movement of the aesthetic of poetry—seduction and the suggestion of something beyond manipulation—confuses, confounds, and invites in the dance between poets and their audience.

W. B. Yeats and Seamus Heaney

Stories have a setting: poems can tell stories and place them in a context that mixes the actual with the possible, shaping a kind of imaginative geography. Tone and character—even of the speaker or narrator—can be imbued in place. The land can be given ideological interpretations, but does poetry try to free it from that or is it just a subtler purveyor of ideology? Lands can be made into a symbolic that makes for nations and states, nationalism and patriotism.

Irish poets, like W. B. Yeats and Seamus Heaney, are good instances of poets who have a noumenal feel for the land but also represent it as a political phenomenon. Yeats wrote in English and is part of an English-speaking tradition of poetry even as he speaks about and learns from a Gaelic Ireland. The first line of "The Song of the Happy Shepherd," the first poem in *Crossways* (1889), is quite consciously in this English tradition, even as it draws from a wider European context. Yeats's pastoral, his Irish georgic, combines the everyday in the first stanza of "The Lake Isle of Innisfree" with the more abstract notions of peace. "No Second Troy" in *The Green Helmet and Other Poems* (1910) employs descriptions of the body to ask questions about a typology between Troy and a present state like Troy. In *Responsibilities* (1914), Yeats uses natural setting in political poetry, for instance, in "September 1913"—with its well-known chorus, "Romantic Ireland's dead and gone, / It's with O'Leary in the grave."[36] The opening of "Easter 1916" sets out the everyday in a poem that is a more general political incantation of Irish martyrs and a people terribly born. "A Prayer for my Daughter" is a meditation on beauty and innocence before arrogance and hatred. The opening stanza of "Sailing to Byzantium," which itself begins *The Tower* (1928), weaves the past of Byzantium with the present of Yeats's Ireland and beyond. The tower where Yeats lived is as symbolic as it is actual, and the poet refines its emblematic significance in *The Winding Stair and Other Poems* (1933), something especially apparent in the first part of "Blood and the Moon." The moon is a world of wisdom found in death free of ideology: whether this is an illusion or a dream that cannot be realized or sustained in life is something the poem raises. The physical stair and the tower become a multitude of symbols lit by emblematic light in a world caught between eternity and change, violence and peace. The tension between being a good maker and a political seer or prophet continues to the end of Yeats's life as a poet. In *Last Poems* (1938–39), Yeats brings together land and mythology. In "Under Ben Bulben," especially in the opening stanza, Yeats connects various figures and landscapes with Ireland. Later in this poem, the speaker implores: "Irish poets learn your trade / Sing whatever is well made." The collection ends with "Politics," which has for its epigraph a quotation from Thomas Mann: "In our time the destiny of man presents its meanings in political terms." The poetic and the political, structural in Yeats's last book, are in tension.

Seamus Heaney also has a gift for enlivening a landscape, of giving phenomena a noumenal quality. The earth and land he chronicles are sometimes strained in the stresses of politics. In "Digging" and "Follower," which appeared in *Death of a Naturalist* (1966), Heaney shows a sureness of description of the land as an actual symbolic, something real and imaginative at the same time. "Thatcher," from *Door into the Dark* (1969), continues this marvelous expression of the physicality of this rural world. An overt political stance in the refusal of being identified as "British" occurs in *An Open Letter* (1983), which ends with "But British, no, the name's not right."[37] The poet defines his identity and nation, what he makes of it and not simply the political divides or boundaries in the actual world. Although not strictly a lyrical poem, *Sweeney Astray* (1983, rpt. 1984) represents the figure of Sweeney through an imagined history that has mythical and literary implications in a way that Cymbeline and Lear interested Shakespeare.[38] Earlier sources are reworked and amplified in poetry. In "Clearances," which appeared in *The Haw Lantern* (1987), Heaney uses physical setting to join personal history with the religious past of his country.[39] A cobblestone thrown at the speaker's great-grandmother has a presence past and present in a typology between ancestor and descendant: it is palpable, a part of nature that is hurled as an element of the religious divide at the heart of Ireland's troubles. The beautiful concrete images in this poem and others by Heaney yoke land as natural place and land as political state. Poetics and politics once more dwell uneasily in the same house, field, or poem.

The revolution of poetry, like that of time, takes on many turns. Poetry turns toward and away from the ideological pressures in which the poets live. Their words embody and flee history. The lyric poem creates a time timeless, but can then break the fold of that myth with a gesture toward history. And so the content of a historical allusion can turn the attention away from form or at least blend the two. The return of ideology threatens the mythology of a pure poetry made for a poetic world but not tarnished with the workaday cares of an actual world. Ways of seeing the land and the scene can be evocative, a suggestion of a descriptive, psychological, political, or symbolic landscape, something diachronic and synchronic, all within the *poiesis* of time and space. Ireland is a place of poetry and politics blended and contentious. Poets see through language and through describing nature. The description of place involves observation, translation, and evocation in a poetic drama of recognition and interpretation. What is more difficult is what truth and beauty and what politics and aesthetics are being recognized and interpreted and by and for whom. Identity is a landscape and an utterance, caught between the practice and theory of language that poetry invokes and evokes. And this was also true of Shakespeare as much as it is of Yeats and Heaney.

Shakespeare

Shakespeare has been many things to many people over the centuries. University students in his day lauded him in a Latin play as if he were the equal of the great Greek dramatists and theory. He wrote sonnets, played at court, and blended thought and feeling in blank verse on the public stage. The dramatic interplay of the language of his characters in various genres— tragedy, comedy, and history—expressed feelings and thoughts in such a way as to make the audience wonder whether there was as much philosophy and history as poetry in this verse for the theater. Shakespeare represented so many ways of seeing that critics and theorists, as well as audiences and readers, have seen so much in him. The German Romantics and Samuel Taylor Coleridge saw Shakespeare as a philosophical poet and the exemplar of an irony that expanded on the Socratic irony that Plato had developed, which itself was a stance or embodiment of a role and method beyond the rhetorical meaning of irony of saying one thing and meaning the opposite (or sometimes something different).[40]

Shakespeare's characters speak of the realm of philosophers and critics. Hamlet himself brings up the nature of philosophy. In a scene where the ghost of his father, Hamlet Senior, appears before Horatio and Hamlet, Shakespeare mixes comedy and debate with the supernatural:

> *Gho.* Sweare.
>
> *Ham.* Well said old Mole, can'st worke i'th' ground so fast?
> A worthy Pioner, once more remoue good friends.

Hor. Oh day and night: but this is wondrous strange.

Ham. And therefore as a stranger giue it welcome.
There are more things in Heauen and Earth, Horatio,
Then are dream't of in our Philosophy. But come,
Here as before, neuer so helpe you mercy,
How strange or odde so ere I beare my selfe;
(As I perchance heereafter shall thinke meet
To put an Anticke disposition on:)
That you at such time seeing me, neuer shall
With Armes encombred thus, or thus, head shake;
Or by pronouncing of some doubtfull Phrase;
As well, we know, or we could and if we would,
Or if we list to speake; or there be and if there might,
Or such ambiguous giuing out to note,
That you know ought of me; this not to doe:
So grace and mercy at your most neede helpe you:
Sweare.

Ghost. Sweare.[41]

Hamlet jokes about the ghost of his father being an old mole, while Horatio, a student at Wittenberg, is struck by wonder. Is seeing believing in this case? Horatio is rational and skeptical and now is dumbfounded. The Ghost frames this reaction with a desire for Hamlet to swear an oath, something that will set the revenge and counter-revenge in motion. Hamlet picks up on Horatio's use of the word "strange" and comments on it and its cognate "stranger" and from that concludes that he himself will make strange, render himself a stranger, as a result of these events, and put on an antic disposition, that is, pretend not to see or know what he does as a defense in a world that is not familiar. This is the world that has more in it than the boundaries of philosophy. Hamlet is constructing his own critique, building his own theory, and will see the world and be seen by others in a way of his making. He will inhabit the riddle that is an ancient theme of literature and philosophy—the nature of appearance and reality.

And in a passage from the Second Quarto of 1604, which is not in the First Folio of 1623, Hamlet also sees philosophy as an agent of inquiry, for at act 2, scene 2, he continues his expatiation on the word "strange":

It is not very strange, for my Vncle is King of Denmarke, and those that would make mouths at him while my father liued, giue twenty, fortie, fifty, a hundred duckets a peece, for his Picture in little, s'bloud there is somthing in this more then naturall, if Philosophie could find it out.[42]

Here, the prince speaks with "Rosencraus and Guyldensterne." Hamlet's philosophy would seek beyond the natural for the truth of the matter. He would like to interrogate the unusual and unsettling events in which he now discovers himself. Seeking or finding is the role of this philosophy. What can be seen on the surface is not enough.

Hamlet comments on ambiguity and language itself and uses conditionals and subjunctives and not a world indicative of ready description and perception. He uses the word "know" amid the oblique and uncertain scene in which he has encountered the ghost of his father, who, it turns out, did not die a natural death, but was murdered. This scene draws out Hamlet's "prophetic soul" and turns his world upside-down. Hamlet must have the wariness of a critic and the role-playing of an actor to test this world against his theory of it. He does much of this through language.

When Polonius tries to smoke Hamlet out about the cause of his madness, Hamlet uses his antic disposition to turn the tables on Polonius. What is actual and antic madness is a central question of the play. Hamlet, the other characters, and the audience attempt to separate the actual in a seeming world. Is it love that has made Hamlet mad or behave like a madman? Is it self-defense? Is it a way to catch Claudius and others in his snare (like the play-within-the play, "The Mousetrap")? Perhaps it is seeing the Ghost and having his world inverted and obscured, the news of murder, and the incestuous marriage his mother is in so unwittingly that drive Hamlet to his antics or madness. The dramatic irony—the gap between what Polonius thinks he knows and what the audience knows—is also a matter of seeing and not seeing. In act 2, scene 2, Polonius tries to outmaneuver Hamlet but to no avail:

> *Pol.* How say you by that? Still harping on my daughter:
> yet he knew me not at first; he said I was a Fishmonger:
> he is farre gone, farre gone: and truly in my youth,
> I suffred much extreamity for loue: very neere this. Ile
> speake to him againe. What do you read my Lord?
>
> *Ham.* Words, words, words.
>
> *Pol.* What is the matter, my Lord?
>
> *Ham.* Betweene who?
>
> *Pol.* I meane the matter you meane, my Lord.

Ham. Slanders Sir: for the Satyricall slaue saies here,
that old men haue gray Beards; that their faces are wrinkled;
their eyes purging thicke Amber, or Plum-Tree
Gumme: and that they haue a plentifull locke of Wit,
together with weake Hammes. All which Sir, though I
most powerfully, and potently beleeue; yet I holde it
not Honestie to haue it thus set downe: For you your
selfe Sir, should be old as I am, if like a Crab you could
go backward.

Pol. Though this be madnesse,
Yet there is Method in't: will you walke
Out of the ayre my Lord?

Ham. Into my Graue?

Pol. Indeed that is out o'th' Ayre:
How pregnant (sometimes) his Replies are?
A happinesse,
That often Madnesse hits on,
Which Reason and Sanitie could not
So prosperously be deliuer'd of.
I will leaue him,
And sodainely contriue the meanes of meeting
Betweene him, and my daughter.
My Honourable Lord, I will most humbly
Take my leaue of you.

Ham. You cannot Sir take from me any thing, that I
will more willingly part withall, except my life, my
life.

Hamlet uses riddles and occasional pregnant replies to impress and confound Polonius, who is wise enough to know there is method in Hamlet's madness but not to what end. Polonius misunderstands that the sole cause of Hamlet's alienation or madness is a thwarted love between Ophelia and Hamlet. Interpretation and misinterpretation, recognition and misrecognition contend in an attempt to understand and construct meaning from verbal exchanges and events. Hamlet's satirical stance and words play with Polonius as the wise counselor who gave his son, Laertes, advice, more than meets his match. Polonius is a man given to words (he makes a living from them and has attained the highest post available to those who advise), but Hamlet is probably the greatest master of language in Shakespeare's plays and perhaps in Western literature. Hamlet and Socrates would have a great debate.

Shakespeare uses the words "philosophy" and "critic" in ways that are telling. These examples should suggest how Shakespeare gives a dimension to knowing and seeing. There is a comic dimension to philosophy, that is, no matter how serious it is, characters in comedy and even comic characters discuss it. In act 1, scene 1 of *Taming of the Shrew*, Lucentio says:

> And therefore, Tranio, for the time I study,
> Virtue and that part of philosophy
> Will I apply that treats of happiness
> By virtue specially to be achieved.
> Tell me thy mind; for I have Pisa left
> And am to Padua come, as he that leaves
> A shallow plash to plunge him in the deep
> And with satiety seeks to quench his thirst.
>   *Tranio Mi perdonato*, gentle master mine,
> I am in all affected as yourself;
> Glad that you thus continue your resolve
> To suck the sweets of sweet philosophy.
> Only, good master, while we do admire
> This virtue and this moral discipline,
> Let's be no stoics nor no stocks, I pray;
> Or so devote to Aristotle's cheques
> As Ovid be an outcast quite abjured:
> Balk logic with acquaintance that you have
> And practise rhetoric in your common talk;
> Music and poesy use to quicken you;
> The mathematics and the metaphysics,
> Fall to them as you find your stomach serves you;
> No profit grows where is no pleasure ta'en:
> In brief, sir, study what you most affect. (lines 17–40)

This exchange represents philosophy in terms of virtue, happiness, appetite, and pleasure. Tranio balances Aristotle with Ovid, and philosophy with logic, rhetoric, music, mathematics, and metaphyics. In act 3, scene 1, Lucentio amplifies this relation between philosophy and music, which occurs through harmony:

> Preposterous ass, that never read so far
> To know the cause why music was ordain'd!

Was it not to refresh the mind of man
After his studies or his usual pain?
Then give me leave to read philosophy,
And while I pause, serve in your harmony. (lines 9–14)

He chides a blind, ignorant and unread attitude and opposes it with his desire to read philosophy. Learning and philosophy become part of a satirical and comic world that tends toward *cognitio*.

Other instances pit philosophy against the ordinary world. In act 1, scene 1 of *Love's Labor's Lost,* Dumain speaks of himself in the third person as if he were a character caught in the world:

My loving lord, Dumain is mortified:
The grosser manner of these world's delights
He throws upon the gross world's baser slaves:
To love, to wealth, to pomp, I pine and die;
With all these living in philosophy. (lines 28–32)

The delights of the world are gross, and philosophy, perhaps ironically given what happens to the cloistered realm proposed in this comedy, seems a higher calling. This comic and civic current of Renaissance philosophy is in the world, so the ideal and real are inseparable. In *As You Like It,* Touchstone is a fool or clown much in the court, so when he finds himself in the green world of the comic countryside, he tells the shepherd about what is good and bad about his country life. At one point, Touchstone asks him in act 2, scene 2: "Hast any philosophy in thee, shepherd?" But philosophy is sometimes made to feel its limitations in the everyday world. In act 3, scene 3 of *Romeo and Juliet*, Friar Laurence, for example, urges philosophy on Romeo, who resists:

I'll give thee armour to keep off that word:
Adversity's sweet milk, philosophy,
To comfort thee, though thou art banished.
    Romeo Yet "banished"? Hang up philosophy!
Unless philosophy can make a Juliet,
Displant a town, reverse a prince's doom,
It helps not, it prevails not: talk no more. (lines 54–60)

For Romeo, philosophy is talk, mere words that cannot affect people and effect real change and action in the world. Philosophy does not solve the hurdles in Romeo's life.

Philosophy also occurs in politics and the councils of war in ancient Greece and Rome. The Roman conspirators against Caesar or champions of the republic as they see themselves talk of philosophy. In act 4, scene 3 of *Julius Caesar*, when a crisis has come upon those who have rid Rome of Caesar, Cassius sees philosophy as a steadying virtue: "Of your philosophy you make no use, / If you give place to accidental evils" (lines 145–146). In act 5, scene 1, Brutus arms himself against a sea of troubles and wonders whether by opposing he should end them. Should he be a Stoic in the face of adversity and dishonor? He says:

> Even by the rule of that philosophy
> By which I did blame Cato for the death
> Which he did give himself, I know not how,
> But I do find it cowardly and vile,
> For fear of what might fall, so to prevent
> The time of life: arming myself with patience
> To stay the providence of some high powers
> That govern us below. (lines 100–107)

Philosophy is used to defy the vicissitudes, fear, and fate that life brings. Cassius and Brutus interpret the past needs and aspirations of Rome quite differently from the way Octavius and Antony do. Men see what they will. The victors do not appeal to philosophy, but their practical realpolitik and strategies in battle win the day. Cicero, a philosopher, dies in such a Rome.

A friction occurs between words and world, thought and action, philosophy and politics in another play about key events in Greek and Roman antiquity. In *Troilus and Cressida* at act 2, scene 2, in a situation given to passion, war, and revenge, Hector appeals to philosophy and reason:

> Paris and Troilus, you have both said well,
> And on the cause and question now in hand
> Have glozed, but superficially: not much
> Unlike young men, whom Aristotle thought
> Unfit to hear moral philosophy:
> The reasons you allege do more conduce
> To the hot passion of distemper'd blood
> Than to make up a free determination
> 'Twixt right and wrong, for pleasure and revenge
> Have ears more deaf than adders to the voice
> Of any true decision. (lines 163–173)

Hector, who will ironically meet a sad end at the hands of Achilles, counsels deep thinking and a determination of what is right. Decisions should not be made in the heat of passion. His remarks, wise as they are, swim against the main current of the play, in which the consequences of the taking of Helen and the betrayal in the love of Troilus and Cressida—the passion of private love—are reflected in the public conflict of war and politics. This is a play of words—Ulysses's speech on degree in act 1, scene 3 probably being the most renowned—about a famous, extended, and extenuated action: the Trojan War. Shakespeare sets up debate in the council of war and brings in philosophy like a Trojan horse.

The word "critic" appears in *Love's Labor's Lost* and in Sonnet 112. Even though theorist and critic are given high regard in the academic culture of the late twentieth century, in Shakespeare's work theorist does not appear in name, and critic appears in unflattering company. In *Love's Labor's Lost* two instances show this comic context. In act 3, scene 1, Biron [Berowne] exclaims:

> And I, forsooth, in love! I, that have been love's whip;
> A very beadle to a humorous sigh;
> A critic, nay, a night-watch constable;
> A domineering pedant o'er the boy;
> Than whom no mortal so magnificent! (lines 174–183)

A critic is sandwiched between a beadle and a constable and leads to a pedant. This is some visionary or prophetic company. This character may, and this playwright does, see the limits of such a persona. Trying to see in the company of love and the blindness Cupid brings is not always easy. In act 4, scene 3, Biron says: "Now step I forth to whip hypocrisy." Then he proclaims in a language full of references to seeing:

> Ah, good my liege, I pray thee, pardon me!
> Good heart, what grace hast thou, thus to reprove
> These worms for loving, that art most in love?
> Your eyes do make no coaches; in your tears
> There is no certain princess that appears;
> You'll not be perjured, 'tis a hateful thing;
> Tush, none but minstrels like of sonneting!
> But are you not ashamed? nay, are you not,
> All three of you, to be thus much o'ershot?
> You found his mote; the king your mote did see;
> But I a beam do find in each of three.

O, what a scene of foolery have I seen,
Of sighs, of groans, of sorrow and of teen!
O me, with what strict patience have I sat,
To see a king transformed to a gnat!
To see great Hercules whipping a gig,
And profound Solomon to tune a jig,
And Nestor play at push-pin with the boys,
And critic Timon laugh at idle toys!
Where lies thy grief, O, tell me, good Dumain?
And gentle Longaville, where lies thy pain?
And where my liege's? all about the breast:
A caudle, ho! (lines 150–172)

Biron alludes to Matthew 7:3–5 to show the blindness of people who see small faults in others (mote) and not their own great shortcomings (beam). The speaker's theme is wisdom and folly among the great, and, in response, the king calls this view Biron's overview. Nestor, the oldest and wisest among the Greeks, as well as strong Hercules, wise Solomon, misanthropic Timon, a critic, like the king, can be reduced to bagatelles, dances, idleness, tops, and tunes. Biron maintains a balance between critical distance and satirical excoriation. This whipping of hypocrisy can be a sport and even Biron can be blinded by Cupid in the lost labor of love. Love and war, here and in the Trojan War (as Nestor knew), can turn passion against the most reasonable, critical, and philosophical man. The women use their wit in *Love's Labor's Lost* to show the folly of these men who would closet themselves from the world in their Academe, which, as Anne Barton notes, "is never in any real danger of succeeding."[43] The wit Biron and his fellows use can be a block to perception or recognition. They are often in love with love rather than with the women of the play. Neither a Platonic nor Plato's academy, this Academe, for which death was the pretext, will not bring philosophy and wisdom because the chaos of comedy needs blindness and deafness to rule, at least in the transgressive middle of things, before the end brings in its new comic order. The women teach with their words and then men, even at the end of the play, have much to learn about the relation of words to the new world in which they find themselves.[44]

Being deaf or blind is a theme of knowing and not knowing in Shakespeare's plays and poems. In the examples discussed in this section, this has been a key thread in the allusions to the philosophical and the critical. The speaker in Sonnet 112 speaks about his beloved's "love and pity," so that emotion becomes a central focus once more for Shakespeare. They brand the speaker's brow through public scandal despite his indifference to their opinion and the state of his reputation. The beloved covers with grass the speaker's faults and approves of his good points, although the quatrain ends with a question mark, so this is a query more than a statement of fact. The speaker says that the beloved or person addressed is all the world to him and speaks with a tongue whose praise and shame the speaker seeks to know. No one else can affect his steeled feelings, right or wrong. And that brings the speaker to these lines:

> In so profound abysm I throw all care
> Of others' voices, that my adder's sense
> To critic and to flatterer stopped are.
> Mark how with my neglect I do dispense:
> You are so strongly in my purpose bred
> That all the world besides methinks are dead. (lines 10–14)

The speaker throws all care in a deep void or chasm, the caring about the voices of others or the care with which they speak. This is a deafness the speaker has taken on knowingly even as it seals him off from a world except in his beloved as a world. Here Shakespeare appeals in his allusion to the adder to Psalm 58:4 in which the adder has deaf ears. The speaker is deaf to critic and flatterer, which is an amplification of line 3 about not caring about reputation. He excuses his own indifference to others and their views. The couplet reinforces what the sonnet has elaborated on, that is, the speaker is so obsessed with, or so dogged in his pursuit of, his beloved that the person addressed is all the world and that the world besides that addressee is, in the speaker's view—"methinks"—dead. Love once more with its passion washes over everything. Here, reason is used to justify emotion and to eclipse the public world with a private world of love.

Ends and Transitions

The critical and the philosophical, then, are important concerns in the poems and plays of Shakespeare. This is but one of the aspects of poetry and poetic worlds discussed here. By looking at the roots of the words, "poetry," "theory," "criticism," or their cognates, it was interesting to observe the role of the senses, especially seeing, in the metaphors of recognition or coming to knowledge. The friction between and the overlap of mythology and ideology, story and argument, complicate the connection between word and world, poetry and poetic worlds (as well as the theory of fictional and poetic worlds). Oscar Wilde, W. B. Yeats, Seamus Heaney, and Shakespeare all suggest something about poetry and poetic worlds, whether in terms of wit and irony, life and art, truth and lies, physical and symbolic setting, understanding and misunderstanding, or wisdom and foolishness. Poetry is a flexible medium that embodies the truth it seeks.

Poetry might share with mathematics and physics forms of intuition and thinking like metaphor, logic, and analogy, but it cannot be checked with a proof. The possible and fictional worlds, such as dream and hypothesis, can be compared to this world and can tell us something about nature and human experience and their interpretation, but they do not have the mathematical precision of the binary language of computers. Leibniz, the coinventor of calculus, was the founder of possible world theory, which has had implications for game theory, literary theory, and other disciplines.[45] Human wishes, aspirations, and frustrations are the truth of poetry. But Hamlet and Werther never die the way Shakespeare and Goethe do. Achilles lives in the text and mind of the reader whether Homer was one poet or many. Literary theory begins in earnest with Plato and Aristotle and owes a debt to Longinus, Aquinas, and others.[46] It is something between philosophy and history (as poetry is) and is and is not connected to literature. Beginning with works like Northrop Frye's *Anatomy of Criticism* (1957), literary criticism and theory declared their independence. Poetry may be now more accessible than ever, through the Internet, but how robust is it? The power of words has always been both great and tenuous. Poetry in an age of theory and technology is a situation that is an intensification of the contexts of earlier ages from ancient Greece onward.

Poetry is a kind of making and theory is a way of seeing. The critic or theorist sees or tries to put into perspective the thing made or the collection of things made for the author or genre or in the context of poetry or literature in general. Sometimes this involves cultural and historical contexts. So making and seeing, text and context, are all complementary and lead writer and reader toward understanding or attempts at recognition and knowledge. Comparative Literature or World Literature often encourage comparative and global contexts more than national literatures usually afford. This can apply as much to theory as to literature itself. There is a dimension to literary studies in Britain, North America, and beyond that came to involve what was once called French theory. Moreover, law, history, sociology, philosophy, and other fields were brought to bear in the areas of literary theory and literary studies.

The subject and his or her relation to ideology and notions of otherness became keys to the study of literature in the English-speaking world. From the 1960s until by the end of the 1980s or beginning of the 1990s, such approaches had become commonplace. Sometimes it is important to examine works that have not found their way much into English but have made contributions to the debates over the status of literature and society. In the next chapter, among other things, I would like to discuss texts in French that concentrate on the stereotype.

CHAPTER 7

Literature, Theory, and After

During the 1960s a move from commentary and New Criticism through structuralism to poststructuralism occurred in the English-speaking world, and this would not have been possible without those theorists working in Paris. The question of the translation of study and language relates to the translation of texts from language to language. English and French have a long relation, their interplay going back about a 1,000 years, and translation between the two languages is of great importance. At one time, I studied the French and English uses of the example of Spain, their translation of Spanish texts, and translation those languages French and English in the representation of the New World from 1492 to 1713.[1] The 1960s and the decades that followed became important for the translation of French texts in literary theory into English. Sometimes significant texts are not translated or are slow to be translated. The texts I begin with were available only in French when I wrote, so part of my task was to "translate" them into the English-speaking sphere through a discussion of the texts and not by direct translation of the texts into English versions.

This is where I begin this chapter. I end it with a brief examination of Terry Eagleton's *After Theory*. If the age of theory was born in the 1950s and the 1960s, then the question becomes whether we are posttheory, just as the poststructuralists were after the structuralists, who came after earlier schools. A supplementary question is whether it is possible to be after theory because theory is a way of seeing, a means into the texts and contexts. In the last chapter, we saw that *kritikos* signified being able to discern, *theoria* suggested contemplation, and *theorein* meant to observe; so if the poet makes, the critic discerns, and the theorist contemplates and observes, at least in their basic operations, then poetry, practical criticism, and theory should exist for as long as literature does. It might be better to say that theory intensified in the 1960s and in its wake, and in recent years the urge to theory has somewhat abated in explicit or institutional forms. Perhaps people are taking a rest or are back to more practical ways of studying literature and culture. Practice and theory are always in a dance in different disciplines and in the way in which they are configured in universities and associations. There is an ebb and flow in the affairs of people.

Translation itself is vexed because poetry is notoriously difficult to translate. In some ways the translator becomes the new author in another language. There is some mediation involved and there is loss and gain. This is so whether it is a matter of translating poetry or theory.

Stereotyping Translation/Translating the Stereotype

In the French tradition there is a discourse that is not easy to translate into English. As hard as the translators of Barthes, Derrida, Foucault, Kristeva, and Cixous have tried, much is lost in translation. The French discourse of theory, whether it dwells on subjectivity, ideology, or the stereotype, loses very little when it is addressed in the United States and Canada in the work of theorists like Shoshana Felman and Daniel Castillo Durante, respectively.[2] They write in French. Translation can also mean gains, and this can also be true of geographic translation, as in the case of theorists like Felman and Castillo Durante, writing in North America in a context that relates to Paris even as it differs from it. This cultural transmission and exchange prevents each national culture from imploding or losing touch with the ever-swirling changes of history.

Translation from language to language is unavoidable in cultural exchange. The French have developed their own Freud just as the Americans have developed their own Derrida. There is nothing wrong with this as long as the host culture realizes that it is changing and reworking the authors and movements it chooses to translate. In fact, the host culture needs to make these adaptations or the exchange would be a kind of dead colonialism. Having said all this, I return to my opening sentence: the discourse of French theory does not quite translate into English.

Since the late eighteenth century, Americans have tried to circumvent London through Paris, and have also ventured to other capitals on the Continent. This exchange with Continental Europe has enriched American cultural and intellectual life, and the English have also made their culture vital through cultural exchange. Sometimes, however, as with the importation of literary theory from Germany and France into Britain, Canada, and Australia, the translation of abstraction does not always do well in the concrete and empirical realm of English. The English sounds like a translation even though the words are in English. Translation is absolutely necessary but it is limited. This is one of the principal arguments for language training in our schools and universities and for Comparative Literature as a discipline. But few are listening to this argument in Canada. Cultural studies, an ally of Comparative Literature, is in danger, at least in English-speaking countries, of flattening out linguistic and generic differences, of reading all languages in amnesiac translation into the lingua franca—English.

The law of genre—as anyone knows who is familiar with the Spanish and English differences from Italian and French theories and practices during the sixteenth and seventeenth centuries—is different in French and in English. In Britain, the neoclassical generic code had to come to terms with Shakespeare. In France, it had to wait for Hugo. The neoclassical had a greater and longer grip on French literary theory and practice than on literary theory and practice in Britain. Having involved a great deal of feedback from the United States to Britain and the Continent, cultural exchange in this century has become more complicated. The globalization of culture, particularly of American popular culture, complicates translation even more. English speakers are sent out messages that English is all they need: Hollywood, popular music, and television spread their images throughout the globe. We forget the dubbing and subtitles and, in forgetting or neglecting other languages, we have nothing against which to contrast our language and therefore our culture.

Stereotypes and Recycling

My task here is to tell an English-speaking audience why a theory of the stereotype in literature, written in French, is important and needs to be translated, while admitting that the very recycling that Castillo Durante discusses means that we can only recycle his theory in English, and that something of the French milieu and expression is lost in translation. In Canada, which is blessed with the collision of French and English, it is particularly important to understand his theory of the stereotype in literature and culture. Nonetheless, this theory would be useful in any country.

Castillo Durante begins *Du stéréotype a la littérature* with an epigraph from Antoine Arnauld and Pierre Nicole in 1662 on how people prefer to load up their minds with all kinds of discourse and maxims and thereby obscure truth with falsity. But Castillo Durante juxtaposes to this a quotation from Roland Barthes in 1973 on the stereotype, where he says that Nietzsche observes that the truth is the solidification of old metaphors, so that stereotype, a kind of solid metaphoricity, is the road to truth. These epigraphs help to focus on the paradox that lies at the heart of Castillo Durante's amplificatory theory of the stereotype in modern literature as the fossilization and the way to truth.[3] They also suggest a cross-cultural translation among German, French, and English as well as the friction between truth as the goal of philosophy and the linguistic relativization of truth in rhetoric. The conflict between philosophy and rhetoric, and accommodations between them, occupies the center of Castillo Durante's argument. He combines an understanding of Barthes's rhetorical unmasking of language as stereotypes expressing mythology or ideology with a reassessment of Aristotle's *Topics* as a means of mediating between rhetoric and its tropes. Castillo Durante thereby effects a comprehension of stereotypes and its rapport with the literary.[4]

The intellectual context of Castillo Durante's theory begins with Barthes and Aristotle. Leaving Aristotle aside for a moment, Castillo Durante's engagement with Barthes leads to other theorists. Barthes's notion of the stereotype in *Le Plaisir du texte* depends on its unmasking as something natural and sufficient for different contexts and not as variable imitations.[5] Elsewhere, Barthes discusses the double sign of realism in the context of the *doxa* and in connection with Brecht's alienation effect. The ideological operation of such a realistic sign is an imitation that erases its imitation of nature and thereby presents itself as natural.[6] Only through estrangement or alienation can art, in Brecht's view, constitute itself properly. The alienation effect distinguishes between past and present, and it does not delude the audience into thinking that human nature is eternal and essential. Louis Althusser is another French theorist who explores the *ideologeme*, the smallest unit of ideology, and, in English, Raymond Williams and Terry Eagleton have examined the nostalgia and aesthetics of ideology. There are, however, French theorists who, like Paul Ricoeur, do not see metaphor as a means of representing ideology. In English, Northrop Frye views metaphor, along with literary form, as embodying counterideology or mythology.[7] The poet breaks up cliché through an innovative use of metaphor and generic convention. Story baffles argument. Castillo Durante's decision to develop a theory of stereotype places him in the thick of the crucial debate over the relation between mythology and ideology, story and argument.

His discussion of stereotypes owes something to Barthes and this ideological context, but it also draws on Jacques Lacan and others for psychological and sociological frameworks. This book is an epistemological study of the stereotype as it applies to the literary text. Castillo Durante thrives on cultural exchange in his analysis of the relation between stereotype and cliché. He points out the use of the word "epistemology" in English before "épistémologie" in French, so that by taking an epistemological approach to stereotype, Castillo Durante is leading French readers through common ground with English-speaking culture.[8] Focusing on the role of repetition in stereotyping, Castillo Durante proposes that we examine the stereotype on several phenomenological levels and not simply according to Genette's narratological approach. While reminding us of Kierkegaard's work in the field, Castillo Durante argues that repetition cannot be reduced to a pure natural function and that the world is like a theater of repetition.[9] In order to explore the complex role of stereotype in literature, Castillo Durante performs several close analyses of literary texts. His hypothesis is that the stereotype as a principle presupposes a regulative role in the economy of discourse. The metaphor of economy pervades Castillo Durante's discussion of stereotypicality. The stereotype presents ways of representing without being taken up in the representations it generates. Castillo Durante envisages the stereotype as the element that assures the system of its transition toward extinction. Stereotypes often pass unperceived.[10] García Lorca's "Ode to Walt Whitman," a Spanish poem on an American poet declaring a Monroe doctrine for English in the New World, serves as a means of demonstrating that stereotypes reactivate a unified borrowed discourse—such as commonplaces, proverbs, and received ideas.[11] Castillo Durante crosses cultural and linguistic boundaries to examine the ideologeme in the stereotype of "blood." He also looks at the autobiographical stereotype in Rousseau's *Confessions*.[12]

Histrionic Borrowing

Stereotypes are monological and not, in Bakhtin's terms, dialogical, but they also relate closely to Kristeva's notion of intertextuality.[13] Castillo Durante calls attention to the histrionic nature of borrowing.[14] He examines borrowing as the play between the subject and the other as well as the play of the other. A thought that cannot overcome the obstacles of a petrified language can only produce copies.[15] In the context of ideology, Castillo Durante discusses the stereotype as an "invariant" of modernity, as something that affirms the paradoxical ontology of the copy, which involves in its repetition usury and echo. Topoi, as Aristotle observes, are thoughts that have individual forms within their combined structure of thought. The logic of the stereotype in relation to the cliché is a dynamic agon between them.[16] Is it not possible that this dynamism makes it difficult to separate stereotype and cliché into an opposition?

Reading is relation to the other, but the pleasure of the text resides in the body of the reader.[17] This kind of autoerotism or onanism in Castillo Durante's reader echoes Rousseau's joy in masturbation, Barthes's literary hedonism, and Derrida's supplement. This onanistic activity determines a suspension between the text and the reader's gaze, a regard that is also a self-regard that helps to decide the accidental nature of his humanity or subjectivity.[18] In speaking about the relation between the stereotype and the cliché, Castillo Durante uses the language of economics, something that Marx did when discussing culture (which he did not do enough), and a way of analyzing culture that was prevalent during the 1980s. Castillo Durante looks to Bourdieu (1982) in this regard, and has affinities with Stephen Greenblatt (1988), whose New Historicism often centers on negotiation and exchange.[19] Here, Castillo Durante uses the example of Baudelaire's *Les Fleurs du mal* to demonstrate the economy of signs.[20] Perhaps, like Flaubert, Baudelaire represents the cliché of the nineteenth-century bourgeois in such a stereotypical manner that he becomes caught up in the ideology and doxology he seeks to expose.[21] While recycling Lacan's Other and Althusser's subject, Castillo Durante seeks a middle way between them. He calls on Michel Pêcheux's notion of a preconstruct as a means of understanding the topoi or structure of the stereotype, and thus of ideology itself. But Castillo Durante questions Pêcheux's tendency to equate or form a homology between Lacan's Other and Althusser's ideology.[22] Whereas Castillo Durante's middle way is one of distinguishing between Lacan and Althusser in order to use them to find a critical path, Pêcheux's is one of likening them to make his own way. Castillo Durante's critical path has something to do with Kant's and the etymological underpinnings of the Greek *krino* as a judge. Judgment requires distance. Perhaps there are criteria that enable one to find a way between subjectivity and ideology.

Borrowed Thought/Loaned Language

What makes a stereotype is the heart of Castillo Durante's book. To understand the relation between the subject and language, we have to comprehend the difference between borrowed thought or loaned language (such as the cliché) and the stereotype.[23] This is the task Castillo Durante sets for himself. He traces the epistemological and critical play of the stereotype from the seminal moment of the publication of Rabelais's *Gargantua* in 1534 through the work of Sade to Sábato and the present. Castillo Durante asks: What does the stereotype wish in saying what it says? He sets up the idea of the metatopic or metatopos as a way of answering that question, which has important implications for the study of ideology. The stereotype is part of the clichéd images it generates because it develops strategies tied to a metatopic economy of discourse. This is the reason, Castillo Durante argues, that the stereotype is confounded with the cliché, which is the product it helps to produce, but the cliché resists all efforts of renewal. Even an attempt to disturb and divert the cliché by calling attention to its ludic and parodic aspects only serves to reinforce its logic.[24] Here, Castillo Durante differs from Barthes by refusing to equate stereotype and cliché. He is interested in the usury of borrowed or preformed thought, how it separates itself from its stereotypical context, and how the stereotype usurps the impersonal as a means of reproducing itself. This impersonality resembles Adorno's analysis of the ideology of the impersonal command and the "it is" construction as a means of underscoring social practice as natural (doxa). In fact, Adorno's critique of Heidegger in terms of jargon and authenticity, no matter how errant it is, helps Castillo Durante frame his inquiry into doxological discourse.[25] Unlike Adorno, Castillo Durante sees that Heidegger understands poetry as a means to depetrify language.

The logic of the subjectivity of the stereotype is that of the copy, which is katoptronic, that is, reflective, reflexive, and mirroring. What is borrowed is reflected as law. Here, Castillo Durante brings together the Althusserian summons and the Lacanian mirror. The subject reflects the stereotypical summons of which it is the object, so that there the ideological character of the clichéd statement discovers its ties to the law. Summoned to exhibit and produce oneself as a copy as long as it conforms to the law, the stereotypical subject loses sight of the direction in which it is moving. Castillo Durante borrows and translates the English phrase, "double bind," to describe the situation of that subject. But the subject is also a multiplier of copies. The void of the law to which its desire is tied (perhaps constrained) determines the stereotypical spiral in which it shuts up its speech. The subject itself delivers the guarantee of its historicity, which is also true for its lack of being. (I use the neuter for his or her in the case of the subject.) Here, Castillo Durante is alluding to the Lacanian castration of male and female in the gaze of patriarchal signification. Behind this lack of being is Heidegger's nothingness, which, paradoxically, reveals our being. This doubly allusive lack also suggests "discharge," which in turn signals a libidinal economy between psychoanalysis and philosophy.[26] Castillo Durante is recalling, at least in the background, Freud's pleasure principle, which depends on repetition.[27] In Castillo Durante, the extreme novels of Sade and Sábato act as the test cases that define the epistemological limits of stereotypical language. Castillo Durante explores the relation between discharge and nothingness in the text.[28] Discharge is orgasm, release, and dumping ground—perhaps a place for recycling—and nothingness is, after Heidegger, a condition of the revelation of being. Castillo Durante plays on puns, such as "la petite mort," orgasm as a shadow of death, so that we live and die in a paradoxical condition between being and nothingness. In English we can excavate this punning that occurs between love and death. On several occasions, Shakespeare evokes the Elizabethan pun on the cognates of "death," which yokes dying with orgasm.

The periphery is also important in looking at the violence articulated through official history. Castillo Durante speaks about Latin America in this context.[29] How are Sade and sadism, even as postmodern texts *avant la lettre*, viewed from the Peru that Rousseau alludes to in his *Confessions*? The Sadian (as opposed to Sadist) enterprise, which involves paradoxical texts, is founded on an epistemological-critical vision of pleasure (joy, delight, and enjoyment). It attempts to break through the armor of presupposition that serves as a base for the flourishing of the stereotyped other. Whether one can get outside of play ("hors-jeu") through an excess of play, if there is enough play in the system, is debatable. "Hors-jeu" might recall, for those of us who have lived with ice hockey in Canada—where "hors-jeu" is an offside and thus a violation of a rule that results in a brief stoppage in the game where the two sides contend in a face-off—that breaking a rule is also a return to the rule in the confines of a system. The same unruly rule might be extrapolated from football or soccer.[30] Without being too playful, we might see what gives with Derrida's famous and much allegorized allegorical declaration that there is nothing outside the text, if we take the text to be play, something done for pleasure itself, something that gives. Is it possible to pass beyond the resistance that blocks a multidisciplinary approach to the problematic of the stereotype?[31]

Irony/Subjectivity

The irony of the novel provides Castillo Durante with a way of analyzing subjectivity. In his view, the literary text, insofar as it is ironic materialization, already presupposes expiation as an inevitable corollary. Castillo Durante shares with Lukács the notion that irony is the interaction between two complex ethics, and he sees the literary text as a struggle between two instances that annul the subjectivity of the creator to the benefit of a complex and polyphonic structure. This irony resembles the kind the Romantics like the Schlegels, Tieck, Solger, and others analyzed in the greatest revolution in irony since the Platonic Socrates. This is an irony that drove Hegel to criticize those chattering after Friedrich Schlegel for continuing his negativity and led Kierkegaard to modify Hegel's critique, and in some ways influence Marx's dialectic and the philosophy of Heidegger. In practice, this is a kind of katascopic or overviewing irony, an objective subjectivity or intersubjectivity, that Aristophanes used in his plays and that, as I have argued, Shakespeare puts into play in his dramatic representations of

English history.[32] Theory often catches up with literature. I was delighted to find that Castillo Durante ended with irony as a way of finding an opening in the ideological machine of discourse. In English-speaking countries, the deconstructive dismissal of irony as a remnant of New Criticism has obscured the contributions of deconstruction to the debate on irony and the range of the ironic in Western culture. Irony can be structural, and it can undo its own structure. It can be neutral in the clash of subjectivities in a representation. In short, it is dramatic.

Another interesting aspect of Castillo Durante's interpretation of Sade is his perception of the connection between irony and fallenness (of the Fall). This position counters that of Pierre Klossowski, who speaks about Sade's remorse.[33] Castillo Durante asserts that irony strives in vain to model the real and not the converse. As this relation is mentioned briefly in terms of the residue or discharge associated with Sade's metatopical text, it is not certain how much Castillo Durante would concede the Augustinian irony of the gap between the City of God and the earthly city as types of the Fall in Eden into history. This tradition is evident in the Middle Ages, as Ernst Kantorowicz demonstrates in his seminal discussion of the political theology of the king's two bodies. Shakespeare explores similar ground in his history plays and nowhere more than in *Richard II*.[34] In our age the sacred and theological aspects of this kind of irony have been displaced into more secular political, social, and literary contexts. Sade transgresses some of the boundaries between the sacred and the profane in ways that would have been apparent to his contemporaries, and that might be said to prefigure or inform postmodern theoretical debates on ideology. Castillo Durante comprehends the need to understand stereotypes and their relation to cliché as a central mechanism in the production and reproduction of ideology. The metatopical text submits language to the test for its own excremental function or discharge. Castillo Durante is well aware of the displacement of the spiritual into the material, and this is one of the grounds on which he differs from Klossowski in the interpretation of Sade.[35]

By subverting instrumental discourse, the metatopical text acts as an epistemological-critical limit. Reified reason is confronted with the agony of the subject under the reign of modernity. The individual is like the refuse of his own desire, is the person in which desire cannot be stereotyped. The novel, which is a kind of metatopical discharge, assigns to itself the role of an evaluator of the cesspool of discourse. The only discharge is writing. The future is the past through repetition. In relation to the other by means of the cliché, the stereotype makes of language a place for recycling where the subject is both the user and the prisoner of language. Here, I have, with some elision, translated parts of the last paragraph of Castillo Durante's book. As in many modern debates on language, from Peirce and Saussure onward, it becomes the center of the world in the human sciences. Is there a way out of the prison house of language or are we caught on the horns of a dilemma? Perhaps the pleasure and wisdom of paradox is where we move as we are tossed on a great ideological sea.[36] But that also leads us to the pleasures of metaphor, which I leave for another time, but, as Philip Sidney and Heidegger knew, poetry can move us in many ways. In the present post-modern debate the diverse movement of poetry is something theory has still to confront fully and perhaps answer to.

The argument and style of Castillo Durante's book are elegant. He sets up a paradigm to explain the dialectical relation between borrowed patterns of expression, of which cliché is the most representative, and stereotypes. Clichés represent the doxa and stereotypes something more flexible. Castillo Durante chooses the middle way between Althusser and Lacan because he finds them both useful but too deterministic. For Althusser, the subject is subject to ideology: the ideological is interpellated in him. For Lacan, the subject is an effect of discourse. Lacan relates ideology to the unconscious and applies the linguistics of Saussure to Freud. Language determines us. Castillo Durante proposes a floating logic of stereotypes. In the context of the changing ideological market, Castillo Durante decides to theorize and demonstrate how stereotypes work without judging them. Unlike Barthes, who equates stereotype and cliché, Castillo Durante differentiates them even as he sets out the way they work together. Castillo Durante is more like Northrop Frye, who saw in mythology the flexible and open possibilities of convention as, paradoxically, a means of overcoming the conventional and the determinism of the teleological, instrumental, and argumentative nature of ideology. Just as Frye observes the close relation between ideology and mythology but distinguishes them, so too does Castillo Durante with cliché and stereotype. Both see the possible subversiveness of literature, and Castillo Durante is particularly interested in a kind of writing that subverts.

The Paradox of the Stereotype

Stereotypes have a paradoxical nature. They allow clichés to hide themselves, but stereotypes can be studied as a means of unmasking the ideological aspect of cliché. Castillo Durante uses texts from Rousseau, Flaubert, García Lorca, and others to illustrate his case. Rousseau's secularization of the Catholic Church's and St. Augustine's genre of confession is interesting because in *Confessions* Rousseau uses the stereotype for his own benefit, as if he were his own priest absolving himself of his sins. In remembering himself as a thief, Rousseau steals himself with virtue. Stereotype allows him to make a positive of a negative experience. Castillo Durante uncovers the truth Rousseau makes for himself from what lies in the past. This unmasking relates to the Greek *kritos* and *aletheia*. The one literally means judgment and the other, uncovering. Figuratively, *aletheia* signifies truth. The critic needs distance to discover truth. A gap occurs between Castillo Durante's search for *aletheia* and what he finds in Rousseau and Flaubert. Castillo Durante argues that Flaubert's notion of the bourgeois is a stereotype. Flaubert is entrapped in stereotype: the stereotype is stereotyped because he does not find a distance between cliché and stereotype. Although Flaubert sees the stereotype behind the activation of clichés about nineteenth-century images of those suffering misery, he is unable to criticize or achieve self-consciousness to escape the stereotype he exposes. In the logic of signs, the known is covered. An accommodation exists between statement and object. Castillo Durante suggests a metatopic, something that uncovers, as a means of achieving that critical distance or self-consciousness. He attempts to show the work of the stereotype in helping to make the cliché mobile.

The central question becomes how do any of us, including Flaubert, Castillo Durante, and me, escape cliché? Another way of phrasing the question is asking, what kind of literature or writing can go beyond topoi? Such an escape or a beyondness is probably not possible, although Castillo Durante holds out the hope that a kind of writing that is able to subvert might serve such a purpose. Except for this hope, Castillo Durante resembles Derrida here, for the Derridean view is that we are caught up in rhetoric in Western poetry and philosophy: all discourse is rhetorical and must therefore call into question the plainness and lucidity of its special truth claims. The metatopic is Castillo Durante's hope because it involves self-consciousness and the ability to unmask the ideological traps of the power of borrowed thought, which cliché most represents. Castillo Durante sets up a hermeneutic community where the worst thing is to accept one perspective of interpretation. He suggests interpretive perspectivism, which is a kind of pluralism. Nonetheless, I would argue that there is for us all a danger of tautology and circularity rather than paradox in the idea of the stereotype because we cannot necessarily escape the trap of the stereotype that we discover (uncover and recognize as in anagnorisis or cognitio) in others. But I think that we have to give this theory of stereotype some play (*jeu*), both in the ludic sense and in that of giving (generosity of spirit, bending). The paradox here is that stereotype helps cliché but allows us to unmask cliché. Perhaps we need to turn for a while from the *doxa* of Barthes, whose encapsulation of dogma has enlisted years of attention, to the *para-doxa* of Castillo Durante. We might, then, find some play in what is beside opinion (para-doxa) and find a postmodern via media between the determinism of public and political ideology found in Brecht, Barthes, and Althusser and the determinism of private psychology represented in Lacan by way of Freud and Saussure.

The ultimate question, if any question can be ultimate, may be the following: Can we translate ourselves between the public and the private into a space free of ideological stereotyping, or is such a desire a dream, Bottom's *translatio*? Castillo Durante's book makes the risk of such a quest worth pursuing. If we are fallen from truth, whether we wander on a dark road with Augustine or Rousseau, is there something that reminds us that truth is before us as well at our backs, something that we can discover about the world and ourselves that in a paradox allows us a critical distance to see a glimmer of things as they are? When the dream is over, if it ever ends, Bottom is restored and rather than an ass, who was the accidental object of love, he is a weaver who might weave many plots of freedom and not settle for yet another shirt of Nessus. The trick, to shift metaphors, is to sit on the unresolved balance of paradox and move forward at the same time. And that is no mean trick. Paradoxically, it may be no trick at all.

After Theory

So whether any space can be free or whether it is always ideological is something Terry Eagleton discussed some time ago and is a question that Castillo Durante raises. One of the issues Eagleton also brought up in the past decade was whether we are after theory—in other words, can we live in a space without theory? The author of a book on the ideology of the aesthetic writes in a way that has an aesthetic dimension, which is one of the ways that books attract attention and endure. That very aesthetic may be seductive and have some negative effects, but traditionally literary studies were in large part about aesthetics, both for the poet and the critic, so that the very people who might lament the shortcomings of beauty and elegance are attracted to them. Theorists, like Northrop Frye, as I argued, have a theoretical imagination, and to that I would say that Frye's style as well as thought helped to gain a readership.[37]

And so I confess that I have a weakness for lively writing and celerity of thought. Those who think that the contracting sales of books on literary criticism and theory is a sign of decline in the discipline, rather than a sign of the times, are not paying close attention. Critical theory in English—whether in Philip Sidney's apologies for poetry in relation to philosophy and history or in Percy Shelley's mediations on poets as unacknowledged legislators of the world; whether in Matthew Arnold's thoughts on poetry as a secular religion or in Virginia Woolf's consideration of women as needing a room of their own; whether in Oscar Wilde's serious and comic play on the decay of lying or in Toni Morrison's comments on the challenges of race; whether in John Dryden's ideas on classical decorum or in Homi Bhabha's exploration of the location of culture—has expressed and continues to express itself with great variety and accomplishment. This range of styles, ideas, and assumptions across centuries is a matter for celebration. The lively commotion of English criticism is something to enjoy and celebrate.

Terry Eagleton is a theorist I have admired for some time: his writing is full of life and engagement, and it always involves the reader in the debate on the relation between literature and society. He is a theorist who has a wide cultural range and brings the vitality and variety of other literatures and cultures into the English-speaking world. Eagleton has a distinct voice that reaches readers and engages them in what matters about the pursuit of fictions and truths, and pleasure and happiness.

After Theory is a teaching book that reaches out primarily to students and general readers; it also has much to offer more specialist readers.[38] Eagleton has hope for the future, but is also nostalgic and elegiac. Although his nostalgia is not for the absolute truths that some earlier theories sought, it can be glimpsed in the opening sentence: "The golden age of cultural theory is long past."[39] Even though the age of theory (the early 1960s to the late 1980s) is now over, he notes that those who think that we can return with relief to "an age of pre-theoretical innocence, are in for a disappointment."[40] Eagleton considers the pursuit of theory and scholarship to be pleasurable, but aptly warns: "Like all scientific inquiry, it requires patience, self-discipline and the inexhaustible capacity to be bored."[41] He uses irony and satiric wit to unmask theories that trivialize culture and politics in the face of starving, underfed, and marginal peoples. Although the art of interpretation can be seen as early as Plato's writings, Eagleton equates the most intense period of cultural theory with the period between 1965 and 1980 in which the political Left became prominent. Cultural and national liberation, as critiques of a dominant capitalism and the conspicuous consumption of wealthy Western cultures, became keys to this brief countering of prevailing trends. The awareness of other worlds and movement between them was part of the spirit of the age.

In the 1980s counterculture turned to postmodernism in a global world where Marxism seemed less and less relevant. Eagleton's satirical insights into the denial of historical events and natural occurrences are cautionary. Theory that is blind to the world is not advisable. Jonathan Swift had wicked fun with that in Book III of *Gulliver's Travels*. Repression and amnesia, unraveled by theory to uncover the antitheoretical nature of humans, might be a survival instinct. Eagleton maintains that cultural theory must be ambitious in trying to make sense of the grand narratives in which it participates. Cultural theory is by necessity abstract, but it needs to engage with the concrete specificity of the art and literature it discusses. Both plain language and conceptual terminology are needed; both close reading and theory share abstraction. Cultural theory, according to Eagleton, "has disabused us of the idea that there is a single correct way to interpret a work of art," but it has also fallen short on many intense human experiences from love through evil to truth.[42] As Eagleton notes, it is important to distinguish truth from dogmatism, and he suggests gnomically: "Other persons are objectivity in action."[43]

Cultural theory might explore the interconnections of politics and ethics more than it has in the recent past. Humans are social animals (or, as Aristotle said, political animals), and therefore encounter ethical choices and decisions in their everyday lives. The movement of history is one in which human life improves in some ways but deteriorates in others. Progress then is neither absolute nor categorical; it has an uneven and partial development. The letter and spirit of texts are an important divide in the world in which revolution, foundations, and fundamentalism have had such an impact in both the past and the present. Fundamentalists try to plug up with dogma "the unnerving vacancy," the open-endedness of human life.[44] What Eagleton advocates is a political order based on "non-being as an awareness of human frailty and unfoundedness" and not of "human deprivation."[45] Cultural theory needs to enter contemporary debates and to engage global history with new resources and topics. He ends the "Afterword," which addresses the world after September 11, 2001, with a satire on American foreign policy and a praise of an "authentic America," that speaks up for justice, humane values, and human liberty.[46] Eagleton goads readers into thought and away from received ideas—theoretical and otherwise. This process of defamiliarization can only be a good thing even if we cannot always agree.

Transitions

Stereotyping has been important in French theories of otherness, and this consideration of alterity has had important implications in the study of the relations between Europeans and other peoples, slavery, colonialism, postcolonialism, and other fields.[47] This kind of theory provided another way of seeing and of discussing aspects of texts and the world that were not given as much play. To speak of life after theory is a useful rhetorical strategy, but there needs to be method to shape instances just as evidence bolsters argument. Practice and theory need each other.

Despite the hermeneutics of suspicion about the seductive nature of literature that characterized one strain of deconstruction, the literary persists in its aesthetic power. The Platonic Socrates showed distrust over the knowledge that the poetry of Homer could convey as opposed to philosophy, and this context seems to have been relived even in the name of an anti-Platonism from the 1960s. Reason would discipline imagination. Another way to attenuate the influence of literature was to put it in a social and historical context and to treat literary criticism and theory as a branch of other disciplines such as sociology and history. While these fields are a key to our knowledge of the human world, they need not obscure or occlude literature. We need all the tools we have to understand the world or actuality. Moreover, the aesthetic is an aspect of all writing—literature, theory, and history. The seduction of argument in ideology, propaganda, or any field can be as strong as the seduction of a story. Rhetoric and poetics have a movement that can entice the audience or reader. In a sense we are all caught between thought and feeling in a mixed world of story and argument. Story-argument is that mixture. In the next chapter, I shall concentrate on the liminal space between poetry and history.

CHAPTER 8

Between History and Poetry

History and poetry share both aesthetics and subjects, and this can especially be seen in the example of epic and in verse drama about history, as in the works of Shakespeare's contemporary, Samuel Daniel. The history play, as the instance of Shakespeare and Schiller attest, is an example of the mixture of the two. This historical dramatic poetry combines the work of the poet and the historian, as Aristotle defined them, the one able to arrange events to the best poetic effect and the other constrained by the sequence of events. As Socrates and Plato were less sympathetic to poetry and much less interested in history than Aristotle was, philosophy became the leading way to find truth and knowledge in the universals of reality. But Homer did not go away so readily.

When Homer wrote about the siege of Troy, he was already part of the tradition stretching back to the epic of Gilgamesh that in its very representation explored the relation between poetry and history. Long before Aristotle would speculate on the connection among, and hierarchy of, history, poetry, and philosophy, Homer was making his epic and representing some of the great themes: love and war, and the clash between cultures. This division between East and West, ages before Orientalism, became a prominent trope even into the Middle Ages and the Renaissance, when Christian crusaders and the Ottoman soldiers fought for the eastern Mediterranean, the cradle of both their civilizations. In addition to discussing the relation between poetry and history as well as between Europe and its rivals, especially through warfare, this chapter, while responding directly to recent scholarship in the field, will in a more oblique way, elaborate on an image that struck me over and again, while a child and then in school and university— Achilles dragging Hector round the walls of Troy. This image involves a poetic and mythical representation of what appears to have been a historical event, a kind of synecdochic emblem of combat, especially between Europe and Asia, that translated into early modern Europe and was displaced in the "conquest" of the New World.

The Genres of History

The epic and the history play are genres that reshape history, and even romance explores the legendary and fictional aspects of the historical. The historical text and the world it describes and interprets are not identical no matter how mimetic or realistic history is thought to be. Like the epic poet or the historical dramatist, historians, at least since Herodotus, have had to select their evidence and their *muthos*—the shape of their narrative. This story-form had to have a beginning, a middle, and an end: history as action and writing shares an open boundary between event and interpretation. Even in historical writing, though perhaps less so than in historical poetry, the quest for what happened becomes by definition a reconstruction of what might have happened. Each present generation reinterprets the past according to the historical changes that have defined that generation.

Having said that, despite the insights of metahistory and New Historicism, such as the importance of genre and aesthetic choice in the one and of the anecdotal, analogical, marginal, and subjective in the other, a knife in the gut is not the text of a knife in the gut. The temptation of textualism and constructivism—both of which are right to bring skepticism to an unbridled and unmediated sense of the empirical because facts, the world, and experience are not self-evident and innocently there—is to think of the world as a book, a kind of translation of the medieval trope to a postmodern metaphor to live by or at least write through. History, like literature, might be easier to prove in practice than in theory, but we need to begin somewhere, as Descartes discovered in his attempt to dismantle philosophy to a first principle. Admittedly, Descartes, who is much maligned in poststructuralist and postmodernist circles, defined his existence according to his ability to think. Aristotle's rational animal, although he had also called "man" a political animal, was still alive in the Cartesian revolution. Had Descartes declared, "I write therefore I am," he would have been more popular with current theorists at the posts to the new millennium. Nor was he interested enough, as Freud was, in the animal in the human, but whatever his assumptions, he did try to go back to a first principle, a premise, something that would have been familiar to Aquinas and to those devoted to scholastic logic. It occurred to me, when I studied logic, and long before I knew anything about the theory of literature and history, that a premise contains a buried conclusion, so that I was sympathetic to and interested in the work of Hayden White, Jacques Derrida, and the generation before me even when they were being denounced by a good number of their mentors and contemporaries.

Still, a fact is a fact even if it soon has a batten of interpretation swathing it (even as it raveled and unraveled from generation to generation). Lenin lived, or he did not. He was born at one time and died at another. There is an "exorable" sequence to his life and to the Russian Revolution. A story exists for novelists and historians, who share both a narrative and an interpretative art, but as Philip Sidney observed, following Aristotle, history is what happened and not what might have happened. The poet can play with sequence: the historian cannot. Even if historians use flashbacks and other novelistic techniques, they should not introduce an invented character (as Shakespeare does with Falstaff in the second tetralogy) or put Lenin's Bolshevik Revolution before Kerensky's Provisional Government in the revolutional sequence.[1] Shakespeare makes Hotspur and Prince Hal the same age, when they were separated by almost a generation, because that way he can identify their rivalry and explore the parallel relations these warriors have with their fathers. Thucydides may have had to construct Pericles's speech on the rhetorical principle, which history and poetry shared under the Greeks, that without evidence of what the leader did say, the writer would produce an oration in keeping with what the character of Pericles would have dictated under the circumstances. Even with this latitude, poetic justice is not as available to the historian as it is to the poet. Cultural historians might lecture according to their politics, but they do have an archive staring them in the face.

History is as much inquiry as it is story even if the boundary between them shifts. The possible world of poetry meets the actual world of history. Poetry, such as the epic, can be historical, and history, especially narrative history, can be poetic, but the two, despite their overlap, in practical terms are not identical. Rhetoric mediates the similarities and differences between the historical and the poetic even in as disparate forms as econometrics and the novel. Even though arguments have narrative aspects and anecdotes, and stories, particularly when they point to a moral, have argumentative qualities, stories and arguments differ practically, especially in their extremes, between the metaphorical and the instrumental. The telos of a fiction is that it moves rhetorically and structurally in a putative space, whereas the end of an argument is to convince someone in the world that things happened, happen, or will happen in a certain way. Historical fiction and metaphysics (in which I include nonempirical theory of any kind) blur those boundaries.

Renaissance Epic

The instance of warfare in the Renaissance epic involves the relation between poetry and history. Michael Murrin's study of this topic allows for a suggestive period between the classical and medieval inheritance and the novel as successor to the epic.[2] The lines between history and fiction change as technology and society alter. The responses to this literary and social transformation vary and bring into focus the discussion of the connection between the historical and the poetic (literary).

Just as the form of history and literature changes, so too does their content. In epic, which is one of the precursors of the novel, the subject of war began to wane in the sixteenth century, so that, as Murrin says, despite Tolstoy and Hemingway, warfare does not preoccupy modern fiction.[3] Murrin's argument about this shift is that to understand it in epic and romance, one must see how warfare changed, and caused these changes through "a slow revolution" that was largely determined by technology.[4] He uses the battle between the Ottomans and the Knights of Saint John of Rhodes, in 1522, as a paradigm shift in warfare, a story about who adapts, and who does not, to changes in warfare. The use of gunpowder changed warfare, and writers had to adjust their genres as much as the warriors did. The romance represented war, particularly between Christian and Muslim, although it was translated to the New World where Natives replaced Muslims as the enemy: "Some tinkered with the old genres, as the Knights did with their medieval walls; others opted for a different form, that of classical epic, which came into Italy along with the star-shaped forts of the new military system."[5] For Murrin, the offensive and defensive phases of the Gunpowder Revolution (1483–1610) affected heroic narrative, and he tries to create more understanding of the background of war and, therefore, of war poetry by discussing field battles, strategy, sieges, guerrilla tactics, and naval wars with galleys and with sailing ships. One of the principal reasons Murrin provides such explanations is to attempt to bridge the historical divide between a post-Vietnam pacifism and distaste for war on the one hand and the early modern fascination with, and extensive practice of, warfare.[6]

Murrin discusses Luigi Pulci's *cantari* in terms of their representation of the battle of Roncevalles, which includes a plan for the Saracen attack, and that is testimony to the endurance of the romance tradition.[7] He reminds us that romance models served as patterns for the lives of quattrocento nobles.[8] Moreover, Murrin suggests that the romancer of the later fifteenth century used abbreviation when he could because of the gap between military practice of the time and the traditional way of narration.[9] Murrin also charts Arthur's rise to power through Sir Thomas Malory, noting that Merlin's strategy relates to the fantasy world that French romancers invented for Britain and that in the book culture of the fifteenth century, people started to design their lives in accordance with their reading.[10] The relation between romance and history, according to Murrin, worked well in tournaments and duels but created strains in military campaigns, so that this connection did not always fit well with all facets of aristocratic life.[11] In representing Agramante's war, Matteo Maria Boiardo did not rework or abbreviate older stories as Malory and Pulci did or model his fictional hero on a historical person. Murrin notes that Boiardo imitated the formal devices of history as opposed to its content.[12]

From Herodotus's description of the defeat of Xerxes, there was a military advantage for Europe for eleven centuries, but, as Murrin observes, by the fifteenth century the Europeans were losing more than winning, so that the fiction that small armies of westerners could defeat multitudes of foreigners came true in life in the western Atlantic after Columbus's landfall.[13] Murrin sees in certain scenes of the *Orlando furioso* a realism that generated a new approach to heroic poetry in the late sixteenth century.[14] Ariosto's innovations affected Torquato Tasso and Ercilla y Zuñiga: the representation of the siege of Paris affected that of Jerusalem and a fort at Penco in Chile. This new realism did not, according to Murrin, do away entirely with the distinction between poetry and history. Sieges became the center of wars, which were in turn the principal subject of epic and of various romances in the Renaissance. From Troy to Paris and beyond, sieges and falls of cities were a major poetic concern.[15] Plots became problematical for all these poets of historical epic and romance, whether the writers began in medias res as in epic or chronologically as in romance. Murrin argues that Tasso's Aristotelian theory covers up his radical experiment.[16] Camões and Ercilla are poetic foils to Tasso.[17] Perhaps Tasso's love of fiction underwrites his love fictions, yet is such love a relief from fighting and killing, or do these love fictions have a grounding in history?[18] Tasso balanced love and war, history and fiction, much more than Ercilla did.[19]

As Murrin observes, the gun created an unprecedented problem for epic poets and romancers: this crisis occurred mainly between 1440 and 1530. In Book 6 of *Paradise Lost* John Milton makes a complaint against the gun similar to that which Ludovico Ariosto had made in the Olimpa episode in *Orlando furioso*.[20] Others, like Camões, Ercilla, and Gaspar de Villagrá, accepted the gun while maintaining the military code of the Middle Ages.[21] These poets celebrated achievements that, owing to the gun, outstripped those of antiquity. Murrin notes Spanish poets–Juan Latino, Hiernonymo Corte Real, and Juan Rufo—who represented the Battle of Lepanto that took place on October 7, 1571, and who did not see the gun as being instrumental to the victory—it was an ornament. Furthermore, Murrin sees in Camões and Ercilla poets of colonialism, who take the gun to be a challenge to chivalry, and thinks that their consideration of technology is a precedent for the later literature of imperialism.[22] Both poets, in Murrin's view, detach the charge of fraud from technology: the Portuguese accuse the Muslims of fraud, who return the accusation, just as the Spaniards and Aracanians exchange mutual recriminations over deceit. These poets reverse history to accuse the enemy of fraud where there was none, so, as in the later imperialist fiction, the Natives are said to deceive their lords from Europe. Because the Iberians fought with so few soldiers but were powerful because of guns, the small numbers helped make the gunner into a hero as part of a small band. The individual hero became part of a tiny collective gunning for its own survival.[23] This notion of the heroic view, as Murrin points out, was given play in the work of Ercilla and Villagrá. The battle at Chile was a case in point for Ercilla: this group hero of the glorious few was a model for the British Square in India, the Foreign Legion in Africa, and the US cavalry in the west.[24] Murrin does not mention the precedence of Greek and Roman battle formations as having a group hero, although whether this topic receives extensive attention in the poetry of antiquity is a matter open to question.

Poets who wrote about Lepanto, like Juan Rufo, made the commanding officer a new hero of the epic narrative.[25] Describing the engagement at Esmeraldas, Pedro de Oña also glorifies the commanding officer.[26] History and poetry, according to Murrin, become one as the commander molds his soldiers just as the poet attempts to form morals in the audience.[27] Boiardo, Tasso, and Ercilla all raised the question of whether there were limits to violence, and the Spaniards in particular paid attention to this debate as it related to limited and total war.[28] Murrin contrasts Boiardo, who mutes violence with humor, and Tasso, who softens details to the same end, with Ercilla, who rejects total war by showing his audience the wounded and the dying. These opposing positions on violence were not resolved.[29] The Spanish victory against great numbers and odds at Ácoma Pueblo in New Mexico raised questions about a massacre of the Natives led by Zutacapan.[30] The poet Villagrá was among this small group, and he presented the evidence differently in his poem from his testimony at the Indian trial after the battle. For instance, in his epic he omits the Indian counteroffer.[31] The issues that arose from this fight helped to affect colonial policy.[32] Murrin ends his wide-ranging and accomplished study with a consideration of Sir Philip Sidney's *Arcadia*, Michael Drayton's *Barons Warres*, and Samuel Daniel's *Civile Wars*, all of them fraught textually owing to the persistent revisions (like the work of their Italian counterparts).[33] Murrin concludes: "All three

English writers prefer imaginative projection to truth."[34] He also observes that Sidney, Drayton, and Daniel limit representations of war, and so go against the common connection in romance and epic. After almost continuous wars from the 1330s to 1485, the Tudors brought peace to England and ruled over a largely civilian population.[35]

This social climate might have affected this poetic practice of downplaying war, which raises the question, "Could there be an epic without war?" Marino in *L'Adone* and Milton in *Paradise Lost* and *Paradise Regained* furthered the limitation or purging of war in the seventeenth century.[36] After the movement from epic to novel, Murrin asserts, much is lost because whereas Renaissance writers engaged in an intense debate over the limits of violence and the technology of war, subsequent writers did much less or fell silent. Perhaps, as Murrin intimates, it was not until the twentieth century that the novel woke up to these issues that epic and romance had debated over so much.[37] A representation and critique of violence and war is an important bond between poetry and history, fiction and the world.

The question of what happened and the chronology of events in history as opposed to the imaginative licence of the poet is a debate that descends from Aristotle's *Poetics*. Sidney himself, not to mention many of the great French poets and playwrights, responded to this Aristotelian division between poetry and history, universals and particulars. Another aspect of history that grew in importance and sometimes blurred the distinction between the poetic and the historical was the use of the archive. Archiving the national or classical past, especially in epic, romance, and the history play during the Renaissance, presented variations on the complications found in the epics of Homer and Virgil and the biography-history-politics of Plutarch's *Lives*. These intricacies gathered a different momentum after the Renaissance.

A Rhetoric of History

The archive and basic facts represent textual constraints on the imagination of the historian. These constraints, like the conventions of a sonnet, can allow the historian to sing of arms and the man in at least as profound a way as Virgil or Bernard Shaw did. These limits shift the ground and the eye, and they present different points of view with which to look at a past battle or revolution. The narrative of events and the interpretation of those events are in a constant flux: during the Enlightenment, Voltaire attacked history as a narrative of events, whereas in the nineteenth century Leopold von Ranke brought events back to the center of historiography. Once again, the debate on narrative is preoccupying contemporary historians: structure and events are the dividing lines. At a practical level, as Peter Burke has suggested, there is a danger of making narrative indistinguishable from description and analysis.[38] Structural historians, who often discuss material and determined conditions, have argued that in historiography, as in fiction, narrative is not innocent, whereas narrative historians, who frequently explain history in terms of individual intention and character, have maintained that, being static, the analysis of structure is therefore unhistorical.[39] Perhaps it is possible to combine narrative and structure and to see them as part of a larger process that addresses discrete events and vast processes.[40]

One of the possible ways of resolving this conflict between the structural and the narrative in historiography is to see the rhetorical connection between history and poetry. Those writing historical narratives could use increasingly (as some have) narrative techniques from fiction, something Hayden White advocated decades ago.[41] Historians write an interpretation of what happened from a given point of view, but still have to examine the facts even if they might do so in terms of fictional techniques. Contemporary historians have addressed, as Burke notes, the problems between the fictional and the factual through microhistory, a narrative about ordinary people in their locality; a shift within the same work between history from above and below; writing history backward; or an examination of the cultural signatures of events, how a culture orders events, that is, how categories and concepts shape the way in which members of a society perceive and interpret what happens during their lives.[42] The structuralist dream of total history was helpful in calling attention to the analysis of something behind the apparent story of events, but the leaving off of narrative left its own kind of gap. In literary studies the arrival of New Historicism, which with its thick structures indebted to Clifford Geertz and its anecdotal to microhistories, like Carlo Cipolla's *Cristfano and the Plague* (trans. 1973) and Natalie Davis's *The Return of Martin Guerre* (1973), followed a similar pattern of trying to bring a new kind of narrative into literary theory and criticism after much attention had been given to structure by critics as diverse as Roman Jakobson and Northrop Frye.[43] These new forms in historiography and literary theory and criticism involve micronarrative, backward narrative, and stories that move between private and public spheres or represent the same events from many vantages. History can employ new techniques similar to those used in literature and in film, but their use is no guarantee of a profound understanding of the connections between events and structure. However, as Burke hopes, an intelligent use of such narrative methods as cross-cutting, flashbacks, and alternation of scene and story might help in the regeneration of narrative in historical studies.[44] Can a postmodernist dissolution of any textual authority, including it would seem historical documents as being as rhetorical as any other text, be incorporated into a new historiography? It is also interesting to speculate what examples or methods postmodernist novels, which have rebelled against the modernist examples Burke sets out, could provide for historians.

It is possible that "postmodernism represents a reformation of temporality" and that it suggests that viewers and points of view are even more subjective and insecure than previously thought.[45] The difficulty in adopting postmodernist views to history is that, for many postmodernist theorists, history is just another text. Elizabeth Ermarth, for instance, says: "The term 'event,' like 'text' or 'self' or 'historical,' retains the essentialism that postmodernism challenges."[46] Rather than give up the realist and humanist view that a world exists that is beyond the text, even if the text represents it in refractory ways, the historian may wish to use and adapt the techniques of postmodernist fiction to show, even in the face of the mimetic fallacy, the difficulty of representing what happened in the past. With some skepticism, the historian need not adhere to the beliefs and assumptions of postmodernists but can, as postmodernists do in their use of citation in architecture, painting, literature, and other endeavors, call upon their methods of narrative as part of a larger archive. If, for the sake of argument, we grant that postmodern narrative, as Nabokov and Robbe-Grillet have argued, places fabrication, invention, and self-conscious fictionality above all else, and that postmodernists' stories subvert time, as Ermarth maintains, then historians would have to use postmodern fictional techniques and theory against themselves as a means of representing the importance and intricacy of time, without textualizing time out of existence or anything but a fictional state.[47] The realism and the humanism of the Renaissance would not, even from a point of view that adapted postmodern techniques in narrative, be entirely a misguided dream from which our culture, so much more able now, is trying to awaken. This kind of presentism or present arrogance, particularly in fields that are not sciences, is something a historian cannot fully accept. If the past is simply a present text, then what is the point of history? Certainly, the present always regards the past with present purposes in mind, but, as Marx and Brecht argued, it ranges from the past. That alienation cannot simply be an identification of past and present in a timeless presence. Time may not simply be linear, but it can, in part, be seen as a road (even if Nabokov and Robbe-Grillet begged to differ), or in terms of many other metaphors we grapple for to describe the linearity, circularity, helixity, or whatever shape of time. Instead, I propose an archeology, a simultaneous archive of narrative and methods from different times: time is so complex that historians need all the help they can in telling a story from the past or analyzing earlier events.

What happened in the world is a necessary and fundamental goal for the historian. It is naive to think, as some literary theorists do, that historians have ever considered this quest to be an easy one. The very existence of the work of historians like Hayden White and Peter Burke demonstrates a current self-examination in the theory and practice of history. Postmodernist time, which includes some of the modernist experiments in the wake of Einstein's theory of relativity, would allow for a history that does not conceive of time as neutral, but where the observer is part of what he or she observes; takes into account the multiple possibilities of the past and not simply a linear or dialectical process or narrative; and demonstrates an awareness of the playfulness and give-and-take (*jeu*) of language and of the view that reality and language cannot be separated, or at least language is not transparent in the ways it produces meaning about the past.[48] History can rediscover its creativity without giving up a similar imaginativeness in science (as Einstein's view of time suggests) while easing away from the positivistic science it hoped to become, especially before the Second World War. This constitutes an emphasis on something that has never left history even though it has been less prominent in historiography during this century: the literary form and the rhetorical nature of history.

Early Modern/Postmodern

As this chapter is about poetry and history, it might serve to shift our focus to postmodernist historical fiction. Historical novels generally, as Umberto Eco has noted, create characters who assert an identity between possible and actual worlds.[49] In Carlos Fuentes's *Terra Nostra* (1975), however, the author does not want to erase the differences between historical fiction and historical world: instead, he emphasizes their differences—Philip II marries Elizabeth I.[50] Not even Shakespeare would do that despite his use of Falstaff and his equating of the ages of Prince Hal and Hotspur. This postmodernist technique emphasizes its own fictionality by calling attention to its difference from the world, and by flouting historical fact, which, paradoxically, stresses the existence of a realm of actual existence and fact. Historical fiction can be realistic, legendary, mythological, fantastic, romantic, and even antihistorical or anachronistic: Shakespeare ranges from the realistic chronicle *Henry VI* plays through the tragic and fantastic *Titus Andronicus*; the melodramatic *Richard III*; the tragic *Richard II*, *Julius Caesar*, and *Macbeth*; the legendary *King Lear* and *Cymbeline*; to the realistic and mythic *Antony and Cleopatra*; and the fantastic and romantic pageant of *Henry VIII*, to name a few of historical methods and moods. In Shakespeare, as much as in Fuentes, unofficial history vies with official history: Shakespeare's very costuming was anachronistic if the De Witt drawing of a performance in 1595 of *Titus* is any measure, and his allusions are full of anachronism, as the apparent references to Essex in *Henry V* attest, so that the anachronisms we find there are not much different from those found in Fuentes. In *Richard II* John of Gaunt prophesies a future that is already past for Shakespeare's audience just as Fuentes's Valerio Camillo, whose theater of memory is a cinema in Renaissance Venice, predicts a future that is already past for the reader. If, as Brian McHale suggests, when postmodernists fictionalize history, they imply that history is a form of fiction, this conflation of poetry and history cuts both ways.[51] To conflate two things as one identity, there has to be some distinction between the two entities, so that history must in some way not be fiction. For more than two thousand years, history has been a rhetorical and literary art, although since the Renaissance it has aspired to a science whose inquiry into the evidence of what happened is not something that can be effaced as readily as constructivists might wish. History has a *muthos*, perhaps many literary and rhetorical shapes, but that does not necessarily mean that interpretation is all. Something that happened, however difficult it might be to discern and represent, is the beginning point. While granting that facts may already contain interpretations, they are not entirely interpretative.

This search for origins may be circular or illusory, just as Descartes's quest for a first principle might have been. Nonetheless, all disciplines begin somewhere even if that beginning seems almost as estranged as distinct ethnological points of view to others from different fields. This estrangement can present observations about another discipline, like history, that are salutary and helpful, but even the vantage of the person who looks from another discipline or set of assumptions is subject to a disappearing disciplinarity or ground in the rearview mirror. Each discipline has to start somewhere, and history has done so with the view that the field is an attempt to find what happened in the past and to interpret it. Postmodernism, from this view, can ask interesting questions about the grounds of history and its relation and possible identity with fiction, but it cannot obliterate history on history's own terms.

Postmodernist explorations of the relation between fact and fiction, such as Umberto Eco's *The Name of the Rose* (*Il nome della rosa*) (1980), call attention to the joint between the factual and the fictional through the use of anachronism (in a way that is much more self-conscious than many uses in Shakespeare, which constituted a view that emphasized historical accuracy and difference as much as historians in our century), the interweaving of fantasy and actuality, and the contradiction of historical events.[52] These techniques, which are hardly new—Shakespeare plays with them in *Henry*

V, particularly in the choruses—are reconstituted in a movement, postmodernism (as well as its modernist precursors), that revives and innovates on the conventions of the novel in the mode of Rabelais, Cervantes, and Sterne before the ascendancy of realism in the nineteenth century.[53] Paradoxically, postmodernist fiction, which may seem to erase the distinction between fiction and history, reinscribes it in two senses: first, it reuses or reorients the archive of premodernist poetics or fictional conventions and, second, it uses an estrangement, like Brecht's alienation effect, to point out the juncture or joint between reality and representation, that is, history and poetry. Postmodern fiction, and I have given only a couple of examples because their authors are interested in medieval and Renaissance texts, might be used as a means of showing how hard and how illusory it can be to say what happened, and the use of fiction and divergent fictional points of view and techniques might help to emphasize the reality of facts and events in the past.

Shakespeare's multiplicity in representing history, as I have argued elsewhere, makes it difficult, if not impossible, for the reader or audience to associate, with any rigor, the author with one point of view, except, perhaps as a textual expression of the polyphony itself. This dialogism or polyphony, which Bakhtin also sees in Dostoevsky's novels and something that occurs elsewhere in the various literary genres, is something Carlo Ginzburg thinks can shed light on some features in inquisitorial witchcraft trials.[54] Like Burke and Ginzburg, then, I am in favor of history learning from the narrative and representational techniques of literature. If modernist and postmodernist fiction can be excavated in such a fashion, then I would add that Joyce learned from Rabelais and Ben Jonson, and Eco read Joyce, so that the techniques of modernism and postmodernism often reshape those of early modern texts in a New Historical context, and that historians, novelists, poets, and playwrights have not exhausted the excavation of fictional texts from the Middle Ages, Renaissance, and Enlightenment in this regard. Fuentes and Eco have shown this to be the case.

Before, during, and after the Modern

This chapter is concerned with the connections between poetry and history in the early modern and the postmodern. Erich Auerbach gave Shakespeare an important place in *Mimesis* when he devoted a chapter to the *Henry IV* plays: he says Shakespeare represents the relation between the real and history in a "multi-layered" manner.[55] Hegel's "dialectic" and Auerbach's "reality" represent the central movement of history for each of these thinkers: the one seeks the essence of reason with which philosophy informs history, whereas the other claims to be more concerned with the specific and the contingent.[56] While I have been arguing for narrative and representational techniques in early modern texts, like Shakespeare's histories, that modernist and postmodernist texts recycle and reorient, it comes as no surprise that Auerbach uses the many-faced Shakespeare to show an advance in realism. In one sense my argument is that realism and self-conscious fictionality need and define each other: words call attention to themselves and therefore to the gap between word and world as much in texts like Cervantes's *Don Quixote* and Shakespeare's *Henry V* as in postmodernist novels like Kurt Vonnegut's *Slaughterhouse Five*. Words can also seek a kind of realism or naturalism as in Falstaff's trashing of honor or Thersites's satirical remarks, no matter how rhetorical the style might seem, or in the novels of Flaubert and Zola or in Truman Capote's *In Cold Blood*. In this sense the real, then, is often a matter of content and is infused with the everyday, which moves away from tragedy and toward comedy and satire.

From a slightly different angle, realism is the content of trying to come to terms with an ever-expanding subject matter, an expansion of consciousness, so that poets, novelists, dramatists, and historians do not have to represent official history from the point of view of the ruler or dominant classes alone, but can, as concerns change over time, represent all classes, different genders and sexual and domestic preferences, various cultures, and not simply that of the writer. It may be that realist and antirealistic techniques, or, more precisely, representational and antirepresentational, or self-reflexive conventions and modes are needed as contrasts that distinguish each other and combine over time in order to represent what the writer or historian considers to be true or to have happened. By saying, as an antirepresentational or self-consciously artificial writer might, that he or she is going to write in a way that is about writing or about art itself, and does not reflect the world, the assumption is that there is a series of realistic conventions and a reality that he or she is trying to ignore, subvert, or obliterate. In time, what appeared to be realistic might seem self-reflexive and, after the revolution of the times, something antirepresentational might appear so much a part of a worldview that it becomes natural. By definition, the changes over time demand that the historical poet and historian find new means of representing truth and reality or even the impossibility of both. What happened in the past is a shifting presence—trying as much to get the present of the past right as the philosopher seeks the presence of truth. To assert the evanescence or constructedness of that past or truth does so from a historical point of view that cannot make that claim absolutely, but as just another contingent sentence in the rhetorical text of the world.

This brings us back to the point where poets, historians, and philosophers have to begin somewhere, even if that somewhere is on a shifting ground or an ever-receding line on the horizon, where even an asymptote is an act of faith that the curve is approaching a line and that the line exists. Historical narrative, as Louis O. Mink once argued, constructs a complex past as a means of understanding the facts and events of the past, which in and of themselves are not intelligible and do not have a structure of meaning that admits understanding in the reader.[57] As historians have known from the beginning, history is events in the past and writing about the past. Constructivists concentrate on the writing as if writing were the event itself or the only event that matters or that can be understood in relation to itself. After providing a reminder that history is what happened and a knowledge of what happened, Bernard Bailyn makes an important observation:

> One needs to understand the reality of what happened—the totality of past events and developments, past circumstances and thoughts—and what, in historical writings and compilations, people represent them to have been. That relationship, it seems to me, is crucial to all historical study and knowledge. The accuracy and adequacy of representations of past actualities, the verisimilitude or closeness to fact of what is written about them, remain the measure, in the end, of good history—this despite all the fashionable doubts that are raised about the attainment of absolute or perfect objectivity and accuracy (which no one pretends to, anyway).[58]

History is partly subjective and constructed because it involves a historian representing knowledge about what happened in the past, which is held up against other interpretations of what happened and of the past itself.

History happens, even for Hegel, who thinks that philosophy brings coherence and understanding to history: the truth is what has happened or what happens.[59] In Hegel's view this use of philosophy has a constructive power for history. Timothy Bahti takes the unpopular view that the university is built on *Wissenschaft*, a teaching and scholarship that history has construed and delimited, so that any return to narrative and to a view of a discipline, like literature, in terms of itself (more like the field of physics) would constitute a challenge to the prevailing interests of the university, a view that flies in the face of the prevalent position that new history, New Historicism, and cultural materialism are attempts to subvert the antihistoricist and totalizing textual dominant of the university.[60] Disciplines in the university are constituted mainly along historical lines, so that, for Bahti, the only two recent literary theorists in the university who challenged this status quo by attempting to understand literature after history, that is, to understand literature and its meaning as emerging from history, without being understood as placing that meaning back within the context of historicism, were Northrop Frye and Paul de Man.[61] Rather than heirs to the New Critics, or to F. R. Leavis, or to the structuralists, all of whom attempted to dwell on the present moment of meaning as opposed to a historicism, Bahti sees Frye and de Man as heretics within "a modern university that has thoroughly institutionalized historical *Wissenschaft*, but theory does not seem to have moved beyond narrative even in these two heresies, or even after the attempts at non-narrative history in Hegel and Walter Benjamin."[62] Frye's attempt at defining the shape of the *muthos* of all of literature in terms of itself and his quest for organic unity in the text and the totality of literature as a text, and de Man's deconstruction of the constructions of meaning in literature based on extratextual historical meaning, challenge the relation between poetry and history, but are once again in the shadow of the very kind of historicism they attempted to displace. With *Anatomy of Criticism*, in the face of "old historicism" and intellectual history, Frye had tried to introduce a new kind of literary theory that was constructed in terms of literature itself as a history of genre and convention, but his influence waned as he faced the heresy from his heresy, if we are to take up Bahti's view for a moment, the textual skepticism and poetics of disunity of Jacques Derrida and Paul de Man.[63]

The larger challenge to Frye's heresy, perhaps, was not deconstruction or metahistory, as Hayden White had used some of Frye's insights on genre, but a larger return to a referential historicism, and with it an appeal to other worldly disciplines not given as much to being so overtly fictional as literature was. New Historicism, cultural studies, and cultural materialism are now dominant models—all historicist—within a university still given to the historical constitution of disciplines. Bahti's view, while not telling some aspects of the story, or analysis, provides a fresh view of textualism as a powerful aberration rather than a dominant. While this insight is important, my primary interest lies elsewhere—I am not interested in choosing among philosophy, poetry, and history, or any of the disciplines that have sprung from them and multiplied, to declare a preference for New Historicism over genre theory. Instead, as Brecht said, we should have as many theories in our pockets as possible: each of these primary disciplines in practice and theory provides us with something, even if they share rhetoric as a bond, the other lacks. In considering the world or past events in the world, in seeking meaning and truth, balanced somewhere among irony, paradox, and allegory, the historian and poet need as many tools as they can borrow from other disciplines as well as the history of their own craft to attempt to understand reality, something whose presence is always past. Time is slippery as is the ground on which we think we stand.

Narrative histories, as Jerome Bruner has suggested, tell stories that "constitute the psychological and cultural reality in which the participants of history actually live," so that stories create an actuality of their own that coincides with paradigms.[64] Charles Taylor makes a similar point in situating his study of the making of modern identity in relation to historical explanation: "One has to understand people's self-interpretations and their visions of the good, if one is to explain how they arise; but the second task can't be collapsed into the first, even as the first can't be elided in favour of the second."[65] Can these historical narratives, which are written in given historical periods, carry transhistorical meaning?[66] Is such understanding possible if the writer of a document and its reader are each separated in a distinct time?

Historiography and Rhetoric

The classical foundations of modern historiography run into the difficulties of rhetoric, which can question the existence of fact or what happened and replace it with a recreation of purpose and motive, an enactment or a reenactment, in R. G. Collingwood's view.[67] Richard Lanham suggests a new literary history and a new conception of history as literary based on a view that dramatic motive or play, rather than purpose, animates history: nonetheless, he then asserts that events are purposive and playful.[68] Although one does not have to be solemn to be serious, the rhetorical play, with its give and take and its sense of audience, can seem frivolous in light of what Stephen Daedalus referred to as the nightmare of history—all those horrors that pervert the sense of play and imagination or obliterate it. At one level, Lanham is making a similar point to Bruner and Taylor that, as hard as it is, history must take into account the mental states and motives of the actors within it.[69] History, as well as historical poetry and drama, is a matter of construction and style, but my argument is that it is not entirely so, as some rhetorical arguments, like Lanham's, seem at times to suggest. It is also debatable whether historiography is unbroken from Herodotus and Thucydides, whether a rupture occurred at the beginning of the nineteenth century when scientific history began in earnest to assert itself.[70] Much depends on how much one takes into account the return to narrative, rhetoric, and style in the new history or, in literary studies, New Historicism. Rhetorical constructivism, since metahistory and deconstruction, has challenged the positivism of scientific history. It is quite possible that new views of science, which emphasize imagination and elegance, might combine with these rhetorical and textual histories to create a new synthesis in historiography.

Ends and Transitions

Perhaps rhetoric, as much as society and technology, lies between poetry and history. In war and peace, the writer—poet, novelist, playwright, and historian—tries to make sense of the world, reflecting and refracting it. A critique of war or the motives of politics are part of an aesthetic of history and poetry even if they were often divided more and more from the late Renaissance. The early modern and postmodern share some important techniques in social critique, satire, and narrative mode. Poets and historians adapt with the times, and the growth of science and technology has thrown curves in the telling of story and history. With each change or crisis, the question is whether literature and history can keep pace and make a difference. Perhaps if "poetry" runs too far from the world, it leaves history to do all the work and does not provide another kind of memory, critique, and protection. Perhaps if history gets too mired in the world, it loses shape and a style to make it memorable or attractive to readers lost in statistics, graphs, and arid discourse. To flee into language or to flee from it is a danger to the world, a danger that has changed shape and will assume new forms worthy of Proteus.

Language is central to representing the world. Mimesis, and even an anti-mimesis, cannot do without the signs of speech and writing. Translation is a key to the movement of cultures and of knowledge. In the next chapter, I return to translation in a comparative context. More specifically, I shall concentrate on a significant instance at a crucial moment in history. My focus will be on Bartolomé de Las Casas, whose father sailed with Columbus on his westward enterprise and who himself became Columbus's editor. Las Casas was a landowner in the West Indies, who held slaves until he became a Dominican and came to try to defend the Natives ("los Indios") from the tyranny and exploitation of the Spanish landowners. As the Portuguese and the Spanish were the first to expand successfully beyond Europe, the French, the English, and the others came to imitate them and to seek to displace them in a double movement. Las Casas's narrative of the New World became a key text in constructing the framework for the European settlement of the Americas, and it came to be a key text in the Black Legend of Spain. In what follows, I shall discuss the theory and practice of translating Las Casas in the classroom, a kind of bringing together of scholarship and teaching. Here is the typology of past and present, where history and language meet in texts that are as rhetorical as they are about history and travel or settlement and exploration.

CHAPTER 9

Translating Las Casas

I mages and texts about the archive in the expansion of Europe into the New World are traces of the great changes that occurred in 1492 and the decades that followed. The Americas were an unexpected place for Europeans bent on expanding south and east or west in search of Asia. Although this expansion first affected Portugal and Spain, it came to bear on other European states. The devastating effects on Native peoples is also something that Bartolomé de Las Casas captured in his work.[1] The encounter texts he produced and the translations of his work and other intertextual productions suggest the complexity of representing the New World. This chapter is designed to show literature, theory, and history in action, that is, how scholarship informs teaching.

Teaching Las Casas in a comparative context means considering notions of translation and intertextuality, as well as questioning how the texts enter the colonial archive (manuscripts and rare books).[2] Spain was to France and England an example, especially, in the colonization of the New World. The national, colonial, and imperial identities of France and England were bound up with the precedence of Spain in the New World and how figures like Columbus and Las Casas permeated their textual and political archive. More specifically, I balance the French and English emulation of Spain with their use of the Black Legend of that country. Texts that emphasized the heroism and riches of the Spanish empire far outweighed those that did not until the seventeenth century. Las Casas is a key part of a course on the comparative studies of the Americas, which should relate him to others—like Columbus, Jacques Cartier, and John Smith—who also came into contact with the indigenous peoples of the New World. My goal is to have North American students see their own colonial and present-day culture in the context of the Atlantic world and to enable them to understand the relation between the Anglo-American colonies and those of the Spanish, Portuguese, French, and Dutch.

As the French and English had to come to terms with Spain in Europe and the New World, they had to consider Spanish texts, and their identities became deeply tied to translations of those works. Translations into French and English early on were closely related: the first English translation of the *Brevísima relación* was from a French text. The revolt in the Netherlands was also a prominent field for the sowing of Las Casas's translations and the rise of the Black Legend. French translations appeared in Switzerland and the Netherlands, and it is on French and other related translations that I concentrate. The "French" translations were at first for French speakers who spread, with the Reformation, into other countries beyond France. Students discuss with me the typology of the Old World and the New (a prefiguration of one in the other, or a double image), in which the cruelty of the Spaniards in the New World was like their cruelty in the Netherlands. The Spanish mistreatment of the Natives from 1492 became a warning for their later abuses in the Netherlands during the Dutch revolt (ca. 1568–1648). My students are surprised to learn that Las Casas and the Black Legend were not simply vehicles for Protestants but were also an influence on French Catholics like Marc Lescarbot (in some ways the Richard Hakluyt of New France). Some of the ideological translation and editing of Las Casas's work is refractory and intricate and does not make for a linear tale. Students see that Las Casas is subject to various interpretations in different languages, by authors who translate and discuss his work among one another in an array of editions and in terms of religious, cultural, and linguistic rivalry. Moreover, students learn that translation is a political and religious instrument as well as a linguistic tool. Las Casas would have been horrified to see some of the uses to which the heretics and other enemies of Spain put his works. The *Brevísima relación* is the text that was chosen for translation into English and French: whether or not it is a fair summary of Las Casas's work, the account was the central focus in these languages, perhaps owing to its brief, polemical, and self-contained nature. This text is the nexus and crux of the representation and misrepresentation of Las Casas in French and English and in some of the European languages.

Teaching this material at the heart of the library or archive is key for students, whatever their level or field of study. I am able to call expert librarians who expose students to a range of editions, translations, and manuscripts. The collection becomes part of the course: its presence is about the students, whose learning is enhanced when they have the actual historical materials before them.

Libraries without the resource of early editions of Las Casas's texts and related works can substitute databases, facsimiles, microfilm, and digital collections. I ask the class to meet in the rare books section of the library so that the students can see various editions, including early Spanish editions of Las Casas (1552, 1553), whose images and typography are always helpful and of special interest for students who know Spanish. With the text at hand, we are able to go over some differences of phrasing between the original and the translations in different languages.

Translations

The first translation we discuss is Jacques Miggrode's 1579 French-language version, *Tyrannies et cruautez des Espagnols, perpetrees es Indes Occidentales, qu'on dit le Nouveau Monde*. Miggrode's translation of Las Casas's *Brevísima relación*—which was printed in Antwerp (1579), then in Paris (1582), and, finally, in Rouen (1630)—emphasizes the tyranny and cruelty of the Spaniards in its title.[3] Miggrode includes in his address "Au Lecteur," a frontal attack on the Spanish. However, he finally confesses that he likes individual Spaniards but not "their insupportable pride" as a nation.[4] In a hyperbolic mode, Miggrode proceeds in his discourse to address the reader directly about the genealogy of Spanish barbarity and cruelty, from the Goths through the Saracens to the Spaniards, all of whom killed millions— especially the Spaniards, who massacred the inhabitants in the West Indies, an area three times as large as Christendom. The slippage occurs when Miggrode speaks of "the nation" but chooses the plural "their pride" ("leur") instead of the singular "its" ("sa"), so that the Spanish nation is constructed as a collection of individuals.[5] This formula is a familiar one: I like the individuals but not the country. Pride was the worst sin for a Christian. In a polemic, logical fallacies were masked in the emotive language of persuasion. If the attack appeared hateful, Miggrode used hatred as a motivation because he was simply calling on a Spaniard, Las Casas, who showed even more asperity in his attack on Spain. The propaganda on both sides of the Wars of Religion was bitter and displayed figuratively and textually what was literally a fight to the death.

Anyone who knows the *Brevísima relación* remembers the chapter on Venezuela, where Las Casas says of the Germans, to whom Charles V had granted this vast territory, "In my opinion, the Venezuela expedition was incomparably more barbaric than any we have so far described."[6] Miggrode left this passage out of his translation of the text, fearing, perhaps, that the Germans might be taken for Protestants (whether they were or not) even more cruel than the Catholic Spaniards. In a more explicit elision, sometimes the word "cristianos" is rendered as "Espagnols."[7] Something I ask my students to consider is whether the example of Spain was as much about staying alive in Europe as it was about death in the New World. Miggrode's address was written to awaken the provinces of the Netherlands from their sleep. Translating Las Casas was a way to draw the attention of the people of the Low Countries to the nature of their Spanish oppressors. Part of the suspicion of the Spanish among the French might have been derived from Miggrode's translation of Las Casas in 1579, which Marc Lescarbot, who questioned the godliness and zeal of the Spaniards, made popular (Lescarbot even inflated Las Casas's number of Native dead).[8] However, the légend noire, or Black Legend, was not the only view in France: two decades before, for instance, André Thevet (*Les singularitez* [1558]) thought that God had rewarded the Spanish with America for taking Granada.[9]

The class also looks at subsequent versions with different outlandish titles that were part of the war of propaganda that surrounded rivalries in Europe, especially the revolt of the Netherlands. Las Casas was reprinted in French in 1620 and 1630. The first of these editions appeared in Amsterdam without any prefatory matter, not even the author's, and the second, in Rouen, reproduced almost all the material from Miggrode's editions of the 1580s, except the "Extract of the Privilege." In 1620, the year the English Pilgrims sailed from Holland, a French edition of Las Casas appeared there, relying largely on copper plates to tell a pictorial story of torture and cruelty on the title page and throughout the text.[10] The publisher, Jan Evertz Cloppenburg (also known as Jan Evertsoon or Jean Everhardts Cloppenburch), presented a typology of Spanish cruelty. He included two title pages set up in identical ways with the same pictures. The first, which introduced the first part of the book, was on the Low Countries, and the second, about halfway through the volume, was about the New World and preceded Las Casas's account. The first title page included writing surrounded by pictures of men, women, and children being tortured. Philip of Spain presided at the top and center above the title, his vassals, "Don Jan" (to the king's right and to the reader's left) and the "duke of Alva" (on the other side), are shown facing the title: the Spanish cruelty in the Netherlands was mirroring that in the New World. Like the readers of the time, the students travel back from Spanish atrocities in Europe to those that happened prior to that.

The volume consists of two parts, each with its own title page: Johannes Gysius's account of the Spanish cruelty in the Low Countries, *Le miroir de la cruelle, et horrible tyrannie*; and Las Casas's account of Spanish cruelty in the New World, *Le miroir de la tyrannie espagnole perpetree aux Indes Occidentales*. This symbolic correspondence was a central typology of the Old World and the New. Cloppenburg was asking the readers to see the

Old World through the New World. This technique resembled the typology familiar to Christians at the time, in which they read the Old Testament through the New Testament. Images were as important as words in these translations, as were intertextuality and a kind of intericonography, all of which combined to affect the reader-viewer. In this version, the first title page introduced visual propaganda of scenes of Spanish brutality, images Cloppenburg arranged in typological correspondence to demonstrate that Spain was a universal tyrant that abused the Dutch in the same way that it had mistreated the Natives.

Cloppenburg's address to the reader illustrates an ideological struggle as well. Here, the publisher says that the Spaniards brought war and tyranny to the Low Countries under the same religious pretext that they used to tyrannize the Natives in the New World a hundred years before. The heretics and the Lutherans in the Netherlands had taken the place of pagans and idolaters in the New World. Cloppenburg catalogued the cruelty and subterfuge of the king of Spain and of the duke of Alba against Dutch Protestants, connecting the abuse of innocent peoples in the New World and the Old. In the service of delivering the people of the Low Countries from the Spaniards, Cloppenburg introduced Las Casas, a Catholic bishop, as a Spanish champion against cruelty and tyranny. In the typology of the Indies and the Netherlands, Las Casas was used as an inspiration in the fight against oppression and for liberty. In some of the engravings in Cloppenburg's edition, the inhabitants of the Netherlands are naked like the Natives. The first part of the book then depicts the Dutch in words, and the second part describes the Natives. The structure of the book is a reverse typology—a movement from present to past. The translation, which is from the Dutch, sometimes elaborates beyond Las Casas's original (to which Miggrode is closer) to make the Spaniards seem even crueler. The engravings of the Flemish artist Theodor de Bry, which had been in the Frankfurt Latin edition of Las Casas in 1598 (*Narratio Regionum*), constituted part of this edition (as they did various Dutch translations), where they reinforced visually the worst atrocities in the text.

The other reprint of *Tyrannies* that we study is the Rouen version from 1630 that reproduces Miggrode's translation, demonstrating that demand for anti-Spanish tracts existed in France even after the Wars of Religion.[11] This version and that of 1642 (also published in Rouen) featured Las Casas on the title page. The 1642 edition presented its own brief preface and bears the permission of the Catholic Church and the "Permission" granted by the king of France. The editor emphasizes "the inhuman cruelties practiced by the Spaniards (who call themselves good Christians and Catholics)" and swears that the narrative is "very certain and true."[12] Like Cloppenburg, this editor addressed the reader with the familiar *tu*, similar to the *thou* in English at the time, thereby creating a familiar bond with the reader, whom he began by addressing as a friend. The editor gave three reasons for the narrative's right to be taken as true: first, Las Casas was greatly respected for his experience in the Indies and his Christian compassion for the ill-treatment of the poor Indians ("pauvres Indiens" [Ã2v]), as well as for his book chronicling the abuses they suffered; second, the Dominican order esteemed Las Casas so much that they wrote several histories of the order that included extensive biographies of him; and finally, the friar's view of Spanish cruelty was corroborated by Girolamo Benzoni (who lived fourteen years in the New World when Las Casas was alive) in his *Histoire nouvelle du Nouveau Monde*, translated from the Italian into the French. Further, the editor noted the *Short Account*'s many translations and its appearance throughout Western Europe: "The Dutch at once translated the book word for word into their language and into French. The Venetians also put it into Italian, and it spread through Italy to Spain in one volume."[13] According to this editor, no one had been able to contradict Las Casas, the authority on the matter of Spanish tyranny. The editor also provided reasons why the Spanish were tyrants in the New World: they wanted to master and settle the lands, and they came from a cruel, haughty, and proud ("superbe") nation.[14] In his address to the reader, however, the book's raison d'être rose to the surface—Spain was the enemy of France: "If you are a good Frenchman, take this warning; if the Spaniard had the power over you that he usurped over the poor Indians, you would not be treated any more gently, and [let] this little book serve as an example to you."[15] Spain's behavior in the New World was a negative exemplum of what Spain might do in France. The Dutch, the French, and the English all used this strategy of reading Las Casas typologically to deploy America as a warning in Europe.

Las Casas was not the only source of the Black Legend: the title page of Urbain Chauveton's 1579 edition of Benzoni's *Histoire nouvelle du Nouveau Monde* (*La Historia de Mondo Nuovo*, published in Venice in 1565) demonstrated that the Italians, too, fed this legend. This page stressed "the rude treatment" that the Spanish showed some of the "poor peoples" in the New World, and indicated that the volume includes a "little history of a massacre" the Spaniards committed against the French in Florida. (See Nicolas Le Challeux's *Discours de l'histoire de la Floride* [1566].) Fifteen years later, Theodor de Bry's illustrations in Frankfurt would indicate the participation of artists and printers in Germany in anti-Spanish tracts.[16] The French used Las Casas and Benzoni as providential scourges of the Spanish colonists in the New World, although even André Thevet, the royal cosmographer in France, attacked Benzoni and "his pal Léry" for lack of proper knowledge and experience of the New World.[17]

With translations came the migration of allusions and ideas among countries. For instance, supplementing Las Casas and Gonzalo Fernández de Oviedo, Richard Hakluyt the Younger, a member of Francis Walsingham's circle and close to the court of Elizabeth I of England, referred in 1584 to Benzoni, using as his source the French preface of Chauveton's edition of Benzoni's text. In so doing, Hakluyt displaced the experienced Benzoni, a severe critic of Spain and one of the contributors to the Black Legend, with his translator, who published in Protestant Geneva. French Protestant views of Spain were influential in Hakluyt's circle, and the Englishman marshaled them in arguments meant to sway the queen into challenging Spain's virtual monopoly in the New World. In Chauveton's version, which Hakluyt attributed to Benzoni (and translated and quoted in making his point), the Indians had logical reasoning without having studied logic, while the Spanish, more furious than lions and more dangerous than wild beasts, were cruel and devilish and had spoiled their country.[18] Montaigne often took a similar view of the Natives, a perspective related to the positive image that Las Casas, the explorer Jean de Léry, the Puritan missionary John Eliot, and Jean-Jacques Rousseau held of the indigenous peoples of the New World. This strand is but one of the textual and intertextual intricacies surrounding translations of Las Casas's *Brevísima relación* and related texts.

We also focus on the 1583 English version of Las Casas, *The Spanish Colonie*, a translation by M. M. S. of Miggrode's French version. (Miggrode's translation, as well as the Dutch version, *Seer cort verhael van d'Indien... uyte Spaensche overgeset* [Antwerp, 1578], served as propaganda against Spain.)[19] The class then explores another context for Las Casas's revival in English: the republican anti-Spanish propaganda campaign in the 1650s. In 1656, John Phillips's version of Las Casas, *The Tears of the Indians*, presented Spanish cruelty as an allegory for Cromwell's era. In it, Phillips stated that his affection for Cromwell had prompted him "to publish this Relation of the Spanish Cruelties," confident that God, "who hath put this Great Designe" in to the protector's hands, would bless the book.[20]

We continue to track this ongoing circulation of Las Casas translations in Europe, discussing versions such as *Popery Truly Display'd in Its Bloody Colours; Or, A Faithful Narrative of the Horrid and Unexampled Massacres, Butcheries, and All Manner of Cruelties, that Hell and Malice Could Invent, Committed by the Popish Spanish Party on the Inhabitants of West-India* (published in London in 1689), which emphasized the horrors of Catholicism to an England that had just undergone a Protestant revolution in 1688. The title page announced that Las Casas had been translated into Latin, High Dutch, Low Dutch, and French and was "now Taught to speak Modern English," and the same old charges of the Black Legend reappeared in the volume (see the headers on pages 76 and 79).[21] The class also learns that the *Brevísima relación* was translated again during the buildup to the War of Spanish Succession and that the anonymous translator presented Las Casas's struggle as one of conscience and humankind's natural right to liberty and property against the inquisition, oppression, and tyranny of his Spain (see the preface in Las Casas, *A Relation* [published in London in 1699, n. pag.]) This edition was translated from the French version of J. B. M. Morvan de Bellegarde.[22] The relation of French and English editions of Las Casas is an intricate maze that has branches in other countries like the Netherlands, creating a sustained intertextuality that endured for centuries.

Intertextuality at Play

As we dig deeper into the issues of translation and politics, the class discussions focus on comparing the colonies of the New World. Las Casas, as an editor of Columbus and as someone who prefigured the work of Léry, Montaigne, and William Shakespeare on European-Native contacts, is an important figure for North American students to locate in relation to their own history and culture as well as to that of the Atlantic basin. A comparative study with Las Casas as centerpiece helps students to gain a better understanding of their own traditions and some of the Hispanic influences then and now. The ethnographic writings of Las Casas, Thevet, Léry, Montaigne, and others use foreign cultures to criticize European culture. (Peter Burke calls the practice the "Germania syndrome," after Tacitus's *Germania*, which uses the manly German barbarians to reproach the effeminate Romans.)[23] Depicting Natives was a way of criticizing European behavior in Europe, the New World, and elsewhere, and the otherness of the past provides a critique that guards against stereotyping or oversimplifications in the present.

Léry's *Histoire d'un voyage faict en la terre du Bresil, autrement dite Amerique* (1578, rev. 1580) was about his voyage to Brazil in 1556. Over time, editions of Léry expanded, especially the section on cannibalism, which came to include Las Casas's description of the Spanish cruelty in the New World. The material from Las Casas had soon grown so much that Léry created a new chapter for it (compare the editions of 1599 and 1611). Sensational cruelty, by the Spanish or the Natives, was obviously in demand and sold books, a profitable (and thus easily overlooked) aspect of the Spanish conquest. In "Des cannibales" (1580), from the *Essays*, Montaigne talks with several New World Natives who traveled to Rouen when Charles IX of France was there, and the essayist asks what they found most remarkable. The Natives then make satirical observations on kingship (wondering why men would obey a boy as a leader), poverty, inequality, and social class (surprised that

the poor do not take the rich by the throats and burn down their houses).
With the students, I discuss Montaigne as developing in part from Las Casas
and Léry, especially in terms of his comments about Spain in "Des coches"
("Of Coaches"), which have been relatively neglected. Whereas Montaigne's
essay on cannibals emphasizes the French and Europeans in relation to the
New World, "Des Coches" represents the Spanish. In it, Montaigne compares the classical world positively to his own day, asking why the new lands
could not have been conquered under the Greeks and Romans, who would
have brought the people virtue instead of teaching them European avarice
and "all sorts of inhumanity and cruelty, to the example and pattern of our
customs."[24] Instead, in search of pearls and pepper, the Europeans extermi-
nated nations and millions of people, which Montaigne deems "mechanicall
victories": Florio, Montaigne's translator in English, rendered the passage
"Oh mechanical victories, oh base conquest."[25]

Montaigne's reference to the New World is meant to chastise the Spanish,
the king of Castile, and the pope, all of whom are mentioned in the description of the usual Spanish ceremony of possession in which the Spaniards,
searching for a mine, tell the Natives that their king is "the greatest Prince
in the inhabited earth, to whom the Pope, representing God on earth, had
given the principality of all the Indies." The Spaniards explain that they want
the Natives to be tributaries: to yield up food, medicine, and gold; believe
in one God; and acknowledge the truth of the Spanish religion.[26] The noble
king of Mexico is subjected to Spanish cruelty and torture, which dimin-
ishes Spain and not the victim.[27] Florio stressed this contrast by applying
the epithet "barbarous mindes" to the Spanish torturers.[28] Strangely, these
and other atrocities were, Montaigne reports, a source of Spanish pride: "We
have from themselves these narratives, for they not only admit but extol and
publish them."[29] According to Montaigne, the Spaniards exceeded the force
necessary in conquest and had met with providential justice in the form of
civil war and the seas' swallowing up some of their treasure.[30] Taken in context, then, Montaigne's comments on the Spaniards and their treatment of
the Natives can be seen in the light of those by Las Casas, Léry, and others
as a critical position Europeans could take in relation to their own colonization, politics of expansion, and relations with other peoples, especially in
the New World. The same can be said about Shakespeare: *The Tempest*,
like Montaigne's essays, is brilliant, but it too is indebted to earlier works.[31]
A couple of examples help students see the importance of context for great
texts. When Gonzalo speaks about an ideal commonwealth in act 1, scene
1, he draws on Montaigne's description of cannibals, which owes something
to the writings of Columbus, Las Casas, and others, although Shakespeare
has Antonio and Sebastian scorn Gonzalo's speech, thus creating friction

between the ideal and the satirical. Caliban opens act 2, scene 2, with a curse on Prospero, who now has power over Caliban and the island that Caliban and his mother, Sycorax, had found and claimed much earlier. (In act 1, scene 1, Caliban tells Prospero, "This island's mine, by Sycorax my mother, / Which thou takest from me.") Whereas Caliban mistakes the English Trinculo for a spirit, Trinculo does not know what to make of Caliban—is the island Native man or fish? In England, Trinculo says, a monster makes a man rich, because there, when people "will not give a doit to relieve a lame beggar, they will lay out ten to see a dead Indian" (1.2.32–34). At this point, students are encouraged to make connections among this key Shakespearean text, Las Casas's writings, and Montaigne's passages about Indians who were brought back to France (similar to those John Cabot and Martin Frobisher took to England). As Frank Kermode states in his edition of Shakespeare's *The Tempest*, in England, as Indians became more familiar, they replaced the wild man in pageants and masques.[32] Caliban performs a parodic first encounter between Natives and Europeans when he asks Stephano if he has dropped from heaven, a recurring trope from Columbus onward among Europeans, who think the indigenous peoples consider them to be gods (2.2.137–40). It is this attitude of superiority that Las Casas, Léry, Montaigne, and Shakespeare were opening up for debate.

Ends and Transitions

Las Casas's *Brevísima relación* and its many translations and appropriations have become a means of understanding European-Native encounters in a comparative setting. Reading Las Casas in comparison to Léry, Montaigne, Hakluyt, Shakespeare, Lescarbot, and others—those we have not had time to discuss include Jacques Cartier, Samuel de Champlain, Samuel Purchas, William Strachey, and Robert Johnson—unveils the process of intertextuality that lies at the heart of the European and Atlantic colonial discourse.

These texts are part of a comparative framework in history, culture, and literature. Comparison has framed the body of this book. As a form of amplification, I would like to furnish some more key parts of this frame. A world history and a world literature are not new ideas, but with the ever-increasing intensification of globalization in the era after the Second World War, these concepts and practices have come to the fore. In the next and final chapter, I shall discuss work in literature and history that addresses comparative and global approaches.

CHAPTER 10

Comparison, Conquest, and Globalization

Perhaps the first great world war was the Seven Years' War (1756–63), and with this conflict Britain began its ascent as a European and global power, which was sealed with its Industrial Revolution and the defeat of Napoleon in 1815. British power was ascendant from that time until the wreckage of the First World War. But no country is an island even if it is an island, and its literature and culture lives in the context of its neighbors and the world. British history and literature cannot be understood fully in isolation. Writing in English, then, I wish to return to Comparative and World Literature and history, and to approach these subjects from yet another angle in order to come to a fuller understanding of them. And so I will begin with Germany and a certain leading writer in the culture of that nation.

Goethe's *Weltliteratur,* or what Harry Levin has called "a loyalty to literature in the aggregate, not a partisanship in favor of who's in and against who's out," is daunting and exhilarating.[1] In reviewing the work in the journals or reviews of Comparative Literature or comparative articles in other journals, it is imperative to discuss the changes and trends in the subject but not to celebrate the ins for being in and dismiss the outs for being out, as if we could divide the world by territories or the study of literature into Big Endians and Little Endians. There is something collective or collaborative about Comparative Literature or World Literature because of the vastness of the subject and the sheer improbability of one person coming to know all languages, literatures, and cultures. Here I would like to survey some suggestive work in the late 1980s, a time that was particularly important in the acceleration of globalization and a critical era in Comparative Literature.[2]

Some of the key topics in this chapter are translation, "Third World" literature, and the interaction of Eastern and Western literatures, and I examine
them at a crucial time during the 1980s, in a kind of move that is back to
the future. What were concerns may or may not persist, and what seemed
pressing in the 1980s and in the decade or so after, one of the concerns of
this book, provides some perspective. What is pressing or predictive at one
point, including now, may or may not be so in time.

What Goethe meant by *Weltliteratur* has, however, long been debated.
During the 1980s, World Literature was extending beyond the principal
European languages on which Goethe founded his canon.[3] This study of
the literatures of the world now includes in earnest the literary works and
culture of the "Orient" and the "Third World." Edward Said has properly
warned of the dangers of Western representations of the Orient, which
began in the French and British views of the Middle East and have extended
to American and European views of this region as well as the Near East
and Far East.[4] In examining Flaubert's *Salammbô* and *Voyage en Orient*,
Lisa Lowe applies Said's perception that the Europeans related to the Orient
as a man to a woman, as well as Teresa de Lauretis's distinction between
woman as historical subject and woman as representation.[5] Paradoxically,
the very impetus to World Literature and widespread comparison can be
an unconscious or conscious attempt at projection, assimilation, subjection,
or, at least, reconstitution. A genuine interplay or exchange between various
cultures is a difficult and necessary task, but it should only be done with
self-conscious examinations of our motives and an examination of how others view us. This cultural interplay can take many forms. Besides a study
of the relation of Eastern, "Third World," and Western literatures, and a
widespread discussion of the translation of languages and cultures, other
critical and theoretical pursuits occur in the various journals: examinations
of genre, convention, rhetoric, reader-response theory, semiotics, narrative,
literary history, the relation of the arts, and representation.

Signs

Genre, convention, rhetoric, and reader response rely on shared assumptions
or conflict between those who send and those who receive signs. As stable as
theorists and critics may wish these terms to be, they cannot avoid historical
change. A cross-cultural study in genre occurs in Earl Fitz's article on the
first inter-American novels in which he discusses examples from Canada,
the United States, Mexico, Québec, and Brazil.[6] Randall Craig relates the
Socratic dialogue to tragicomic novels because of their realism, balance of
contending attributes, and self-conscious role-playing, and finds a precedent

for doing so in Kierkegaard, Ortega, and Bakhtin.[7] Convention relates closely to genre, to the role of convention in the production and reception of literature, and to contexts.[8] If rhetoric is the art of persuasion, it is also the study of figures, of schemes and tropes, and how they work conventionally. Using rhetoric, the speaker or author attempts to affect the listener or reader either through persuasion or by communication, while the receiver depends on a knowledge of rhetoric to interpret the manipulation or message. In discussing interpretation, in the context of narrative and language, in the mid-1980s Steven Mailloux asserted that formalist rhetoric still dominated literary studies.[9] According to Kevin McClearey, rhetoric derived from pro-torhetoric, which is the production of symbols for occasions and which followed on the presymbolic.[10]

Readers

The relation between writers and readers is a central part of genre, but there are other aspects to the connection, including reception. Reader-response theory, a reaction to authority and intention, continues to generate theoretical work. Alcorn and Bracher argue that reading literature can reform the self through projection and identification, as such reading resembles transference in psychoanalysis.[11] There are other aspects of the role of readers that were being debated during the 1980s. For instance, the cognitive powers of metaphor, Paul B. Armstrong says, are important for the reader because metaphor effects semantic innovations by breaking and stretching the rules of language.[12] Joanne M. Golden also relates reader-response theory to cognitive psychology and advocates a pluralistic approach.[13] A different approach occurs in Reed Hoyt's comparison of the reader of literature to the listener of music. More specifically, Hoyt relates Stanley Fish's reader-response theory to Eugene Namour's implication realization model, both of which, he maintains, descend ideologically from Gestalt psychology, which concentrates on the tendency of the mind to make patterns of stimuli.[14] In a particular application, Victoria Kahn argues that the active role of the reader in the production of meaning occurs in classical, medieval, and early Renaissance texts, not beginning with texts of the sixteenth century. She focuses on Petrarch's *Secretum* as an example of the dramatization of the will as an interpretative faculty.[15] Joëlle Mertes-Gleize argues that in novels before realism, the narrator pays little attention to reading, whereas Lance Olsen thinks that the individual reader must define fantasy within general personal and cultural limits.[16] When arguing for the rights of readers, most of these theorists do not wish for nihilism or arbitrary meaning. It is as if the reader's response cannot escape the influence of genre, convention, and rhetoric. Perhaps in the tension or interplay between those who send and receive signs, we can locate or trace energy, pleasure, and knowledge.

Semiotics and Narrative

Semiotics, in Kaja Silverman's view, produces readerly and writerly texts. The first is more classical and rhetorical and includes identical intents and motives for writer and reader, whereas the second is heterogeneous, multiple, and contradictory and enables the reader to participate in an archeological dig in the anarchy and incoherence of the text.[17] Silverman's readerly text corresponds to rhetorical communication, and her writerly text to lectional freeplay. Nevertheless, a reader always responds to authorial texts, which if not authoritarian and entirely intentional represent a pattern against which the most rebellious reader rebels. Even the subversion of a text can lead to parodic homage, which may be homage nonetheless. The reader's power is no more likely to be absolute than any author's, and in sheer terms of cultural influence, it tends to be less. If Roland Barthes's proclamation of the death of the author attempted to revive the millions of buried readers lying obediently in obscure graves, he probably realized that the author was nearly as hard to kill as God.[18] Semiotics, the science of signs, is not partisan—Jonathan Culler's definition of critical work makes this claim: "Criticism is the pursuit of signs, in that critics, whatever their persuasion, are incited by the prospect of grasping, comprehending, capturing in their prose, evasive signifying structures."[19] Although the present participle "capturing" is unfortunate for its association with the hunt, warfare, and the denial of freedom, it may refer analogically to wrestling Proteus. Whatever the intent or the effect, Culler rightly calls attention to the indirection and evasion of literature, and it is the work of semiotics or semiology to know more about literary signs. Maja Boskovic-Stulli, for instance, discusses Kowzan's semiological systems in terms of theater and oral tale telling.[20] More specifically, David Robey examines how formalist, structuralist, and semiotic approaches to *The Divine Comedy* have helped illuminate the nature of the structure and the language of Dante's poem.[21]

Semiotics includes an investigation of the nature of narrative as well as the relation between story and discourse, theme and structure, literary work and interpretation. A special issue of *Poetics*, "Narrative Analysis: An Interdisciplinary Dialogue," attempts to extend the study of narrative beyond literature to history, social research, therapy, education, artificial intelligence, social sciences, public discourse, conversation, and other areas.[22] The study of narrative can, however, turn away from the world and toward itself. Genette's narratology, Cees J. Van Rees says, credits the reader with an undetermined knowledge of phenomena external to the text—the "hypostatization of the reader"—and assumes that the text determines how it will be read—the "hypostatization of the text"—so that Genette implies that language embodies all narrative phenomena.[23] Narrative can also relate to reader-response theory, psychology, and psychoanalysis.[24] Peter Hunt suggests that misreading in children's literature is necessary, and that developmental psychology may be a more useful approach to the problem than narrative grammar.[25] Whereas Peter Brooks's discussion relates narrative and psychoanalytical constructions, critic and psychoanalyst, Lynne Layton discusses the use of post-Freudian psychoanalytical theories of the development of the self, such as the self-object and narcissism in relation to studies of content and form as well as to contemporary literary theories.[26] While, according to David Novitz, Derrida denies literal language in favor of metaphorical language, Donald Davidson does the opposite: both fail in their arguments.[27] Gerald Prince differentiates between the narratee, addressee, and receiver and asserts that a text is about many things other than themes, which constitute a part of the study of interpretation and cognition.[28] A topical or special issue of *Poétique*, which includes one of Prince's articles, examines the question of theme. In this issue, Claude Bremond distinguishes concept from theme and observes that themes mutate and are perceived as a referent both inside and outside the text; Menachem Brinker discusses theme and interpretation and maintains that a theory of literature cannot furnish criteria for identifying themes; for Peter Cryle, thematics and semiotics are two types of knowing that are articulated in different ways; and Shlomith Rimmon-Kenan says that the relevance of linguistics in elaborating a theory of "theme" is limited because the meaning of that term differs between that discipline and literary studies.[29]

Literature and History

In literary history we can observe a complex relation between word and world and a variety of methodologies. Asking how textual history is and how historical the text is generates a productive exploration of the boundaries between literature and history. The mid-1980s was also a critical time in this debate. A special issue of *Poetics*, "On Writing Histories of Literature," examines various aspects of literary history: theoretical foundations, historical narrative as a present construction, history of communication and structures in textual production and reception, a historiography of literature based on discourse as well as an examination of the relation of power and the literary, the connection between base and superstructure, an explication of the underlying constructions of historiography, the agent-text-context syndrome, an interdisciplinary approach, and the relation between semiotics and linguistics.[30] A topical issue of *Revue d'Histoire Littéraire de la France* on the sublime explores the historical development of an idea. Jacques Bompaire, for instance, looks at the role of historical writing in *Du Sublime* (*Peri Hypsous*), which he says relates to poetry through figures of thought and tropes, and Paulette Carrive examines the sublime in Kant's aesthetics, which she says is already Romantic.[31] *New Literary History* also devotes an issue to the sublime. David B. Morris looks at the shift from eighteenth-century to Romantic sublime in view of Freud's theory of terror, whereas Charles Altieri discusses the sublime in Plato and the ends of reading.[32] Other matters of literary history concern theorists and critics. According to Jean Weisgerber, a historical perspective is important for an understanding of the avant-garde.[33] Yuri B. Vipper sets out the principles of the *History of World Literature* by the Gorky Institute of World Literature.[34] More generally, Hans Ulrich Gumbrecht argues for a "history of literature" within a larger idea of history, so that it does not become a fragment.[35] The interaction of history and literature in literary history resembles the interplay of literature and the other arts as both raise questions about the relation between signifier and referent, and about mimesis.

The Arts

The relations among the arts as well as their means of representation, subjects that Plato presented with such controversy in *The Republic*, continue to generate interest. Music, for instance, resembles literature because it is a temporal representation whose score may be read silently, but whose performance often involves voice. Musical notation and writing are symbolic representations that may reflect nature but may also subvert, refract, supplement, telescope, or recombine it. Both music and literature are interpretations that are interpreted, and both rely partly on silences, rests, and subtexts. Analogies are imperfect. Poetry set to music and music placed in a literary text are recontextualized. The composer and audience, writer and reader, find themselves translated, sometimes through a singer, at other times through an actor, or through the actual voice of the poet at a reading. Translation becomes refractory and many-sided. To speak of translation and recontextualization as monolithic and static ideas, no matter how much the various types of symbolic codes and contexts share with one another, is to ignore the great differences among specific comparisons and applications. The danger is to say what a metaphor is by using another metaphor. Nor can an example of metaphor be composed into a comprehensive generalization about metaphor. Here, once more, is a perspective from the mid-1980s.

Metaphor, as David Langston argues, possesses with other tropes social and historical attributes and involves the exercise of power.[36] A special issue of *Mosaic* examines various aspects of the complex relations between music and literature. Peter Rabinowitz argues that reader-response theory can be helpful in musical analysis, and says that authorial, fictional, and actual circumstances affect the acts of reading and listening.[37] Whereas J. Russell Reaver examines how musical literature is, John and Ursula Rempel maintain that two areas are particularly important in the study of the relation between music and literature: poets who regard themselves as musicians (often using musical themes) and composers who interpret poetry when they set texts to music.[38] Garrett Stewart looks at Streisand's *Yendl*, an adaptation of Singer's story.[39] Rose Zak asserts that in *L'Histoire du soldat* Stravinsky represents a text at once in terms of music, dance, and theater.[40] Examining *Between the Acts*, Jack Stewart says that Virginia Woolf plays with words self-reflexively and so foregrounds literary surface in a manner similar to the Cubist technique of collage.[41] Other journals explore the interaction of the arts: articles examine Schiller's *Die Räuber* in light of Tolstoy's idea of art; Runge's view that poetry and art coalesce in its reception; the relations among the *Partisan Review*, the surrealists, and Trotsky; the use of fact and imagination in the literary portraits of Mozart in Puskin, Mörike, Shaffer, and Hesse; Proust's artistic debt in *Recherche* to Wagner; the stability and instability of the photograph and the relation of this paradox to intention and reception; cinematic parallels in Ernesto Cardenal's documentary poetry prior to 1960; Hawthorne's ambivalent concept of sculpture; the transposition of the figurae of classical mythology in the Western; the notion of originality in the paintings of Church, Turner, and Cole; and how the sublime reveals the necessity of ambiguity and intertextuality in narrative.[42] Luiz Costa Lima examines social representation and mimesis and suggests that representations identify with, while they are alienated from, themselves.[43] If mimesis turns to and from the world, the different media of representation do so, perhaps, in like ways but with different materials.

Translation

A literary history of World Literature also depends on translation, which involves new contexts for texts, an interpretation of interpretation. Translation between languages in literature can be as radical as that between the arts, particularly when the translator must decode and recode from one tradition to another or one alphabet to another. If translation between European languages is difficult enough, translating "Third World" or Eastern texts can sometimes seem presumptuous or a caricature. What we carry across the boundaries to and from other cultures can lead as much to misrepresenta-tions as to representations. If there are no true synonyms in one language, it is hardly surprising that there is none between languages. Although rep-resentation is not identity, the representation of a representation, the trans-lation of a literary work, remains full of peril. The layers of interpretation increase, so that hermeneutic choices—foregrounding and backgrounding, stressing and repressing—come between the reader and the represented sub-ject, for better or for worse. The translated literary text becomes culturally, socially, politically, and interpretatively more complex while being recast in another voice that is often incomprehensible to the original author and audience. The translation unites and divides, stabilizes and destabilizes cul-tures. It turns them inside out and outside in but never entirely so because literary and cultural texts and contexts are not reproducible even if they can be represented.[44]

Translations within Europe can represent cultural crisis and difference as well as harmonious cultural relations or a pan-European ideal. Europe has had and continues to have many contending views, languages, and symbolo-gies. Literary texts can indicate cultural contention as well as productive interaction. Once again, I am concentrating on the period of the mid-1980s. Intertextuality occurs, as Laurel Boone argues, in twelfth-century France because Marie de France's Anglo-Norman works, *Lais* and *Fables*, and William of Guilford's English work, *The Owl and the Nightingale*, use the same material, so that a more general cultural translation occurs after the Norman conquest.[45] From another point of view, W. Rothwell says that from the end of the twelfth century to Chaucer's time, speakers of *francien* imposed it as a cultural norm and mocked those who spoke Anglo-Norman and other dialects.[46] Studies of translation also analyze the reinterpre-tation of classical Greece and Rome. Virgil Nemoianu notes the transla-tion of Xenophon's *Anabasis* in modern European languages and suggests its connection with the picaresque tradition and with Defoe.[47] Rosemary Nielsen and Robert Solomon look at a modern reconstitution of a classical text, Housman's translation of Horace's *Ode* IV.7, and call the translation an interpretation and not an imitation, a defiance of convention in poetry and morality.[48] Whereas H. B. Nisbet discusses the translation of Lucretius by Goethe and other eighteenth-century German writers, Norbert Oellers examines Goethe's translation of a contemporary French story.[49] Goethe translated *De rerum natura* in Lucretius's hexameter, and later without it, an indication, perhaps, that the German poet was changing his views of translation and the relation between classical and modern Europe. Reginald Gibbons applies Ezra Pound's heuristic categories of poetic form in translat-ing Spanish poems into English.[50] Another tendency is to extend Nietzsche's good European to the good Westerner. Paradoxically, the assertion of the worthiness of a minority culture in a multicultural country like Canada also appeals to a pan-Western culture or sometimes a world culture: the claim of difference is founded on an underlying similarity or shared culture. Joseph Pivato examines Italian-Canadian women writers who write in Italian, French, and English about their experience as immigrants.[51] Conversely, Carla Fratta discusses Italian translations of Québécois literary works from the first translation in 1924 to 1983.[52] Both articles reveal a mutual interest between Italy and Québec even if Italians know little about the works of this area of Canada. Translation may, as Sandra Gilbert and Susan Gubar affirm, rely as much on gender and sexuality as on language.[53] European culture is a construct of past and present that can deny differences between language and gender, although it would be unwise to negate some shared aspects of culture among men and women living in Western countries or those who have learned about that culture.

Third World?

The "Third World" may also be an unwieldy construct even if many of these countries share a decolonization from the Western European imperial powers. These countries are various and distinct and often possess long and complex histories. Their literary production is too vast and intricate to be generalized. Western definitions of "Third World" culture can be a form of containment or an attempt at marginalization. This was a topic for debate in the 1980s. Jack Corzani argues that elaborating a literary history of the Caribbean raises many methodological questions, including the inadequacy of the idea of marginal literatures and the necessity of centering that history on the Caribbean itself.[54] Focusing on two African texts that represent the same early Muslim leader, one from Tunisia and the other from Nigeria, Tijani El-Miskin discusses how each text struggles against its own originality but in different ways.[55] Whereas Norbert Hopster and Ulrich Nassen outline the colonial policy of the Nazis, Pierrette Herzberger-Fofana sets out the development of children's and youth literature in Senegal during the 1970s.[56] Mineke Schipper tries to move toward a definition of realism by discussing the African realist novel and by examining Sembene Ousmane's *Les bouts de bois de Dieu*.[57] In studying realist fiction in Africa, it is also helpful to consider Edward Said's observations on the marginalization of non-European cultures and on Conrad's novels as well as Fredric Jameson's discussion of the realist novel as an ideological process or form.[58]

Mohammad Shaheen asserts that a complicated relation exists between Tayeb Salih and Conrad.[59] Various interests are apparent in the following four articles. The oppression of girls and of "Third World" children, Aritha Van Herk says, is reflected in their marginalization in children's literature.[60] According to Richard Bjornson, the term "national literature" is useful in approaching the diverse literary production in Africa and, to prove this point, he uses the case of Cameroon.[61] In exploring the relations among literature, anthropology, and popular culture in Brazil, Roberto Ventura asks questions about the role of identity that results from cultural synthesis and conflict.[62] Adele King maintains that Boubacar Diop's *Le temps de Tamango* is the first Franco-African novel to use narrative techniques to demonstrate the difficulties of an art that attempts to establish a historical or an ideological truth, and that the real hero of the novel is the narrator who is pulled between historical exactness and the need to create his own myth of African history.[63] Most of these articles on literature of the "Third World" come from *Komparatistische Hefte*.

A difficulty in the studies of so-called marginal literature arises when interest from Western journals, universities, and libraries threatens to smother the scholarship and criticism in "Third World" countries. If Western countries ignore these important cultures, then they do so at their own peril, but the very interest they should have can recolonize, inadvertently or not, the decolonized cultures. The economics of education and the literary institution may mean that many intellectuals and scholars from the "Third World" write about their homelands in the West and may be in danger of viewing them increasingly from a Western point of view. The dilemmas for Westerners interested in other cultures and for those from the "Third World" living, studying, or publishing in the West are neither simple nor easy. One response has been subaltern studies, an example of which is Guha's and Spivak's *Selected Subaltern Studies* (1988).[64]

East-West

China and the "Orient" represent a distant other to the West. The Western view on the East can be ambivalent. Whereas for Francis Bacon, the Chinese "write in characters real, which express neither letters nor words in gross, but things or notions," for Dr. Johnson, the Chinese are rude because they lack an alphabet.[65] We may still find ourselves discovering China, looking into the distance into the ambiguities, thinking with Montaigne: "In China, in whose kingdom the government and the arts, without any contact with and knowledge of ours, surpass our examples in several kinds of excellence, and whose history teaches me how much wider and diverse the world is than either the ancients or ourselves can conceive, the officials punish those who mismanage their duties [and] reward those who have been successful in them."[66] If Zhang Longxi commends the views of Henri Cordier and George Steiner on the Chinese language, he warns against those misguided opinions of others like those expressed by Ernest Fenellosa, Ezra Pound, and Jacques Derrida. According to Zhang, "Contrary to popular misconceptions, Chinese writing is not pictographic because the characters are signs of concepts and ideas of things rather than of things themselves .. . . to see Chinese characters as minipictures of a myriad of things is a perennial Western misconception that simply refuses to die."[67] Zhang aptly asks us to see China not as a projection of our society but as an actual other that is in and of itself as well as being like and unlike us. If the translation of classical and modern European languages is difficult, the reinterpretation of Chinese language and literature is more so. Two fine translators of classical texts tell how they made their decisions in translation. In translating *The Iliad* Richmond Lattimore "allowed anapests for dactyls, trochees and even iambs for spondees" while trying to recreate Homer's rapidity and his plain and direct expression and substance, whereas in translating three of Plautus's comedies, Erich Segal reproduced the iambs and trochees but had to take liberties with the rhythms of the polymetric lyrics.[68] As Zhang implies, the difficulty of faithful reproductions of Chinese literature into English arises because of the great difference between our languages, so that to achieve what Lattimore and Segal have accomplished in recasting the classics may be improbable, and the only way to attempt to achieve a similar end is to recognize the distinction and the in-and-of-itselfness of the Chinese language and culture.

In the 1980s, it seemed that more needed to be done on translating Chinese. When translating seventeenth-century Chinese short stories, Cyril Birch is interested in the literary techniques of the original authors, and does not say much about his own problems and solutions in translation. Kai-Yu Hsu discusses the *Wenjen* or the traditional literary elite of China, reveals the complex development in the language of Chinese literature such as the allusory classical style and the modern vernacular or *pai-hua*, examines the influence of the West on modern Chinese poetry, and thinks that a rich new language for poetry is developing in China. Briefly and generally, in the foreword, he explains his translation: "I have tried to keep the translations as close to the original Chinese as possible, but often I have had to depart from the literalness in order to convey the meaning of a line or stanza in clear English." A more extensive and specific discussion of translation occurs in Arthur Cooper's translation of Li Po and Tu Fu. Besides examining the calligraphy and the sound of the Chinese language, he talks about Coleridge's idea of "poematic" translation and the revolution in Western translations of Chinese poetry that occurred in Ezra Pound's *Cathay* (1915) and Arthur

Waley's *170 Chinese Poems* (1918). Cooper also includes the Chinese calligraphy of Shui Chien-Tung, agrees with Paul Demieville's view in his introduction to *Anthologie de la poésie chinoise classique* (1962) that each syllable in short Chinese poems gives out powerful visual and aural resonances, and sets out his reasons for selecting verse translation, for changing Chinese meters into specific English meters, for almost always veering away from the Chinese rhyme schemes, for the sad but inevitable omissions in any translation, and for the lack of some equivalents between the two languages.[69] As important as China is in the Orient, it cannot subsume the entire region, which is complex and varied. Japan, India, and other countries are ancient and dynamic societies, and the Middle East has long been an obsession of the West.

Those who study the literary relations between East and West are as apt to find similarities as differences between the "two" cultures, whether the authors of the articles come from Eastern or Western countries. Some translators have illustrated through their practice and theory the complexities that Sanskrit, Korean, Japanese, and other "Oriental" languages contribute to intricate literatures. Kenneth Rexroth writes eloquently about the literary language of Japan, such as its economy, oral presentation, and puns, while suggesting the relation to Chinese.[70]

During the 1980s, in the United States, there was much talk of the Japanese economy overtaking the American economy. A fascination with and fear of Japan was much in the air when in the mid-1980s I was living in Cambridge, Massachusetts. Japanese culture at all levels seemed to be a matter of interest. Still, there was always room for more interest in comparisons with Asian literatures in Comparative Literature in the 1980s. In discussing Japanese literature, Masauki Ayiyama observes similarities in James's and Nanboku's use of ghosts in supernatural stories.[71] Margaret Berry thinks that Artaud's *Le Théâtre et son double* is a good beginning in comparing the drama of the East and the West, such as Beckett's plays and Noh drama or Marlowe's *The Jew of Malta* and a kabuki play.[72] By examining Japanese literature from a more cosmopolitan point of view, which includes the writings of immigrants and emigrants, Matoshi Fujisawa expands our notion of that literature beyond *kokubungaku* or "native literature."[73] Yoshinobu Hakutani looks at the Japanese American poet, Yone Noguchi, who wrote in both English and Japanese and showed both Western and Eastern influences—from Whitman to Zen.[74] The influence of Dostoevsky and Kropotkin on Takuboiku's poetry interests Yukinori Iwaki.[75] Yoshiko Takita argues that Wakamatsu Shizuko's Japanese translation between 1890 and 1892 of Francis Hodgson Burnett's *Little Lord Fauntleroy* was an important event in the literary history of Japan because it introduced modern, realistic, juvenile literature from the West when the first works of Japanese children's literature were initially appearing.[76]

South Asia, and particularly the largest nation of that area—India—as considered in the 1980s, inhabited a position in an ambiguous geography, somewhere within the "Third World" and the "Orient." Here is a place that has long been fascinating but that was less considered in Comparative Literature and literary studies generally during the 1980s than it is now. India is also on the rise economically. In Jaishree Odin's view, Poe makes sense in light of the Sanskrit aesthetic philosophers Anandavardhana and Abhinavagupta.[77] Uwanda H. J. Sugunasiri gives an overview of writing in English, Punjabi, and Gujarati in Canada by those Canadians of South Asian origins: from India, Pakistan, Bangladesh, Sri Lanka, as well as those from the West Indies, East and South Africa, and the United Kingdom.[78] In the movement of peoples, we can see that Western literatures and South and East Asian literatures interpenetrate, and are similar and distinct. This is an example, perhaps, of a new World Literature, which changes the configurations of that which Goethe envisioned.

During the 1980s, China generated interest in the West, but it was surprising that Western curiosity was not even greater, as China was more isolated under Mao than it was then. So, while concentrating on the mid-1980s here, it is instructive to see the difference between the near obsession with China now and the almost obliviousness or benign neglect of the 1980s, at least in Comparative Literature. Here is an example of then and now, in literature and the world, that perhaps helps to justify my typological method of then and now, and moving backward and forward, and forward and backward, in matters of literature, theory, and history, here and throughout my book. A great deal of work in Chinese and other Eastern literatures needed to be done even by the 1980s. We could not compare our own literatures to those of the East without a better understanding of their languages and literary works. Some basic groundwork was being performed in the 1980s. Gloria Bien examines the oblique relation between Baudelaire and the Tang poets, and says that this connection would have encouraged Chinese symbolist and modernist poets of the 1920s and 1930s to use Baudelaire as a model.[79] Creative imitation is how Carolyn T. Brown describes Hung Shen's "translation" of Eugene O'Neill, so that, in Brown's view, Chinese borrowings from the West in the 1920s and 1930s are stimulating and not traumatic.[80] Patricia J. Howard analyzes the influence of Lao-Tse on Hermann Hesse.[81] In China, Dore J. Levy argues, the cultural hero occurs in historiography and not, as in Persia, Greece, Rome, and Britain, in the epic, although the characteristics of the hero are similar in both cultural groups.[82] Goethe's interest in China, Ingrid Schuster says, is not as uncritical as most European views in his time, which she outlines.[83] Even though the comparisons between authors is valuable, a more comprehensive study of Eastern languages and literatures, along the lines of the humanist retrieval of the classics in the Renaissance, may be needed in the West, so that we can build on the work already done by scholars over the centuries and make an informed view of the "Orient" widespread. This program may or may not be utopian, but it is worth a try. It is time to become more aware of the traps of cultural and gender stereotypes and to exercise our reason and imagination in more fruitful and complex ways, to observe the complexities of our biases, and to attempt to overcome them, as much as is humanly possible, in order to observe the complex Orients for what they are. Our project is not merely a narcissistic projection but a stretching of our imaginations to meet other great traditions, which change as we do in a vast flux.

When I wrote in the 1980s, I observed that World Literature, it seems, is constantly undergoing redefinition, so that it would be appropriate if literary theory and criticism changed configurations. Even now, I maintain this view. Thus far, in this chapter, I have drawn on special issues of journals and articles published mainly in 1985 and 1986, as a kind of Wordsworthian spot of time. This was a journey into a moment at the heart of the archive—the world of scholarly journals in various countries. At the beginning of the book, I started with a view of Comparative Literature just before and after the millennium, and toward the end I backed into the heart of the 1980s, a time of great change. Some of the articles to which I have referred in this overview examine genre and convention, rhetoric and narrative, which involve the relation between author and audience. The production and reception of literature alter over time, and this change concerns a few of the articles on literary history. Part of the alteration may arise from practical as well as theoretical developments that will continue, as I said in the 1980s, to bring about a literature and literary studies that are increasingly worldwide, that rely on a collective project, which compares with care and empathy the literatures of the West, the "Third World," and the "Orient." Perhaps then we can really translate ourselves.

The 1890s

If the 1980s were part of an intense era of globalization, so too were the 1890s. I shall discuss the War of 1898, and discuss briefly one study of that conflict as a reminder that the history of globalization is full-on conquest, and is not always about a building of mutual understanding through culture and literature. This point is important as part of a transition in the English-speaking world and in the world generally from a century of British power to one of American power. Here and in the next section, I shift to scholarship of the past decade. This is another perspective in looking forward and backward, and backward and forward.

The events surrounding the War of 1898 were a turning point for the United States and for the world. This country, which took some time to overcome the catastrophe of the Civil War and which would continue to wrestle with the legacy of slavery, had been arising from its own pain and ashes. The World Columbian Exposition in Chicago in 1893 was, like the World Exposition of 1851 in Britain and the European expositions that followed, an assertion of knowledge and power, even if it was more applied and on a vaster scale than Francis Bacon could have imagined. The English colonies in North America had struggled to expand as part of the first British Empire until the great break occurred between the thirteen colonies and Great Britain. Here was a peeling away of Canada, Acadia, Newfoundland, and the Caribbean, and what remained was to be a new United States. The new nation's situation was precarious for a long time even though it expanded, and it relied grudgingly on Britain culturally, politically, and economically while other influences from the continent, such as those of France and elsewhere, counterbalanced the influence of the mother country. Britain itself had close ties with the country that France had helped to create from the former core of British America. In time, the former colonies would come to rival Britain. The Spanish-American War, fulfilling Alexis De Toqueville's earlier predictions, would signal the beginnings of the translation of empire from Britain to the United States, which would end in the period from the 1940s through the 1960s.

This transfer is more readily apparent now than it was even after World War II, when books were written about the "big three"—Britain, the United States, and the Soviet Union. Soon there were only two superpowers, and after 1991, only one. The British Empire had been a blend of many types of states and combined, especially in its last hundred years, informal and formal control. The United States, once it expanded into a continental "empire" or nation, as Russia had been from the sixteenth century, moved from a formal consolidation to an informal one, based more directly on economic interests than on political rule over territories. The absorption of British liberalism and notions of liberty and the United States' continental evolution allowed for economic benefits without long-term worries over governing places afar. This matter of empire, as Walter LaFeber notes in his foreword, makes Thomas Schoonover's book so vital for scholars, students, and general readers.[84] What is impressive about Schoonover's study is its blending of the general and the specific. He provides five chapters as a context for the War of 1898, which he discusses in a single chapter, and then ends with a discussion of the legacy of the crises of the 1890s. The war itself, then, becomes part of a larger pattern, and even during the 1890s, Schoonover sees this conflict in terms of the Depression of 1893, China, and Cuba. Globalization has been in evidence for perhaps as long as human trade and culture, but American globalization, although built on the networks of formal Western European empires, is, according to the author, something different. The heart of the empire, informal or not, lies in the Americas. Schoonover's tracing of the expansion of the United States from the 1780s was an apt decision. Just as the reconquering of the Iberian peninsula allowed Portugal and Spain the institutions, attitudes, and energy to expand further, the continental expansion of the United States as part of its manifest destiny permitted it to go out into the world as well. There was a new twist, however, because this set of former colonies became the imperial center, something that never happened to any of the former settler colonies of Portugal, Spain, France, or the Netherlands.

Schoonover notes that the activities of the United States in the Caribbean and Central America in the late nineteenth and early twentieth centuries were largely motivated "by the same vision, greed, competitiveness, and curiosity that drove European adventurers who quested for a route to Asia in the fifteenth century."[85] He argues that when fighting Spain in 1898, the government of the United States expected the insurgents in Cuba and the Philippines to lend support but did not expect such a push for self-government as they encountered, which American biases opposed just as Spanish prejudices had.

One of the key aspects of Schoonover's book is his understanding of the United States in terms of the North Atlantic world, so that even as he sees the distinctiveness of this new power, he provides a context for it that promoted greater wisdom. The leaders of the United States, for example, distinguished themselves from their Japanese and European rivals by asserting "a 'special relationship' with China and Asia, a manifest destiny, which supposedly summoned the United States to Asia."[86] Schoonover also points out that one major consequence of the promotion of the political and economic interests of the United States has been not simply to create trade and investment and to extract raw materials but "constant involvement in conflict around the world."[87] The three crises of the 1890s led the United States to "conduct that was more harbinger than solution to international relations in both the Caribbean and Pacific basins," so that expansionist policies based on abundant raw materials, cheap food, open markets, and military force did not always have long-term success.[88]

Just as Schoonover presents the beginnings of the expansion of the United States as part of this new globalization to be an important aspect of understanding the events of 1898, so too does he examine the legacy of the crises of the 1890s, which culminated in the war with Spain. The Western European empires had trouble coming to terms with the nationalist uprisings in their territories, especially but not exclusively (the Boer War attests to that) from those inhabitants who were not European; the United States did as well. Among the many virtues of this book, the author's frank discussion of dissent and controversy in the United States is significant. The American attitudes toward people of color created a typology between the domestic and the foreign (the Philippines, Cuba) and created a debate in white and black communities.[89] Boldly and aptly, Schoonover sees American expansion as an extension of Columbus's Western "intrusion" in search of "value," which caused reaction and revolution, so "Mao Zedong and Ho Chi-Minh did not create the tensions in Asia."[90] This is a strong ending to a wide-ranging and learned study. Schoonover more than manages the dilemma among historians between the specifics of evidence and the general shape of argument or narrative.

Conquest

"Conquest" and "expansion" are terms that are generally received with suspicion in the humanities in the universities of the West, as might well be said of "conversion." The English themselves suffered a conquest in 1066, and the Normans, Spaniards, Portuguese, and other western Europeans continued to speak of conquest in the Middle Ages, the Renaissance, and beyond. In the age of decolonization, which was most intense from 1945 to 1975, the idea of conquest, given the horrors of the Scramble for Africa (1870 to 1914) and the two world wars, was associated with aggression and the dark side of imperialism. Still, the subject is vital to our understanding of culture and history, and I would like to discuss briefly a recent book in the area.

David Day's study of conquest takes up an old theme and attempts to see it in a comparative and global context.[91] In recent decades, Anthony Pagden, Stephen Greenblatt, and Patricia Seed have discussed conquest comparatively, and Day has drawn on their fine work, as well as early scholarship by Annette Kolodny and Edward Said. Day provides a new perspective as well as an Australian point of view to the debate on conquest—a discussion that tends to use European examples, especially in relation to the New World or Americas.

The structure of Day's *Conquest* is enlightening, as he begins with legal claims and proceeds to discuss maps, naming, supplanting, right of conquest, defending what is conquered, foundational narratives, farming, genocide, and populating the land. He ends with the suggestion that conquest is a journey without end. The virtue of this thematic approach is that the reader can see the connection that Day makes among his key interests, for instance, the relations between the Greeks, Turks, and Macedonians; the Spanish conquest of the New World; the westward growth of the United States; the European incursions into Africa; the British claiming of Australia and New Zealand in competition with the Dutch and French; the Japanese domination of the Ainu in Hokkaido; the Russian expansion into Siberia; and the Chinese move into Tibet. Although this sometimes leads to repetition, the effort is worthwhile in terms of proving a comparative and global historical approach.

Particularly interesting is the kind of enduring typology of conquest that Day identifies, despite historical and cultural differences. There is the legal claim set out de jure and de facto, by means of occupation. Ceremonies, maps, and the renaming of conquered lands were used to legitimize the claims made by conquerors and to project power. Day draws on Patricia Seed's view that the English colonies in North America used surveyors most extensively to establish legal possession of the land. One irony, as the author points out, is that the British created India by creating it as an entity on the map. Day also makes distinctions: unlike the Spanish, the English did not think that naming was an effective mode of claiming—for example, the British were slow to change the name of New Holland to Australia. Use of indigenous names did not really represent recognition of the Native peoples, but was a way for settlers to claim a connection with the long tradition of the peoples that they had dispossessed. Supplanting these peoples was a primary aim of conquest. The notion of superiority is an ideology and form of rationalization that the conquerors use to dispossess the original inhabitants, who are viewed as savages and barbarians. This dehumanization was a way to displace the inhumane actions of the colonizing power. Enslaving the original inhabitants or others to take to the supposedly unoccupied lands was another ploy.

Day also shows that the conquerors were not as well received as they hoped, whatever myths were constructed of their glory, civilization, and triumph. Captain Cook recognized that the Aborigines wanted him and his men gone. But Noble Savages soon became savages if they got in the way of land, resources, and nation-building—even the Irish, arguably cousins of the other peoples of the British Isles. In the conquest of Korea, the Japanese also made the Koreans less than themselves. Justification is everywhere. Day places Hitler's views on the rights of conquest into a long line, and he comes out sounding not always too different from other conquerors. A tension between natural and moral laws comes up over and over again in this study. Day also raises the problem faced by Israel, a state identified with survival of the Holocaust but also caught in the dilemma of possession and dispossession. Conquerors build forts to defend their conquered territory. The Romans and Normans did this long ago, and this practice was central to the possession of North America by European powers. Another kind of construction is the foundation story, the myths conquerors live by to justify conquest of a certain place. Constantine laid this foundation with Constantinople in images and texts. Archaeology became a key way to contest myths of origin.

A few more aspects of the typology of conquest remain. One is farming and the creation of gardens. Efficient farming represents occupation of lands which nomads, in the views of settled cultures, do not occupy. The British liked to establish their hold through fencing. The Japanese denied that the Ainu tilled the soil.

Genocide is at the heart of conquest and thus of Day's book. He uses Poznan in Poland as a contested city in the middle of the genocidal imperative, reminding us of Polish lawyer Raphael Lemkin's definition of genocide as "a coordinated plan of different actions aiming at the destruction of essential foundations of the life of national groups, with the aim of annihilating the groups themselves."[92] Day cites the German action against the Herero in South-West Africa as an example, but the genocidal urge has been present in many places in conquest, including in North America. Ecological imperialism, to use Alfred Crosby's term, or the American Holocaust, to employ David Stannard's term, underlines the fact that epidemics can aid the awful intentions of conquerors. To claim lands, the conquerors need to people the land. This is true in all imperial expansion, such as the Russians in Siberia. Sometimes, as in Canada and Australia, land, usually nonarable, has been given back to indigenous peoples. Day, perhaps taking his cue from Benedict Anderson, thinks about moving away from notions of homelands as imaginary communities toward a shared past and future in a small world of mutual dependence, where societies are more sensitive to justice for existing inhabitants than before.

The virtue of Day's book is that it brings together wide-ranging examples of conquest in a well-defined argument. The volume is an important contribution to the ongoing debate on empires and colonies in the various fields that examine this subject such as history, literature, ethnology, law, and politics.

Comparing different contexts in literature, culture, and history allows for a dialogue among disciplines. The separation of text and context is often artificial as is the division among the literary, the theoretical, and the historical. We need all the tools we can muster in trying to recognize and understand our world. It is hubris to think that history, literature, and other subjects from a comparative or global perspective should not be approached or given a place in the institution. Learning languages and codes and translating them have been something humans have done along trade routes since they began to travel and to keep records and to make literature and to write annals and chronicles. Words share rhetoric, but each discipline or even genre within literature provides another way to write about the world and to read about it. Interpretation is what joins the various fields, and it is to this and other related matters that I turn in the conclusion.

Conclusion

In writing to Harriet Munroe, the editor of *Poetry* in Chicago, Ezra Pound thought that England and France had remained cultural models because they had not yielded to the "yelp" of race and nationality, and Pound recommended to her "a universal standard which pays no attention to time or country—a Weltlitteratur standard."[1] The idea of a World Literature goes back through writers and critics like Pound to Goethe. This global or comparative view of literature is suggestive even if one were to agree with Gertrude Stein's view of Pound "as a village explainer, excellent if you were a village, but if you were not, not."[2] Rather than be a village explainer myself, I have tried, as I think Pound did, to be open to a world of literature, theory, and history beyond English, and to call attention to perspectives that provide wider and more multiple views.

With Tom Conley, whose discussion of the theory of cartography of film and maps in films raises so many suggestive questions about mimesis and history, I have an interest in imaginary relation to modes of production and, looking into Borges's *Dreamtigers*, assume that a map is not a territory.[3] Fictions, otherness, and making are the symbolic maps of represented language in literature, theory, and history. Texts call attention to their making whether they are historical or not because words, like maps, attest to their own truth and their shaping into mythical forms or plots. As Hayden White has pointed out, history takes on the forms of fiction in its emplotment. Theory, as a way of seeing, mediates between word and world and the verisimilitude and fictions that literature and history share. Whereas theory grew out of philosophy with Plato and Aristotle, criticism developed from the commentary on sacred and secular books. Both are made of language and, more specifically, of rhetoric. Rhetoric and the shapes or genres of writing have some overlap in literature, theory, and history. Our mental maps can be both virtual and virtuous, and referential and self-referential. This discourse can be the verbal equivalent of Borges's maps of empire and Conley's maps within film, pointing outward and inward at once. As Borges's story suggests, this is a geography in time that can be abandoned and lie in ruins.

The nature of plots or *muthoi*—as J. Hillis Miller says in his discussion of the late Derrida and, more particularly, in Derrida's remark that he could not tell a story—is not simply a matter of the Aristotelian plot with a beginning, a middle, and an end, but the swerve away from chronological order found in Cervantes, Sterne, Conrad, and Faulkner.[4] In *Poetics*, Aristotle foresees such divergence and says the poet plays with events whereas the historian must set down events as they happened. Rhetoric, like poetics and philosophy, is a key to the overlapping disciplines I have discussed in this book. In advocating for literature in this monograph, I am not detracting from these or other fields, nor am I trying to create an encomium, as Gorgias (483–376 B.C.), a contemporary of Socrates, did for Helen, to clear her name.[5] Part of what I have attempted to do is to stress the comparative aspects of literature, theory, and history, and this emphasis is as much a matter of teaching and education as it is of research and scholarship.

The three fields I have examined here have their own elegance and power. Although literature seems vulnerable, along with the teaching of many languages in the English-speaking world, which is a worrying trend for the general health of culture in those countries, the literary continues to delight and instruct. English-speaking countries are nations more given to immigration than other states, and are open in so many ways, seeming to assimilate, perhaps for unity and coherence, other peoples and their languages. English has long borrowed from many languages even before the expansion of England into Britain and the British Empire and the rise of the United States, from colony to nation to superpower. Yet, students in the schools and universities in much of the English-speaking world appear to be taking fewer courses in languages, except perhaps those that associated with money, power, and influence. With the demise of the Soviet Union, fewer students take Russian, and with the rise of China, more take Mandarin. Still, many do not pursue languages beyond that which is required, and languages appear, in most places, not to be required. So as the world becomes more global, English-speaking places become more parochial, at least for their host culture and not the immigrants, many of whom are bilingual or multilingual.[6] Comparative history and literature and world history and literature can stress those languages, and if not the language at least foster some kind of perspective and cultural understanding. In all this, it is important to heed the warning of Isocrates (436–338 B.C.), who founded a school of rhetoric in Athens a few years before Plato's academy, about teachers and rhetoricians promising too much from education: "If all who are engaged in the profession of education were willing to state the facts instead of making greater promises than they can possibly fulfill, they would not be in such bad repute with the lay-public."[7] So my book really discusses aspects of literature, theory, and history in a comparative context as one way of seeing the texts and their temporality or contexts, of interpreting past, present, and future. This one way, with all its limitations, is a means of suggestion for the reader, who will have his or her own interpretative grounds. Each of us teaches and writes in a particular way, and we are overheard in what we do. Taken together, our work in the classroom and in the library constitutes part of a larger conversation now and over a long time.

Argument

In this book, which is its own particular conversation, I examined changes in Comparative Literature and literary studies in the crucial time from the mid-1960s onward while stressing literature and its interpretation. Then I argued for the benefits of comparison as a way of finding the contours of a subject. This study seeks a wider context in which culture and literature are considered comparatively, each approach leading, amid difficulty, to new insights or recognition. Narratives of European exploration and expansion are an example of texts that open up debate and widen perspective. A moment of recognition involves a movement from ignorance to knowledge, although misrecognition is a constant danger.

Communication across time depends on language and, more specifically, the common ground of rhetoric. The drama of meaning or the theatrical model of text emphasizes the rhetorical relation between speaker and audience, writer and reader. The present embodies and acts out past and future, and this drama is both fulfilled and unfulfilled. My discussion of literature also occurred in relation to systems, law, theater, nature, stereotype, and other subjects. Moreover, I examined "discovery" of the New World as a key for exploring otherness and authority. Texts from Columbus through Vitoria and Montaigne to Aphra Behn and beyond raised issues about authority in the context of relations with Natives and slaves. Once more, my emphasis was on a comparative point of view, including the typology of the Old and the New World. In discussing theory, I also concentrated on New Historicism and deconstruction in the context of feminism as these ways of seeing provided other means to think about literature, reading, and interpretation.

Rather than take one side, my view of literature, theory, and history was plural, and I argued that many kinds of texts are part of discourse. Furthermore, I examined poetry and poetics in a few contexts from Aristotle to W. B. Yeats. The relation between fact and interpretation was one of the questions that I raised. The book also maintained that whatever the period or changes, meaning, genre, character, language, and structure are principal matters for debate. Those central elements in literature and culture endure and enrich the discussion. I also looked briefly at the possibility of post-theory and discussed some aspects of translation, which is so important to literature, theory, and history. Questions of subjectivity, ideology, or the stereotype from the French also benefit English and its intellectual milieu.

In the last third of my book, I returned to the ancient relation between poetry and history, and did so in part by concentrating on epic and warfare with observations about the history play and romance. Historical writing involves a quest for what happened, while historical poetry explores the legendary. In this context, I found metahistory and New Historicism suggestive while assuming that history, like literature, has an intricate relation to the world. I returned to accounts of the New World to explore this relation between history and the fictional in accounts of exploration and encounter and their translation. To this end, I discussed teaching Bartolomé de Las Casas in a comparative context and considered translation, intertextuality, and the colonial archive. Here, I examined writers and translators in France and England who came to terms with the example of Spain in the New World in a double movement of emulation and displacement. Moreover, I tried to place Las Casas in the context of Columbus, Jacques Cartier, John Smith, and others. Finally, I came back to the *Weltlitteratur* that Goethe discussed and to Comparative Literature, with which I began the body of the book. I ended with variations of themes that ran through the monograph: translation, "Third World" literature, and the interaction of Eastern and Western literatures. In my argument at its conclusion, I maintained that comparing different contexts in literature, culture, and history permits a dialogue among disciplines and between text and context. It is this understanding of and between disciplines that lies at the heart of this study.

Endings

In literature, theory, and history, imagination is as important as the knowledge and inquiry of narrative and the logic and evidence of argument. This is one reason that I spoke of story-argument in discussing the work of New Historicism earlier because the two overlap at times and lead to a kind of recognition or knowledge.[8] Hayden White draws attention to another element that is important for historical work, and that is the matter of interpretation or what R. G. Collingwood calls "constructive imagination."[9] Just as Northrop Frye's work on literary narrative is helpful for an understanding of White's view of historical narrative, so too is Collingwood's idealist philosophy an interesting ground from which to view Frye and White. Collingwood's view of culture in *Speculum Mentis, or the Map of Knowledge* (1924) elevates history beyond the place Aristotle and Philip Sidney had given it behind both philosophy and poetry, although these have a different order in *Poetics* and *The Defence of Poetry*. History involves the mind as it comes to know and interpret, and this self-consciousness takes on different cultural shapes.[10] Recognition and misrecognition, as I have suggested in this book and elsewhere, are bound up with each other.[11] Arguments, narrative, and interpretation in literature, theory, or philosophy, and history cannot keep logic, myth, and rhetoric entirely separate. In following from Erich Auerbach's view that to write history is to make concessions to legend, White comes up with his own memorable statement: "The fall into legend is the price science pays to myth for the use of language."[12] This melding of philosophy and history also occurs in the work of Benedetto Croce as they share awareness and inquiry, and Croce thinks that moral choices in the world are made between blindness and insight.[13]

History, theory, and literature also have their blind spots. As this book has discussed various eras, it is important to remember, as Margaret W. Ferguson says in her study of Dido's daughters, of literacy, gender, and empire in early modern France and England, "that historical eras overlap in complex ways and that change is always uneven."[14] In this monograph, I have sometimes made a three-way comparison of the literary, theoretical, and historical, but at other times the comparing has been two-way. I wished to open up discussion, to bring out different writers, theorists, and historians in order to call attention to diverse views as well as affinities among their subjects. Poetry and history, for instance, was a two-way comparison, and even in such a double analysis, there is never room enough. For instance, E. P. Thompson's view on this relation between the poetic and the historical, in his consideration of commitment in poetry, is suggestive:

> All that I am arguing is that our sense of political reality, in any generous historical sense, has become lost within faded rhetoric and threatening abstractions, and that poetry, most of all, is what we now need. And this must be poetry more ambitious, more confident of its historical rights among other intellectual disciplines, than any that is commonly presented to us today.[15]

Thompson is not simply seeing poetry in ideal terms; he also knows the limitations of those who make it. Poetry, as in the work of William Blake, is important. Thompson also recognizes that poets have made a habit of becoming "lost in mazes of misrecognition," but that being said, he sees poetry as a place of the realignment of values and reverses the usual question of the commitment of poetry to people (perhaps the people) by asking "about the commitment of people to poetry."[16] For this historian, the world of poetics is anything but irrelevant or without value to the world. A commitment to poetry and a poetry of commitment are mutual relations that are as desirable as they are difficult.

Poetry has long been controversial, and Plutarch, contrary to Thompson, who seeks some truth and commitment in poetry, speaks of the saying that "poets tell many lies."[17] For Plutarch, poets tell deliberate lies because they think truth is drier than fiction, and that whereas truth is real and follows its course no matter how unpleasant, fiction turns from pain to what is pleasing. Socrates, according to Plutarch, strove for truth and so could not write the lies of poetry, and thus turned Aesop's fables into verse when he wrote poetry, "on the principle that where there is no fiction, there is no poetry."[18] Plutarch warns against the involuntary errors of poets.[19] Teaching through instances of ill deeds is something that joins philosophy and poetry, despite the one pursuing truth and the other fiction: "Philosophers use examples, admonishing and instructing from given facts, while poets do the same thing by inventing facts and spinning tales on their own."[20] Moreover, Plutarch has to admit that poetry cannot abandon a likeness to reality if its imitation is to be convincing, so that the young men who read should be reminded that in poetry as in life, as his quotation of Euripides points out, the good and the bad mix together.[21] Theodor Adorno takes an opposite tact in his view of art, which he sees as autonomous and not, because it is of itself but also a social fact: "Artworks participate in enlightenment because they do not lie: They do not feign the literalness of what speaks out of them. They are real as answers to the puzzle externally posed to them. Their own tension is binding in relation to the tension external to them."[22] Poetry and art lie and do not lie: they are of themselves but also of their contexts. The controversy and conversation of art have continued over time, and it seems that they are not near resolution.

In a book about literature, theory, and history, it is important to remember, as Terry Eagleton has noted, that in eighteenth-century England, the idea of literature "meant the whole body of valued writing in society: philosophy, history, essays and letters as well as poems."[23] While time moves on and there is no such thing as a return, I would like to see in this earlier view of literature the very reason why I have to speak about literature, theory, and history rather than merely subsuming these disciplines under "literature." History, like literature, repeats with variations, and in recent times, as Peter Burke has observed, a tension exists between historians who emphasize structure and those who focus on narrative.[24] Although Burke takes into account Hayden White's and Lionel Gossman's calling attention to literary innovation in history, he thinks that historians should avoid some experimentation in literature.[25] Burke does suggest that cinematic and literary techniques, if used in a way that steers clear of superficiality, can help historians to reveal connections between events and structures and present various points of view. Natalie Zemon Davis's *The Return of Martin Guerre*, for instance, appeared after a collaboration with Michael Vigne, as a film.[26]

To return to an earlier image in this conclusion—that of maps—I turn to Robert Darnton, who says that in *The Great Cat Massacre* (1984), "the inquiry leads into the unmapped territory known in France as *l'histoire des mentalités*."[27] Darnton explains that this kind of cultural history depends on studying the otherness of one's own culture, of producing a history against the ethnographical grain, just as an anthropologist might examine another culture. He advocates putting questions to the archive just as the anthropologist does to the Native informant.[28] The anxieties of policing disciplinary boundaries and of the dangers of transgression in interdisciplinary research are something that Darnton addresses head-on. For instance, he notes: "The anthropological mode of history has a rigor of its own, even if it may look suspiciously like literature to a hard-boiled social scientist."[29] Interpretation is what ties this history and its literary and anthropological dimensions together.

History, like literature and theory, is a way of seeing, and that is not come by easily. Here, I wish to return to a passage I referred to in chapter 8 in which Bernard Bailyn sums up the problem of history well:

> The accuracy and adequacy of representations of past actualities, the verisimilitude or closeness to fact of what is written about them, remain the measure, in the end, of good history—this despite all the fashionable doubts that are raised about the attainment of absolute or perfect objectivity and accuracy (which no one pretends to, anyway).[30]

The question of word and world, of representation of the world in literature, theory, and history, never quite goes away in the subject-object of writing and reading, if not in the intersubjective drama of meaning. I have discussed comparative history and literature, but the comparison between periods and between disciplines, the ways in which one field enriches the other, also enables new perspectives. How attractive and powerful the representations are, depends on the reader who weighs truth and fiction, considers the relation between language and the world, and wonders whether a given way of seeing leads more to recognition or misrepresentation. As Euripides knew, so much more is mixed than the good and the bad.

Notes

Introduction

1. See, for instance, Jonathan Culler, *Literary Theory: A Very Short Introduction* (Oxford: Oxford University Press, 1997), 72–73—Culler mentions White in this context—and his "The Turns of Metaphor," *The Pursuit of Signs: Semiotics, Literature, Deconstruction* (London: Routledge & Kegan Paul, 1981), 188–209. See Hayden White, *Tropics of Discourse: Essays in Cultural Criticism* (Baltimore: The Johns Hopkins University Press, 1978). See also Jacques Derrida, "White Mythology: Metaphor in the Text of Philosophy," *Margins of Philosophy* (Chicago: University of Chicago Press, 1982), 207–71.
2. Northrop Frye, *Anatomy of Criticism: Four Essays* (Princeton: Princeton University Press, 1957, rpt. 1973).
3. *Longinus on the Sublime*, trans. W. Rhys Roberts (Cambridge: Cambridge University Press, 1899), ch. 2, ch. 9.
4. See *Plotinus: The Enneads,* ed. and rev. B. S. Page and trans. Stephen Mackenna (London: Faber & Faber, 1962), ch. 1.
5. Stanley Fish, "Rhetoric," *Critical Terms for Literary Study*, ed. Frank Lentricchia and Thomas McLaughlin (Chicago: University of Chicago Press, 1990), 220–21. See, for instance, Richard Rorty, *The Consequences of Pragmatism* (Minneapolis: University of Minnesota Press, 1982).
6. Antoine Compagnon, *Literature, Theory, and Common Sense*, trans. Carol Cosman (Princeton: Princeton University Press, 2004), 7. The French original has a more provocative title: *Le Démon de la théorie: Littérature et sens commun* (Paris Editions du Seuil, 1998).
7. Compagnon, 10.
8. Compagnon, 11. See Julien Gracq, *En lisant en écrivant* (Paris: José Corti, 1981), esp. 174.
9. Compagnon, 11–12.
10. Compagnon, 12–13. See René Wellek and Austin Warren, *Theory of Literature* (New York: Harcourt, Brace, 1949).
11. "False perceptions" is Compagnon's term (14) and "false dilemmas" is Pierre Bourdieu's in *The Rules of Art: Genesis and Structure of the Literary Field*, trans. Susan Emanuel (Cambridge: Polity Press, 1996), 193.

12. Patricia Waugh, "Revising the Two Cultures Debate," *The Arts and Sciences of Criticism*, ed. David Fuller and Patricia Waugh (Oxford: Oxford University Press, 1999), 33–34. See Jonathan Hart, "Introduction," *City of the End of Things: Lectures on Civilization and Empire* (Toronto: Oxford University Press, 2009), 1–34.

13. David Lodge, "Literary Criticism and Literary Creation," *The Arts and Sciences of Criticism*, ed. David Fuller and Patricia Waugh (Oxford: Oxford University Press, 1999), 152.

14. *Bertolt Brecht Diaries 1920–1922*, ed. Herta Ramthun and trans. John Willett (London: Eyre Methuen, 1979), 42–43.

15. In *Bertolt Brecht: Chaos According to Plan* (Cambridge: Cambridge University Press, 1987, rpt. 1994), 174, John Fuegi ends with "lots of theories," and in the "Introduction" to *Encyclopedia of Contemporary Literary Theory: Approaches, Scholars, Terms*, ed. Irena R. Makaryk (Toronto: University of Toronto Press, 1993), vii, Irene Makaryk ends with "newspapers."

16. *Bertolt Brecht Journals* [1935–1955], trans. Hugh Rorrison and ed. John Willett (London: Methuen, 1993), 90–91.

17. *Bertolt Brecht Journals* [1935–1955], 91.

18. *Bertolt Brecht Journals* [1935–1955], 91.

19. Walter Benjamin, *Selected Writings Volume 1 1913–1926*, ed. Marcus Bullock and Michael W. Jennings (Cambridge MA: Belknap Press of Harvard University Press, 1996), 219.

20. Benjamin, 218.

21. Benjamin, 226.

22. Hayden White, *The Fiction of Narrative: Essays on History, Literature, and Theory 1957–2007*, ed. Robert Doran (Baltimore: John Hopkins University Press, 2010), 271.

23. W. J. T Mitchell, " Critical Inquiry and the Ideology of Pluralism," *Critical Inquiry* 8 (1982), 612–18; White, *Fiction*, 223–25. In the chapter "Historical Pluralism and Pantextualism," White discusses Mitchell's view of theory and history.

24. White, *Fiction*, 225.

25. White, *Fiction*, 310–17.

26. Lodge, 138; White, *Fiction*, 315.

27. See James Clifford, *Routes—Travel and Translation in the Late Twentieth-Century* (Cambridge, MA: Harvard University Press, 1997).

28. *Bertolt Brecht Diaries 1920–1922*, 21.

29. *Bertolt Brecht Journals* [1935–1955], 422–23.

30. White, *Fiction*, 316.

Chapter 1

1. The original reads: "Dès son origine, . . . elle est toujours définie comme une discipline en crise." Armando Gnisci, "La Littérature comparée comme

discipline de décolonisation." My translation here and below unless otherwise indicated. *Canadian Review of Comparative Literature/Revue Canadienne de Littérature Comparée*[CRCL/RCLC] 23 (1996), 67. I would like to thank Wladimir Krysinski, Amaryll Chanady, and their colleagues in Littérature Comparée at l'Université de Montréal for their invitation and hospitality in 2005 and for the bilingual session that surrounded my original paper. It was good to be back in one of the cities of my youth. My thanks also to Wladimir Krysinski and to Jean Bessière of the Sorbonne Nouvelle (Paris III) for reading and encouraging this article and to the editors and readers of *Revue de littérature comparée* for their suggestions, interest, and support. For an earlier version of this chapter, see Jonathan Hart, "The Futures of Comparative Literature: North America and Beyond," *Revue de littérature comparée* 2006/1—N317, 5–21. My thanks to the editors and to the publishers, Klincksieck, for permission to reprint.

2. The original reads: "une discipline véritablement mondiale." Gnisci, "La Littérature comparée," 77. See also *Letteratura comparata: Storia e testi*, ed. Armando Gnisci and Franca Sinopoli (Roma: Sovera, 1995).

3. Tania Franco Carvalhal, *Literatura Comparada* (São Paulo: Ática, 1986).

4. *Revue Canadienne de Littérature Comparée CRCL/RCLC* 23 (1996), 75. The original reads: "La littérature comparée existe au Brésil depuis longtemps: en réalité, dès le temps où on a commencé à réfléchir sur la formation de la littérature Brésilienne et sur la création d'un project de literature nationale."

5. Walter Moser, "La Littérature Comparée et la crise des études littéraires," *Revue Canadienne de Littérature Comparée* [CRCL/RCLC] 23 (1996), 43. The original reads: "Une discipline nomade."

6. Moser, 44. The original reads: "La précarité du statut de leur discipline peut même se tourner en avantage."

7. See Alvin Kernan's *The Death of Literature* (New Haven, CT: Yale University Press, 1990) and Susan Bassnett's *Comparative Literature: A Critical Introduction* (Oxford: Blackwell, 1993), especially 47.

8. Gayatri Chakravorty Spivak, *Death of a Discipline* (New York: Columbia University Press, 2003), xii.

9. Spivak, xii.

10. Spivak, 1.

11. Spivak, 3.

12. Spivak, 5.

13. Spivak, 6.

14. Spivak, 8–9.

15. Spivak, 13.

16. Spivak, 23.

17. Spivak, 26–34.

18. Spivak, 52.

19. Spivak, 55.

20. Spivak, 65.

21. Spivak, 66.
22. Spivak, 96, 101.
23. Spivak, 102.
24. See, for instance, Marshall McLuhan, *The Mechanical Bride: Folklore of Industrial Man* (New York: Vanguard Press, 1951) and his *The Gutenburg Galaxy: The Making of Typographic Man* (Toronto: University of Toronto Press, 1962); Roland Barthes, *Mythologies* (Paris: Editions du Seuil, 1957). For a discussion of Roland Barthes, Marshall McLuhan, Northrop Frye, and others in regards to mythology, ideology, technology, and culture, see also Jonathan Hart, *Northrop Frye: The Theoretical Imagination* (London and New York: Routledge, 1994), and Hart, *Interpreting Cultures: Literature, Religion, and the Human Sciences* (London and New York: Palgrave Macmillan, 2006). For related debates, see Jonathan Hart, "Introduction," *City of the End of Things: Lectures on Civilization and Empire* (Toronto: Oxford University Press, 2009), 1–34.
25. *The Republic of Plato*, trans. Francis MacDonald Cornford (1941; New York and London: Oxford University Press, 1945, rpt. 1968), especially, book 10.
26. Philip Sidney, "An Apology for Poetry," in *English Critical Texts: 16th Century to 20th Century*, ed. D. J. Enright and Ernst de Chickera (London: Oxford University Press, 1962, rpt. 1975), 3–49.
27. See, particularly, Percy Bysshe Shelley, *A Defence of Poetry*, ed. Mrs. Shelley, reprinted from the edition of MDCCCXLV (Indianapolis, IN: The Bobbs-Merrill Company, 1904), "Part First."
28. Karl R. Popper, "Die Logik der Sozialwissenschaften," (1972), in *Der Positivismusstreitin der deutschen Soziologie* by Theodor W. Adorno et al., 3rd ed. (Darmstadt: Luchterhand, 1974), 108, in Douwe Fokkema, "Comparative Literature and Canon Formation," *Canadian Review of Comparative Literature/Revue Canadienne de Littérature Comparée [CRCL/RCLC]* 23 (1996), 53.
29. Fokkema, "Comparative Literature and Canon Formation," *Revue Canadienne de Littérature Comparée [CRCL/RCLC]* 23 (1996), 53.
30. Linda Hutcheon, "Comparative Literature's 'Axiogenic' State," *Revue Canadienne de Littérature Comparée [CRCL/RCLC]* 23 (1996), 35.
31. Hutcheon, p. 39.
32. Hutcheon, p. 40.
33. These reports of the American Comparative Literature Association can be found at http://www.umass.edu/complit/aclanet/Levin.html for the American Comparative Literature Association Report on Professional Standards (First or Levin report, 1965); http://www.umass.edu/complit/aclanet/Green.html for the (Second or Greene report) (Submitted to the American Comparative Literature Association by the Committee on Professional Standards, September, 1975); http://www.umass.edu/complit/aclanet/ Bernheim.html for the (Bernheimer report, 1993). The Bernheimer report was later published as *Comparative Literature in the Age of Multiculturalism*, ed. Charles Bernheimer (Baltimore: Johns Hopkins University Press, 1995). The Saussy report, 2003–4, has been

posted at http://www.stanford.edu/~saussy/acla. It later appeared as a book—see *Comparative Literature in an Era of Globalization,* ed. Haun Saussy (Johns Hopkins University Press, 2006).

34. The quotations are from the draft version of the report at the Stanford University website (as listed in note 33). All page numbers refer to the numbers in the draft of each article—numbers are not continuous throughout the draft. This draft report occurred in 2003–2004. The book appeared as cited in note 33. I have kept the analysis I did of the draft report for its historical context as it was not a response to the book that later appeared.

35. Haun Saussy, "Exquisite Cadavers Stitched from Fresh Nightmares: Of Memes, Hives, and Selfish Genes," in the "Saussy Report" (in draft), 1.

36. Saussy.

37. Saussy, 31.

38. Alain Badiou, *Petit manuel d'inesthétique* (Paris: Seuil, 1998), 85, in Emily Apter, "Je ne crois pas beaucoup à la littérature comparée:" Universal Poetics and Postcolonial Comparativism," in the "Saussy Report" (in draft), 1.

39. Apter, "'Je ne crois pas beaucoup à la littérature comparée:' Universal Poetics and Postcolonial Comparativism," in the "Saussy Report" (in draft), 1.

40. Ibid., 6–7.

41. Bernheimer, ix, in Djelal Kadir, "Comparative Literature in an Age of Terrorism," in the "Saussy Report" (in draft), 1; this is also noted in the "Saussy Report" itself.

42. Kadir, "Comparative Literature in an Age of Terrorism," in the "Saussy Report" (in draft), 9.

43. Steven Ungar, "Writing in Tongues: Thoughts on the Work of Translation," in the "Saussy Report" (in draft), 1.

44. Walter Benjamin, "The Task of the Translator" (1921), in *Selected Writings, vol. 1: 1913–1926*, ed. Marcus Bullock and Michael W. Jennings (Cambridge, MA: Harvard University Press, 1996), 257, in "Writing in Tongues: Thoughts on the Work of Translation," in the

45. Ungar, "Writing in Tongues," in the "Saussy Report" (in draft), 7. See William H. Gass, *Reading Rilke: Reflections on the Problems of Translation* (New York: Basic Books, 1999), 55.

46. David Damrosch, *What Is World Literature?* (Princeton, NJ: Princeton University Press, 2003).

47. David Damrosch, "World Literature in a Postcanonical, Hypercanonical Age," in the "Saussy Report" (in draft), 1.

48. Damrosch, 9.

49. Christopher Braider, "Of Monuments and Documents: Comparative Literature and the Visual Arts in Early Modern Studies, or The Art of Historical Tact," in the "Saussy Report" (in draft), 1.

50. Michael Baxandall, *Patterns of Intention: On the Historical Explanation of Pictures* (New Haven, CT: Yale University Press, 1985), introduction and chapter 4, cited in ibid., 13.

51. Gail Finney, "What's Happened to Feminism?" in the "Saussy Report" (in draft), 1.
52. Finney, 8.
53. Lynne Pearce, *The Rhetorics of Feminism: Readings in Contemporary Cultural Theory and the Popular Press* (London and New York: Routledge, 2004).
54. See Finney, "What's Happened to Feminism?", 8.
55. Fedwa Malti-Douglas, "Beyond Comparison Shopping: This is Not Your Father's Comp. Lit.," in the "Saussy Report" (in draft), 11.
56. Caryl Emerson, "Answering for Central and Eastern Europe," in the "Saussy Report" (in draft), 7.
57. Marián Gálik, "Comparative Literature in Slovakia," *Revue Canadienne de Littérature Comparée* [*CRCL/RCLC*] 23 (1996), 101–112; Richard Teleky, "Towards a Course on Central European Literature as Translation" [*CRCL/ RCLC*] 23 (1996), 115–23.
58. Franco Moretti, "Conjectures on World Literature," *New Left Review* 1 (January– February 2000), 57–67, p. 54, quoted in Katie Trumpener, "World Music, World Literature: A Geopolitical View," the "Saussy Report" (in draft), 1.
59. Trumpener, "World Music, World Literature: A Geopolitical View," in the "Saussy Report" (in draft), p. 1. See Johann Gottfried Herder, *Stimmen der Völker in Liedern. Volkslieder. Zwei Teile* (Stuttgart: Philipp Reclam, 1975).
60. Trumpener, "World Music, World Literature," 9–10.
61. Trumpener, 10.
62. Richard Rorty, "Looking Back at 'Literary Theory,'" in the "Saussy Report" (in draft), 10. See Michel Foucault, *Les mots et les choses: Une archéologie des sciences* ([Paris]: Gallimard, 1966). Jacques Derrida, *De la Grammatologie* (Paris: Éditions de Minuit, 1967).
63. Rorty, "Looking Back at 'Literary Theory," 2.
64. Rorty, 2.
65. Rorty, 2.
66. Rorty, 2.
67. Rorty, 2.
68. Rorty, 2.
69. See Rorty, 3.
70. Rorty, 3.
71. Wang Ning, "Toward a New Framework of Comparative Literature," *Revue Canadienne de Littérature Comparée* [*CRCL/RCLC*] 23 (1996), 91–100.
72. King or Captain Ludd were imaginary names or nicknames for the leader of the rioters (Luddites), mainly mechanics and their friends, in the Midlands of England in a critical time during the Industrial Revolution (1811–16), who destroyed manufacturing machines. At critical moments, it is easy to turn on the tools or instruments of change. Kicking in a television set or trashing a computer will not stem the tide of change. Literature will find itself in new relations in new configurations as media for words and images change. The *Oxford English Dictionary* notes the following story about the etymology of "Luddite":

"According to Pellew's *Life of Lord Sidmouth* (1847) III. 80, Ned Lud (Ludd) was a person of weak intellect who lived in a Leicestershire village about 1779, and who in a fit of insane rage rushed into a 'stockinger's house, and destroyed two frames so completely that the saying 'Lud must have been here' came to be used throughout the hosiery districts when a stocking-frame had undergone extraordinary damage. The story lacks confirmation." For the most accessible form (and something Luddites might not want access to themselves), see http://dictionary.oed.com/

73. Aristotle's *Poetics*, trans. George Whalley (Montréal and Kingston: McGill-Queen's Press, 1997), 81, 83 (1451a–b).

Chapter 2

1. See James Clifford, *Routes—Travel and Translation in the Late Twentieth-Century* (Cambridge, MA: Harvard University Press, 1997), 3. This chapter is based on a paper presented at the Congress of the International Comparative Literature Association in Rio de Janeiro in 2007 and revised and published as "Comparative Literature and the Comparative Narratives of European Expansion," *Beyond Binarisms: Discontinuities and Displacements: Studies in Comparative Literature*, ed. Eduardo F. Coutinho (Rio de Janeiro: Aeroplano Editora, 2009), 183–94. I would like to thank Eduardo F. Coutinho, principal organizer of the Congress and the editor, for granting permission on behalf of the publisher to reprint this revised version. Some recent books continue the long-standing and ongoing debate about encounters in the New World. See, for instance, Susan Castillo—who speaks about the staging of encounters between Native and European characters in dramatic dialogues, plays, lexographical studies, and travel narratives—in *Colonial Encounters in New World Writing, 1500–1786: Performing America* (London: Routledge, 2006), 3–4. Christine Johnson discusses the relation between the Renaissance and European expansion and does so in the particular case of Germany in *The German Discovery of the New World: Renaissance Encounters with the Strange and Marvelous* (Charlottesville: University of Virginia Press, 2008), 1–2. In discussing ways of encountering death, Erik K. Seeman says: "Residents of the early modern Atlantic world combined inclusivity and exclusivity—a recognition of similarity and difference—when they interacted with outsiders"; *Death in the New World: Cross-Cultural Encounters, 1492–1800* (Philadelphia: University of Pennsylvania Press, 2010), 4. Drama and recognition are never too far from the representation and interpretation of empire from the late Middle Ages onward, as these books together suggest.

2. Terence Cave, *Recognitions: A Study in Poetics* (Oxford: Clarendon Press, 1990), 1–9; see Northrop Frye, "'The Argument of Comedy' (1948)," in *Theories of Comedy*, ed. Paul Lauter (Garden City, NY: Doubleday, 1964), 450–60 and Northrop Frye, *Anatomy of Criticism: Four Essays* (Princeton, NJ: Princeton University Press, 1957, rpt. 1973).

3. Aristotle, "On the Art of Poetry," in *Classical Literary Criticism*, ed. T. S. Dorsch (Harmondsworth: Penguin, 1975), 33–75; Bertolt Brecht, *Brecht on Theatre: The Development of an Aesthetic*, ed. and trans. John Willett (New York: Hill and Wang, 1964); Jonathan Hart, "Alienation, Double Signs with a Difference: Conscious Knots in *Cymbeline* and *The Winter's Tale*," *CIEFL Bulletin* (New Series) 1 (1989), 58–78. A revised version of this article appears in Jonathan Hart, *Shakespeare and His Contemporaries* (New York: Palgrave Macmillan, 2011).

4. See the *Oxford English Dictionary* [*OED*] (1989), 2nd ed. (Oxford: Oxford University Press, 1989).

5. Michel de Certeau, *Heterologies: Discourse on the Other*, trans. Brian Massumi (Minneapolis: University of Minnesota Press, 1986), 68, 70; Anthony Pagden, *The Fall of Natural Man: The American Indian and the Origins of Comparative Ethnology* (Cambridge: Cambridge University Press, 1986), 175, 195.

6. See J. de Acosta, *The Natvrall and Morall Historie of the East and West Indies*, trans. Edward Grimstone (London 1604), and Michel de Montaigne, *The Essays of Montaigne*, trans. E. J. Treichmann (London: Oxford University Press, 1953).

7. Herodotus, *The Persian Wars*, trans. G. Rawlinson (New York: Modern Library, 1942). For the eyewitness report, see (II, 99), and belief, (VII, 152).

8. Arnaldo Momigliano, *The Classical Foundations of Modern Historiography* (Berkeley: University of California Press, 1990), 36–39.

9. Herodotus, IV, 18.

10. Herodotus, IV, 106.

11. Herodotus, IV, 64.

12. Herodotus, IV, 64.

13. Herodotus, IV, 110.

14. Herodotus, IV, 111.

15. Herodotus, IV, 111.

16. Herodotus, IV, 113.

17. Herodotus, IV, 113.

18. Herodotus, IV, 114–16.

19. Margarita Zamora, *Reading Columbus* (Berkeley: University of California Press, 1993), 3–20, 211; Felipe Fernández-Armesto, *Columbus on Himself* (London: Folio, 1992), 9–16, 101–03.

20. Cecil Jane, "Introduction," *The Four Voyages of Columbus*, ed. Cecil Jane (New York: Dover, 1988), vol. 1, esp. xcvii–xcviii.

21. Las Casas wrote many key texts, the most substantial of which may be Bartolomé de Las Casas, *Historia de las Indias*, ed. Gonzalo de Reparaz, 3 vols. (Madrid: M. Aguilar, 1927).

22. Christopher Columbus, *Four Voyages*, ed. Cecil Jane (New York: Dover, 1988), 2.

23. Columbus, 4.

24. Columbus, 6; "la Española es maravilla" [7].

25. Columbus 6, 8.
26. Columbus, 10.
27. Columbus, 14.
28. Columbus, 14.
29. Columbus, 16.
30. On monsters, see Jacques Le Goff, *La Civilisation de L'Occident medieval* (Paris: B. Arthaud, 1964).
31. Columbus, 14, 16.
32. Columbus, 6–11.
33. Jacques Cartier, *The Voyages of Jacques Cartier*, trans. H. P. Biggar with corrections to the translation and an Introduction by Ramsey Cook (Toronto: University of Toronto Press, 1995), 21.
34. Cartier, 26, 27.
35. Jean de Léry, *History of a Voyage to the Land of Brazil*, trans. Janet Whatley (Berkeley: University of California Press, 1990), 26.
36. Léry, 26.
37. Léry, 67.
38. Léry, 67.
39. Montaigne, 114.
40. Walter Raleigh [Ralegh], *A Report of the Trvth of the fight about the Isles of Açores, this last Sommer. Betwixt The Reuenge, one of her Maiesties Shippes, And an Armada of the King of Spaine* (London: William Ponsonbie, [1591], 1967); *The Discouerie of the Large, Rich, and Bewtiful Empyre of Guiana, with a Relation of the great and Golden Citie of Manoa (which the Spanyards call El Dorado) And of the Prouinces of Emeria. Arromaia, Amapapaia , and other Coun-tries, with their riuers, as-ioyning* (London: Robert Robertson, 1596, rpt. Leeds: The Scholar Press, 1967), A3ᵛ.
41. Ralegh, A5v.
42. Ralegh, 101, see 96.
43. Quoted in Pagden, 162.
44. Pagden, 162.
45. Anthony Grafton with April Shelford and Nancy Siraisi, "Introduction," *New Worlds, Ancient Texts: The Power of Tradition and the Shock of Discovery* (Cambridge, MA: Harvard University Press, 1992), 1, 5.
46. Jonathan Hart, *Representing the New World: The English and French Uses of the Example of Spain* (New York: Palgrave, 2001), and *Empires and Colonies* (Cambridge: Polity Press 2008). Some of this chapter overlaps with work in these books of mine as well as in my other works: *Interpreting Culture: Literature, Religion, and the Human Sciences* (New York and London: Palgrave Macmillan, 2006); *Contesting Empires: Promotion, Opposition and Slavery* (New York: Palgrave Macmillan 2005); *Columbus, Shakespeare, and the Interpretation of the New World* (New York: Palgrave Macmillan, 2003); *Comparing Empires: European Colonialism from Portuguese Expansion to the Spanish-American War* (New York: Palgrave Macmillan, 2003).

47. Seymour Phillips, "The Outer World of the European Middle Ages," in *Implicit Understandings*, ed. Stuart B. Schwartz (Cambridge: Cambridge University Press, 1994), 23–63; J. R. S. Phillips, *The Medieval Expansion of Europe*, 2nd ed. (Oxford: Oxford University Press, 1998), ch. 9.

48. See William McNeill, *Plagues and Peoples* (New York: Anchor Books, 1976) and Jared Diamond, *Guns, Germs, and Steel: The Fates of Human Societies* (New York: Norton, 1999).

49. See Lewis Hanke, *Aristotle and the Indians: A Study of Race Prejudice in the Modern World* (Chicago, IL: H. Regnery, 1959).

50. S. Phillips, 45–47.

51. *A Chinese Bestiary*, ed. and trans. Richard E. Strassberg (Berkeley: University of California Press, 2002), 56.

52. *Anti-Foreignism and Western Learning in Early Modern Japan: Selections of the New Theses of 1825,* ed. Bob Tadashi Wakabayashi (Cambridge, MA: Harvard University Press for the Council on East Asian Studies, Harvard, 1986), 49–51, 200.

53. Jonathan Hart, "A Comparative Pluralism: the Heterogeneity of Methods and the Case of Possible Worlds," *Canadian Review of Comparative Literature* [*CRCL/RCLC*] 15 (1988), 320–45.

54. Aristotle; a suggestive discussion of literary representation occurs in Erich Auerbach, *Mimesis: The Representation of Reality in Western Literature*, trans. Willard Trask (New York: Doubleday, 1957); for alternative view of writing history, see Karen Hellekson, *The Alternate History: Refiguring Historical Time* (Kent, OH: Kent State University Press, 2001).

Chapter 3

1. This brief section was from something I wrote for the *Canadian Review of Comparative Literature/Revue Canadienne de Littérature Comparée* [*CRCL/RCLC*] in 1999. Any work that I have revised and included here or elsewhere in the book appears with thanks for permission from the editor of *CRCL/RCLC* on behalf of the Canadian Comparative Literature Association.

2. Harry Levin, "Literature as an Institution," *Accent* 6 (1946), 159–68.

3. Hendrik Van Gorp, Anneleen Masschelein, Dirk de Geest, and Koenraad Geldorf have brought together articles in a special issue. Hendrik Van Gorp has divided the essays into three sections. This part of the chapter is a revision of Jonathan Hart, "Afterword—System and Anti-System: Shaking up the Paradigms," *Canadian Review of Comparative Literature/Revue Canadienne de Littérature Comparée* [*CRCL/RCLC*] 24 (1997), 190–92. In this issue, see, for instance, Van Gorp's " Introduction: The Study of Literature and Culture—Systems and Fields," 1–5; De Geest's "Systems Theory and Discursivity," 161–75; Geldof's "Du champ (littéraire). Ambiguïtés d'une manière de faire sociologique," 77–89; there are—besides those of the editors—important contributions to the debate in this special issue, including, Douwe Fokkema,

"The Systems—Theoretical Perspective in Literary Studies: Arguments for a Problem Oriented Approach," 177–85; "Factors and Dependencies in Culture: A Revised Outline for Polysystem Culture Research," 15–34; Elrud Ibsch, "Systems Theory and the Concept of 'Communication' in Literary Studies," 115–18; José Lambert, "Itamar Even-Zohar's Polysystem Culture Research," 7–14; Siegfried J. Schmidt, "A Systems-Oriented Approach to Literary Studies," 119–36.

4. I have mentioned this special issue above.

5. Hans Bertens, *Literary Theory: The Basics,* 2nd ed. (Abingdon: Routledge, 2008), esp. vii–ix, 12–14, 24–25.

6. Plato, *The Republic of Plato,* trans. Francis M. Cornford (New York: Oxford University Press,1941, rpt. 1968), 605c, 337.

7. Dennis D. Kezar, ed., *Solon and Thespis: Law and Theater in the English Renaissance* (Notre Dame, IN: University of Notre Dame Press, 2007). Thanks to the editors for allowing me to use here a revised version of my contribution to *Renaissance Quarterly* 60 (2007), 1028–30.

8. A. G. Harmon, *Eternal Bonds, True Contracts: Law and Nature in Shakespeare's Problem Plays* (Albany: State University of New York Press, 2004). My thanks to the editors for allowing me to use here a revised version of my contribution to *Renaissance Quarterly* 58.3 (2005), 1043–45.

9. Although I first argued this in the early 1980s, the argument can be found in different revised forms and contexts in my *Theater and World: The Problematics of Shakespeare's History* (Boston, MA: Northeastern University Press, 1992) and *Shakespeare: Poetry, History, and Culture* (New York: Palgrave Macmillan, 2009).

10. See, for instance, Margaret Scott, Peter Alscher, and Clara Mucci.

11. Harmon, 161.

12. Harmon, 163.

13. George Steiner, *Lessons of the Masters* (Cambridge, MA: Harvard University Press, 2003). My thanks to the editors for allowing me to use here a revised version of my contribution to *Harvard Review* 26 (2004), 225–27.

14. Steiner, 29.

15. Steiner, 141.

16. Steiner, 183. In 1971, Steiner said: "We cannot turn back. We cannot choose the dreams of unknowing." See George Steiner, *In Bluebeard's Castle: Some Notes Towards the Redefinition of Culture* (New Haven, CT: Yale University Press, 1971), 140. On Lacan as a master, not surprisingly in a psychoanalytical context, see Friedrich A. Kittler, *Literature, Media, Information Systems: Essays,* ed. and trans. John Johnston (Amsterdam: OPA, 1997), 50–52.

17. Eva Kushner, *The Living Prism: Itineraries in Comparative Literature* (Montreal and Kingston: McGill-Queen's University Press for Carleton University, 2001). I thank the editors for allowing me to use here a revised version of my contribution to *University of Toronto Quarterly* 72.1 (Winter 2002/3), 350–52.

18. Kushner, 3.

19. Kushner, 17.
20. Kushner, 29.
21. Kushner, 37.
22. Kushner, 51.
23. Kushner, 68
24. R. G. Collingwood, *The Idea of History* (Oxford: Clarendon Press, 1946), 282, quoted in Kushner, 91.
25. Kushner, 105.
26. Kushner, 116.
27. Kushner, 200.
28. Kushner, 256–57.
29. Kushner, 275.
30. On the question of the other, see Martin Buber, *Ich und Du* (Berlin: Schoken Verlag, 1923) and, in translation, *I/Thou* (1937; rev 1958; London: Continuum, 2004), Tzvetan Todorov, *La Conquête de L'Autre* (Paris: Éditions de Seuil, 1982); Kushner, 180. Kushner also discusses Todorov.
31. Wladimir Krysinski, *Carrefours de signes: essays sur le roman moderne* (La Haye: Mouton, 1981).

Chapter 4

1. Otherness is a vast field. Here, I mention briefly some pertinent discussions of otherness. The discussion of the stranger and otherness stretches back to Herodotus and beyond as I argue in this chapter. Montaigne is another important figure. In 1943, in *Les Cahiers du sud*, Jean-Paul Sartre wrote on Albert Camus and the idea of the stranger in his novel by that title. For a recent translation of this and on his work on existentialism and humanism, see Jean-Paul Sartre, *Existentialism is a Humanism*, introduction by Annie Cohen-Solal; preface and notes by Arlette Elkaïm-Sartre (New Haven, CT: Yale University Press, 2007). For work related to my chapter, which discusses otherness in the colonial, see Jean-Paul Sartre, *Situations V* (Paris: Gallimard, 1964) and his *Colonialism and Neo-Colonialism,* trans. Azzedine Haddour, Steve Brewer, and Terry McWilliams (London: Routledge, 2001), an English translation of that work. See also Emmanuel Levinas, *Le temps et l'autre* (Paris: B. Arthaud, 1947). On otherness and Europe's bad conscience, see Emmanuel Lévinas, *Entre Nous, Essais sur le-penser-à-l'autre* (Paris: Editions de Bernard Grasset et Fasquelle, 1991) and his *Entre Nous*, trans. Michael Bradley Smith and Barbara Harshav (1998; London: Continuum, 2006), 164–66. See also Jacques Derrida, *Psyché: inventions de l'autre* (Paris: Galilée, 1987) and—the translation—Jacques Derrida, *Psyche: Invention of the Other* (Chicago: University of Chicago Press, 1993). Derrida relates psyche, allegory, fable, and truth to the invention of the other and appeals to Paul de Man's rhetoric of temporality. See also Jacques Derrida, *Adieu à Emmanuel Levinas* (Paris: Galilée, 1997), translated as *Adieu to Emmanuel Levinas*, trans. Pascale-Anne Brault and Michael

Naas (Stanford: Stanford University Press, 1999). On otherness in a feminist context, see Verena Andermatt Conley, *Hélène Cixous: Writing the Feminine, Expanded Version* (1984; Lincoln: University of Nebraska Press, 1991), 100–102. For a discussion of the relation between otherness and subjectivity in light of Freud see Jean Laplanche, *La révolution copernicienne* (Paris: Aubier, 1992) and Jean Laplanche, *Essays on Otherness* (London: Routledge, 1999). On the relation between alterity and Husserl's notion of intersubjectivity, see Bertrand Bouckaert, *L'idée de l'autre: la question de l'idéalité et de l'altérité chez Husserl des "Logische Untersuchungen" aux "Ideen 1"* (Dordrecht: Kluwer Academic Publishers, 2003), especially 1–16. I would like to thank Rajnath, the editor, for permission to reprint in this revised form "Recognitions, Otherness and Comparing Literatures and Histories," *Journal of Literary Criticism* 12.1–2 (June/December 2008), 130–59. Many thanks to my colleagues in Comparative Literature at the Sorbonne-Nouvelle—Jean Bessière, Philippe Daros, Stéphane Michaud, and Alexandre Stroev—and the students in my doctoral seminar on otherness, in the spring of 2009.

2. Quoted in Colin Heywood, *A History of Childhood: Children and Childhood in the West from Medieval to Modern Times* (Cambridge: Polity, 2001), 26.
3. Herodotus, *The Persian Wars*, trans. George Rawlinson (New York: Modern Library, 1942), 4.110.
4. Herodotus, 4.110.
5. Herodotus, 4.111.
6. Herodotus, 4.111.
7. Herodotus, 4.111.
8. Herodotus, 4.111.
9. Herodotus, 4.111.
10. Herodotus, 4.111.
11. Herodotus, 4.112.
12. Herodotus, 4.113.
13. Herodotus, 4.113.
14. Herodotus, 4.114.
15. Herodotus, 4.114.
16. Herodotus, 4.114.
17. Herodotus, 4.114.
18. Herodotus, 4.114.
19. Herodotus, 4.114.
20. Herodotus, 4.115.
21. Herodotus, 4.116.
22. Herodotus, 4.117.
23. Herodotus, 4.117.
24. Herodotus, 4.117.
25. Christopher Columbus, *The Four Voyages of Columbus: A History in Eight Documents, Including Five By Christopher Columbus, In the Original Spanish, With English Translations*, trans. and ed. Cecil Jane (New York: Dover, 1988), 6.

26. Columbus, 6.
27. Columbus, 6.
28. Columbus, 14.
29. Columbus, 16.
30. Columbus, 16; see Jonathan Hart, "Images of the Native in Renaissance Encounter Narratives," *ARIEL* 25 (October 1994), 55–76.
31. "Letter by Pedro Vaz de Caminha to King Manuel Written from Porto Seguro of Vera Cruz the 1st of May 1500," *The Voyage of Pedro Álvares Cabral to Brazil and India from Contemporary Documents and Narratives*, trans. with an intro. by William Brooks Greenlee, Second Series No. 81 (London: Hakluyt Society 1938 for 1937), 5.
32. See Caminha, "Letter;" Jonathan Hart, *Comparing Empires: European Colonialism from Portuguese Expansion to the Spanish-American War* (New York: Palgrave Macmillan, 2003, rpt. 2008).
33. See *Les Français en Amérique pendant la première moitié du XVIe siècle*, ed. Charles-André Julien, René Herval, and Théodore Beauchesne (Paris, 1946); *Voyages au Canada avec les relations des voyages en Amérique de Gonneville, Verranzano et Roberval*, ed. Charles-André Julien, René Herval, and Théodore Beauchesne (Paris, 1981).
34. Richard Eden, *A treatyse of the newe India, with other new founde landes and Ilandes, as well eastwarde as westwarde, as they are knowen and found in these our dayes, after the descripcion of Sebastian Munster in his boke of universall Cosmographie: wherein the diligent reader may see the good successe and rewarde of noble and honeste enterpryses, by the which not only worldly ryches are obtayned, but also God is glorified, and the Christian fayth enlarged. Translated out of Latin into Englishe. By Rycharde Eden* (London, 1553).
35. Jean Ribault, *Discovery of Terra Florida*, trans. Thomas Hacket (London, 1563); Nicolas Le Challeux, *A true and perfect description, of the last voyage or nauigation, attempted by Capitaine Iohn Rybaut, deputie and generall for the French men, into Terra Florida, this yeare past. 1565. Truely sette forth by those that returned from thence, wherein are contayned things as lame[n]table to heare as they haue bene cruelly executed* (London, 1566).
36. Richard Hakluyt, *Discourse of Western Planting* (London: Hakluyt Society, 1993), 56.
37. Hakluyt 59; see Jonathan Hart, *Representing the New World The English and French Uses of the Example of Spain* (New York: Palgrave, 2001).
38. See Jonathan Hart, "Strategies of Promotion: Some Prefatory Matter of Oviedo, Thevet and Hakluyt," *Imagining Culture: Essays in Early Modern History and Literature*, ed. Jonathan Hart (New York: Garland, 1996), 73–94, 201–2.
39. See Jonathan Hart, *Contesting Empires: Opposition, Promotion, and Slavery* (New York: Palgrave Macmillan, 2005).
40. See Hart, *Contesting*, ch. 3.
41. Bartolomé de Las Casas, *A Short Account of the Destruction of the Indies*, trans. Nigel Griffin. London: Penguin, 1992), 3–4.

42. Michel de Montaigne, *Les essais: reproduction typographique de l'exemplaire annoté par l'auteur et conservé à la bibliothèque de Bordeaux* (Paris, 1906–31), I, 169.

43. Michel de Certeau, "Montaigne's 'Of Cannibals': The Savage 'I,'" *Heterologies: Discourse on the Other*, trans. Brian Massumi (Minneapolis: University of Minnesota Press, 1986), 69–70; see Hart, *Contesting*.

44. Tzvetan Todorov, *The Conquest of America: The Question of the Other*, trans. Richard Howard (1982; New York: Harper, 1984, rpt. 1992), 148, 151.

45. J. H. Elliott, *The Old World and the New 1492–1650* (Cambridge: Cambridge University Press, 1970, rpt. 1992), 11, 20–21, 32, 40, 43. See J. H. Elliott "Cortés, Veláquez and Charles V," Hernán Cortés, *Letters from Mexico*, trans. Anthony Pagden (1971; New Haven, CT: Yale University Press, 1986).

46. Anthony Pagden, *The Fall of Natural Man: The American Indian and the Origins of Comparative Ethnography* (Cambridge: Cambridge University Press, 1982, rev. 1986), 11, and Anthony Pagden, *European Encounters with the New World: From Renaissance to Romanticism* (New Haven: Yale University Press, 1993), 56.

47. See Hart, *Contesting*.

Chapter 5

1. Peter Burke, "Overture: the New History," *New Perspectives on Historical Writing,* ed. Peter Burke (1991; University Park: Pennsylvania State University Press, 1992), 2.

2. Burke, 3–6. Other historians have called attention to historiography and theory in history as well as to new methods. For instance, Michael Bentley says that some historians are terrified of theory and historiography and assume that those interested in such questions, which touch on the assumptions behind how historians treat "knowledge, understanding, imagination, explanation, analysis, narrative," are postmodernists. See Michael Bentley, *Modern Historiography: An Introduction* (London: Routledge, 1999), viii. According to Aviezar Tucker, "Philosophy of historiography is simply the philosophical examination of all the aspects of our descriptions, beliefs, and knowledge of the past." See Aviezar Tucker, "Introduction," *A Companion to the Philosophy of History and Historiography*, ed. Aviezar Tucker (Oxford: Blackwell, 2009), 4.

3. Stephen Greenblatt, *Renaissance Self-Fashioning from More to Shakespeare* (Chicago: University of Chicago Press, 1980), 1–4 and his *Shakespearean Negotiations: The Circulation of Social Energy in Renaissance England* (Berkeley: University of California Press, 1988), 6. For a detailed discussion on Greenblatt and the New Historicist use of analogy, see Jonathan Hart, "Stephen Greenblatt's Shakespearean Negotiations," *Textual Practice* 5 (1991), 429–48.

4. *The New Historicism*, ed. H. Aram Veeser (New York: Routledge, 1989). My thanks to the editors for giving me permission to include here a revised version of "The New Historicism: Taking History into Account,' *ARIEL* 22 (1991),

93–107. For articles on New Historicism and related topics during the 1980s, see Jonathan Goldberg, "The Politics of Renaissance Literature: A Review Essay," *ELH* 49 (1982), 514–82; Jean E. Howard, "The New Historicism in Renaissance Studies," *ELR* 16 (1986), 13–43; Edward Pechter, "The New Historicism and Its Discontents: Politicizing Renaissance Drama," *PMLA* 102 (1987), 292–303; Walter Cohen, "Political Criticism in Shakespeare," in *Shakespeare Reproduced: The Text in History and Ideology*, eds. J. E. Howard and M. F. O'Connor (New York: Methuen, 1987), 18–46. For a study that combines the British and American versions of a new way to discuss history in literary studies and for an annotated bibliography, see John Brannigan, *New Historicism and Cultural Materialism* (New York: St. Martin's Press, 1998). In their introduction, Catherine Gallagher and Stephen Greenblatt say that writing their book has convinced them "that new historicism is not a repeatable methodology or a literary critical program" and they hope that what they do cannot be summed up, that is, they "cannot bear to see the long chains of close analysis go up in a puff of abstraction." See Catherine Gallagher and Stephen Greenblatt, *Practicing New Historicism* (Chicago, IL: University of Chicago Press, 2000), 19.

5. Michael McCanles, "The Authentic Discourse of the Renaissance," *Diacritics* 10 (1980), 77–87; Stephen Greenblatt, "The Forms of Power and the Power of Forms in the Renaissance," *Genre* 15 (1982), 1–4. Stephen Greenblatt in Veeser, 1–14.

6. Fredric Jameson, *The Political Unconscious: Narrative as a Socially Symbolic Act* (Ithaca, NY: Cornell University Press, 1981), 20, and his "Postmodernism, or the Cultural Logic of Late Capitalism," *New Left Review* 146 (1984), 53–93. Jean-Francois Lyotard, "Judiciousness in Dispute, or Kant after Marx," in *The Aims of Representation*, ed. Murray Krieger (New York: Columbia University Press, 1987), esp. 37.

7. Greenblatt in Veeser, 2–6.

8. Greenblatt, 8.

9. Greenblatt, 11–13.

10. Jane Marcus and Judith Newton in Veeser, 132–67.

11. Marcus, 133.

12. Marcus, 133–34, 148.

13. Newton in Veeser, 153.

14. Newton, 153. For related feminist criticism of the 1980s, see *Rewriting the Renaissance: The Discourses of Sexual Difference in Early Modern Europe*, ed. Margaret W. Ferguson et al. (Chicago, IL: University of Chicago Press, 1986); Carol Thomas Neely, "Constructing the Subject; Feminist Practice and New Renaissance Discourses," *ELR* 18 (1988), 5–18. For studies of other periods, see Catherine Gallagher, *The Industrial Reformation of English Fiction* (Chicago, IL: University of Chicago Press, 1985); Nancy Armstrong, *Desire and Domestic Fiction: A Political History of the Novel* (New York: Oxford University Press, 1987); Mary Poovey, *Uneven Developments: The Ideological Work of Gender in Mid-Victorian England* (Chicago, IL: University of Chicago Press, 1988).

15. Newton, 166.
16. Gayatri Spivak in Veeser, 280.
17. Spivak, 285–86.
18. Spivak, 290–1, see 279–82.
19. Richard Terdiman in Veeser, 225, see 226–30.
20. Catherine Gallagher in Veeser, 37.
21. Gallagher, 37–38.
22. Gallagher, 40–45.
23. Gallagher, 43.
24. Gallagher, 43–44. See Louis Althusser, *For Marx*, trans. Ben Brewster (London: Allen Lane, 1969); Pierre Macherey, *Pour une theorie de la production litteraire* (Paris: Maspero, 1966); translated by Geoffrey Wall as *A Theory of Literary Production* (London: Routledge & Kegan Paul, 1978); Etienne Balibar and Pierre Macherey, "On Literature as an Ideological Form," in *Untying the Text: A Post-Structuralist Reader*, ed. Robert Young (London: Routledge, 1981), 79–99; Michael Sprinker, *Imaginary Relations: Aesthetics and Ideology in the Theory of Historical Materialism* (New York: Verso, 1987).
25. Gallagher, 45.
26. Gallagher, 46–47.
27. Joel Fineman in Veeser, 49–76, see n. 34.
28. Fineman, 56–57.
29. Fineman, 60.
30. Fineman, 61.
31. Fineman, 61.
32. Fineman, 62.
33. Fineman, 63.
34. Fineman, 64.
35. Jon Klancher in Veeser, 77–88.
36. Klancher, 77–78.
37. Klancher, 78. For a key text of the 1980s in this "school," see *Political Shakespeare: New Essays in Cultural Materialism*, ed. Jonathan Dollimore and Alan Sinfield (Ithaca, NY: Cornell University Press, 1985).
38. Stephen Bann in Veeser, 102–15.
39. Jonathan Arac in Veeser, 116–31.
40. Arac, 117.
41. Jean Franco in Veeser, 204–12.
42. Franco, 205.
43. Aram Veeser in Veeser, ix–xvi.
44. Veeser, ix–xvi.
45. Louis Montrose in Veeser, 15–36.
46. John Schaeffer in Veeser, 89–101.
47. Schaeffer, 89, 99–100.
48. Frank Lentricchia in Veeser, 231–42.
49. Lentricchia, 241–42.
50. Gerald Graff in Veeser, 168–81.

51. Graff, 169–71.
52. Graff, 172.
53. Graff, 175.
54. Graff, 179.
55. Graff, 180.
56. Vincent Pecora in Veeser, 243–76.
57. Pecora, 245–46.
58. Clifford Geertz, *The Interpretation of Cultures* (New York: Basic Books, 1973), and his *Local Knowledge* (New York: Basic Books, 1983).
59. Pecora, 272.
60. Brook Thomas in Veeser, 187, see 182–203.
61. Thomas, 194–95.
62. Thomas, 200–01.
63. Elizabeth Fox-Genovese in Veeser, 216, see 213–24.
64. Fox-Genovese, 222.
65. Hayden White in Veeser, 293–302, and Stanley Fish in Veeser, 303–16.
66. White, 297, 301.
67. White, 301.
68. White, 302.
69. Fish in Veeser, 303.
70. Fish, 305.
71. Fish, 307–09.
72. Fish, 311–15.
73. Bann, 102-03.
74. Fineman, 63
75. Louis Montrose in Veeser 32, n. 6. For a variety of views for and against difference, see *Exploration in Difference: Law, Culture and Politics,* ed. Jonathan Hart and Richard W. Bauman (Toronto: University of Toronto Press, 1996).
76. Barbara Johnson, *The Critical Difference: Essays in the Contemporary Rhetoric of Reading* (Baltimore, MD: Johns Hopkins University Press, 1980); *A World of Difference* (Baltimore, MD: Johns Hopkins University Press, 1987); *The Feminist Difference: Literature, Psychoanalysis, Race and Gender* (Cambridge: Harvard University Press, 1998). This revised section on Barbara Johnson was written originally for the *Canadian Review of Comparative Literature/Revue Canadienne de La Littérature Comparée.* Gayle Greene and Coppélia Kahn assert: "Feminist scholarship undertakes the dual task of deconstructing predominantly male cultural paradigms and reconstructing a female perspective and experience in an effort to change the tradition that has silenced and marginalized us." See Gayle Greene and Coppélia Kahn, "Feminist Scholarship and the Social Construction of Woman," *Making a Difference: Feminist Literary Criticism,* ed. Gayle Greene and Coppélia Kahn (London: Methuen, 1985), 1. On feminist historiography and poststructuralism, see R. Radhakrishnan, "Feminist Historiography and Post-structuralist Thought: Intersections and Departures," *The Difference from Within: Feminism and Critical Theory,* ed. Elizabeth Meese

and Alice Parker (Amsterdam: John Benjamins, 1989), 191–95. Radhakrishnan maintains that "post-structuralist thought opens up an entire field where the feminist intervention may enable and empower its projects to the fullest" (192), See Susan Strickland, "Feminism, Post-Modernism and Difference," *Knowing the Difference: Feminist Perspectives in Epistemology*, ed. Kathleen Lennon and Margaret Whitford (Abingdon: Routledge, 1994), 265. On feminism and the problem of essentialism, which was a crucial debate during the 1980s, see Ellen T. Armour, *Deconstruction, Feminist Theology, and the Problem of Difference: Subverting the Race/Gender Divide* (Chicago, IL: University of Chicago Press, 1999), 16–22. In a discussion that begins an examination of the problem of difference and locates Simone De Beauvoir's *The Second Sex* (1949) as the start of modern feminism, and views her contribution as an exploration of the question of the Other, see Susan J. Hekman, *The Future of Differences: Truth and Method in Feminist Theory* (Cambridge: Polity Press, 1999), 1–7. For a discussion of some of the challenges of difference for feminist theology in the 1960s and 1970s in a world dominated by men, and in the 1980s and since concerning internal divisions within feminism, see Margaret D. Kamitsuka, *Feminist Theology and the Challenge of Difference* (New York: Oxford University Press, 2007), 3–4. For an examination of sameness and difference, particularly in relation to the work of Betty Friedan, beginning with *The Feminine Mystique* (1963), see Rosemarie Tong, *Feminist Thought: A More Comprehensive Introduction,* 3rd ed. (Boulder, CO: Westview Press, 2009), 27–34.

77. Johnson, *Feminist Difference*, 2; see hooks in Johnson, 3.
78. Johnson, 12.
79. Johnson, 13.
80. Johnson, 13.
81. Johnson, 13.
82. Johnson, 17–36.
83. Johnson, 19.
84. Johnson, 37, 45, see 37–60.
85. Johnson, 73, see 61–72.
86. Johnson, 61–87. For another point of view, see Terry Eagleton, *The Ideology of the Aesthetic* (Oxford: Blackwell, 1990).
87. See *The Richard Wright Reader*, ed. Ellen Wright and Michel Fabre (New York: Harper and Row, 1978).
88. Johnson, *Feminist Difference*, 100.
89. Johnson, *Feminist Difference*, 101–02, see 103–28. See Simone de Beauvoir, *The Second Sex*, trans. H. M. Parshley (New York: Alfred Knopf, 1953). Johnson also calls attention to Elizabeth Spellman, *Inessential Woman* (Boston, MA: Beacon Press, 1988).
90. Johnson, 114.
91. Johnson, 127.
92. Johnson, 153, see 129–52.
93. Johnson, 154–64.

94. Johnson, 182, see 165–81.
95. Johnson, 194.
96. Johnson, 194.

Chapter 6

1. For two of my various discussions of poetics, see Jonathan Hart, *Northrop Frye: The Theoretical Imagination* (London and New York: Routledge, 1994), and my *Interpreting Cultures: Literature, Religion, and the Human Sciences* (New York and London: Palgrave Macmillan, 2006). Many thanks to Rajnath, the editor, for giving me permission to include here a revised version of "Poetics and Poetic Worlds," *Journal of Literary Criticism* 10 (2004), 35–63. For a discussion of the relation between neo-Latin and vernacular poetry and the diverse theory and practice of poetry in the Renaissance, see Philip J. Ford, *George Buchanan: Prince of Poets* (Aberdeen: Aberdeen University Press, 1982). On the relation between rhetoric and poetics in neo-Latin and seventeenth-century Dutch and French poetry, which includes a consideration of the role of argument in poetics, see Marijke Spies, *Rhetoric, Rhetoricians, and Poets: Studies in Renaissance Poetry and Poetics* (Amsterdam: Amsterdam University Press, 1999). In his introduction, Louis Armand says that the authors in his collection are not trying to create a kind of poetics in the tradition of Aristotle or present a current state of poetry, but rather they examine poetics of the here and now, a practice of writing that engages with what it means to be contemporary, since the time of Stéphane Mallarmé. See Louis Armand, "Editor's Introduction: Transversions of the Contemporary," *Contemporary Poetics*, ed. Louis Armand (Evanston, IL: Northwestern University Press, 2007), xiii–xiv. On poetry and poetics, see *12 x 12: Conversations in 21ˢᵗ-Century Poetry and Poetics*, ed. Christina Mengert and Joshua Marie Wilkinson (Iowa City: University of Iowa Press, 2009), which mixes interviews and poetry. My own approach includes texts from theory and practice, here and there, then and now.

2. Plato, *The Republic of Plato*, trans. Francis M. Cornford (New York: Oxford University Press,1941, rpt. 1968), especially Book 10; Aristotle, "On the Art of Poetry," in *Classical Literary Criticism*, ed. T. S. Dorsch (Harmondsworth: Penguin, 1965, rpt. 1975), 33–75.

3. Philip Sidney, [*Defence of poetry*]. *An apologie for poetrie. Written by the right noble, vertuous, and learned, Sir Phillip Sidney, Knight* (At London: Printed [by James Roberts] for Henry Olney, and are to be sold at his shop in Paules Church-yard, at the signe of the George, neere to Cheapgate, Anno. 1595); William Shakespeare, *Mr. William Shakespeares comedies, histories & tragedies: published according to the true originall copies* (London: Isaac Iaggard and Ed. Blount, 1623); for Keats, I have in mind the culminating lines of "Ode on a Grecian Urn,"—"'Beauty is truth, truth beauty,'—that is all / Ye know on earth, and all ye need to know" (lines 49–50). I have left out the quotation marks in these lines in keeping with the first printing of the poem in *Annals of*

Fine Arts (James Elmes, ed.), January 1820; William Butler Yeats, *The Collected Poems of W. B. Yeats*, Definitive ed. with the author's final revisions (New York: Macmillan, 1956, rpt. 1960). See, for instance, *Ars Poetica*, in Horace, *Satire, Epistles, Ars Poetica*, trans. H. R. Fairclough, Loeb Classical Library (Cambridge, MA: Harvard University Press, 1936), 333–65. Perhaps the key line is "Omne tulit punctum qui miscuit utile dulci, / lectorem delectando pariterque monendo" (343–44). This can be loosely translated as: "He wins every vote who can mix the useful and the sweet, at once delighting and teaching the reader" (my translation).

4. See "poetry" and its cognates in the *Oxford English Dictionary*, 2nd ed., 1989.
5. Jacques Derrida, *Of Grammatology*, trans. Gayatri Spivak (Baltimore and London: Johns Hopkins University Press, 1976), esp. 158–64. See Gregory Ulmer, "Op Writing: Derrida's Solicitation of Theoria," *Displacement: Derrida and After*, ed. Mark Krupnick (Bloomington: Indiana University Press, 1983), and Michael J. C. Echeruo, "Derrida, Language Games, and Theory," *Theoria: A Journal of Social and Political Theory* 86 (1995), 99–115.
6. Friedrich Wilhelm Nietzsche, *The Birth of Tragedy* [*Geburt der Tragödie.* English], trans. Douglas Smith (Oxford: Oxford University Press, 2000); Roland Barthes, *Mythologies* (Paris: Éditions du Seuil, 1957) and his *Le plaisir du texte* (Paris: Éditions du Seuil, 1973); Marshall McLuhan, *The Mechanical Bride: Folklore of Industrial Man* (New York: Vanguard Press, [1951]). See also James J. Murphy, "The Metarhetorics of Plato, Augustine, and McLuhan: A Pointing Essay," *Philosophy and Rhetoric* 4 (1971), 201–14; Hwa Jung, "Misreading the Ideogram: From Fenollosa to Derrida and McLuhan," *Paideuma* 13 (1984), 211–27; Nicholas Harrison, "Camus, écriture blanche and the Reader, between Said and Barthes," *Nottingham French Studies* 38 (1999), 55–66; Dorothea B. Heitsch, "Nietzsche and Montaigne: Concepts of Style," *Rhetorica* 17 (1999), 411–31; D. A. Miller, "Foutre! Bougre! Ecriture!," *Yale Journal of Criticism: Interpretation in the Humanities* 14 (2001), 503–11.
7. *Oxford English Dictionary*, 2nd ed., 1989.
8. See the etymologies available in OED.
9. The word "theory" and its cognates in OED.
10. The term "poetry" and its cognates in OED.
11. More specifically, the etymology of "read" is as follows: "[Comm. Teut.: OE. raédanÿ OFris. reda using, OS. radan (MLG. raden, MDu. and Du. raden), OHG. ratan (MHG. raten, G. raten, rathen), ON. ráqa (Sw. rada, Da. raade), Goth. -redan: OTeut. *ra[d an, prob. related to OIr. imrádim to deliberate, consider, OSl. raditi to take thought, attend to, Skr. radh- to succeed, accomplish, etc." See ibid.
12. See ibid. for the cognates of "interpret."
13. See ibid for "culture" and its cognates, as well as my *Interpreting Cultures* for this more detailed discussion.
14. On story-argument, see Jonathan Hart, "Stephen Greenblatt's *Shakespearean Negotiations*," *Textual Practice* 5 (1991), 444, and *Theater and World: The*

Problematics of Shakespeare's History (Boston, MA: Northeastern University Press, 1992), 259.

15. Hayden White, *The Content of the Form: Narrative Discourse and Historical Representation* (Baltimore and London: Johns Hopkins University, 1987, rpt. 1992), 185–213.

16. Doreen Maitre, *Literature and Possible Worlds* (London: Middlesex Polytechnic Press, 1983), esp. 66–70. See Jonathan Hart, "A Comparative Pluralism: The Heterogeneity of Methods and the Case of Possible Worlds," *Canadian Review of Comparative Literature* [*CRCL/RCLC*] 15 (1988), 320–45, esp. 324. Two key books in the field are Jerome Bruner, *Actual Minds/Possible Worlds* (Cambridge: Harvard University Press, 1986), and Thomas Pavel, *Fictional Worlds* (Cambridge: Harvard University Press, 1986). A more recent study, which relates the possible to fictionality, is Ruth Ronen, *Possible Worlds in Literary Theory* (Cambridge: Cambridge University Press, 1994), esp. 18–20.

17. See the culminating lines of "Ode on a Grecian Urn" and the edition quoted from in note 3 earlier. On the debate over the quotation, see Dennis R. Dean, "Some Quotations in Keats's Poetry," *Philological Quarterly* 76 (1997), 69–85.

18. *The Republic of Plato*, trans. Cornford, esp. Book 10. On Plato and Augustine, see Murphy, 201–14.

19. Plato, *Republic*, Book 10,

20. Oscar Wilde, "The Decay of Lying," *Essays by Oscar Wilde*, ed. Hesketh Pearson (London: Methuen, 1950), 70–71.

21. Wilde, 72.

22. Pavel, esp. 55.

23. Pavel, esp. 144–48; Jonathan Locke Hart, *Breath and Dust* (Edmonton and Melbourne: Mattoid/Grange, 2000).

24. On story-argument, see note 14 above. See Bruner, 5–14.

25. Bruner, 24–26.

26. For studies, from the mid-1940s into the 1990s, of Shakespeare's history or history plays that are readily accessible to students, see E. M. W. Tillyard, *Shakespeare's History Plays* (London: Chatto and Windus, 1944); Herbert Lindenburger, *Historical Drama: The Relation of Literature to Drama* (Chicago: University of Chicago Press, 1975); Jonathan Hart, *Theater and World: The Problematics of Shakespeare's History* (Boston, MA: Northeastern University Press, 1992).

27. On the relation between ideology and music, see, for instance, Gregory B. Lee, *Troubadours, Trumpeters, Troubled Makers: Lyricism, Nationalism, and Hybridity in China and Its Others* (Durham, NC: Duke University Press, 1996), esp. ch. 6; Leslie David Blasius, *Schenker, Argument and the Claims of Music Theory* (Cambridge and New York: Cambridge University Press, 1996); *Music/Ideology: Resisting the Aesthetic: Essays*, ed. Adam Krims (Amsterdam: G *Music and Ideology in Cold War Europe* (Cambridge and New York: Cambridge University Press, 2003), esp. 1–21.

28. Aristotle, *The Poetics/Aristotle. On the sublime/"Longinus." On style/Demetrius* (Cambridge, MA: Harvard University Press, 1927); Greek and English texts

29. See "'The Politics of the English Language'" (1946); George Orwell, *The Collected Essays, Journalism, and Letters of George Orwell*, ed. Sonia Orwell and Ian Angus (London: Secker & Warburg, 1968). See also Raymond Williams, *Orwell* (London: Flamingo, 1971) and Stephen Ingle, *George Orwell: A Political Life* (Manchester: Manchester University Press, 1993), ch. 5; Roland Barthes, *Mythologies*; *Barthes, au lieu de roman*, ed. Marcielle Macé and Alexandre Gefen (Paris: Desjonquères, 2002) and *R/B, Roland Barthes*, ed. Marianne Alphant and Natalie Léger (Paris: Seuil, 2002). Many American writers engage the French on ideology in the nineteenth century. John Adams expressed his skepticism about the ability of the fledgling United States to establish a free republican government as Thomas Jefferson had envisioned. In a letter to Jefferson of July 13, 1813, Adams expresses this doubt and notes: "Napoleon has lately invented a Word, which perfectly expresses my Opinion at that time and ever since. He calls the Project Ideology"; see *The Founders' Constitution*, ed. Philip B. Kurland and Ralph Lerner (Chicago: University of Chicago Press, 1987, 2000), ch. 15 (Equality), document 59. Thomas Jefferson had outlined, in an undated document (*Elements [Of] Ideology*), his own view of the word, which he took to mean "our means of obtaining knowledge" in an outline for what would appear to be a projected study or book (*The Thomas Jefferson Papers Series* 1, Library of Congress, ms. 1 p.) During the 1790s, Destutt de Tracy conceived of "ideology" as a science or system of ideas, but the word could also mean abstract speculation, idealism, and the way ideas are expressed. *The Oxford English Dictionary* (2nd ed. 1989) sets this out clearly.

30. On the history of ideology, beginning with Destutt de Tracy, see J. Plamenatz, *Ideology* (London: Macmillan, 1985). A recent brief study is Michael Freeden's *Ideology: A Very Short Introduction* (Oxford: Oxford University Press, 2003); ch. 3 discusses theory and ideology.

31. In particular, see Northrop Frye, *Anatomy of Criticism: Four Essays* (Princeton, NJ: Princeton University Press, 1957, rpt. 1973).

32. Narrative and argumentation were often seen as being opposed to each other. Plato opposes philosophy to poetry, whereas Plato's philosophy involved a good deal of narrative, especially in the form of allegory, so that the actual foundation of philosophy was narrative as well as dialectical and dialogical. The usefulness of knowledge is one of the reasons Plato places philosophy above poetry. Oscar Wilde, who used his wit to create plays and stories, wrote: "Arguments are to be avoided; they are always vulgar and often convincing."

33. In *Mythologies*, Barthes attacked mythology in 1957, the same year Frye was defending it in *Anatomy*. In some ways, Barthes idea of mythology is similar to Frye's notion of ideology. This relation between mythology and ideology is a central concern of my *Northrop Frye: The Theoretical Imagination*, esp. ch. 7 (see 194–95 for the discussion of Barthes and Frye). Terminology can change

and blur and cause misapprehension in the connection between mythology and ideology.

34. Plato, *Republic*, Book 10.

35. Buffon's most celebrated discussion of style may be found in Georges Louis Leclerc, comte de Buffon, *Discours sur le Style; texte français avec version latine de J. A. Nairn* (Paris: Société d'édition 'Les belles letters,' 1926). The original text is 1753. For Buffon, style was integral to the person. In "An Essay in Criticism," Alexander Pope wrote: "For diff'rent Styles with diff'rent Subjects sort," defining decorum. Pope begins this poem musing on whether a poet or critic suffers most in his craft: "'Tis hard to say, if greater Want of Skill / Appear in Writing or in Judging ill"? Matthew Arnold's use of the phrase "grand style" is in keeping with his notion of the high aims of poetry and poetry as something that would take the place of religion and philosophy and would be a kind of knowledge that would supplant dogma. In Arnold's view, poetry might have had a higher use, but it had a use. See his essay from 1864, "The Function of Criticism at the Present Time."

36. All quotations from the poetry of Yeats are from W. B. Yeats, *The Poems: A New Edition* (New York: Macmillan, 1983). On Yeats, Heaney, Paul Muldoon, and others, see Jonathan Hart, "Some Thoughts on Irish Lyric Poetry," *New Delta Review* 19.1 (Fall/Winter 2001), 92–107 and, in the same issue, my review of "*Poems 1968–1998* by Paul Muldoon," 113–16. See also Deborah Fleming, "Landscape and the Self in W. B. Yeats and Robinson Jeffers," *Ecopoetry: A Critical Introduction*, ed. J. Scott Bryson (Salt Lake City: University of Utah Press, 2002), 39–57.

37. All references to Heaney's poetry are, unless otherwise specified, to Seamus Heaney, *New Selected Poems 1966–1987* (London: Faber and Faber, 1990), 1–2, 10; Seamus Heaney, *An Open Letter* (Derry: Field Day Theatre Company, 1983), stanza 33, p. 13. For work on Heaney germane to this discussion, see Michael Cavanagh, "Tower and Boat: Yeats and Seamus Heaney," *New Hibernia Review/ Iris Éireannauch Nua* 4 (2000), 17–38; Eugene O'Brien, "The Question of Ireland: Yeats, Heaney, and the Postcolonial Paradigm"; and Raphael Ingelbien, "Decolonizing Ireland/England? Yeats, Seamus Heaney and Ted Hughes," *W. B. Yeats and Postcolonialism*, ed. Deborah Fleming (West Cornwall, CT: Locust Hill, 2001), 51–70 and 71–100 respectively.

38. Seamus Heaney, *Sweeney Astray* (1983; London: Faber and Faber, 1984).

39. Seamus Heaney, "Clearances," *The Haw Lantern*, Poem I, ll. 1–4, p. 225.

40. On irony, see, for example, Friedrich Schlegel, *Literary Notebooks, 1797–1801*, ed. Hans Eichner (Toronto: University of Toronto Press, 1957), 114; Bishop Connop Thirlwall, "On the Irony of Sophocles," in *Remains Literary and Theological of Connop Thirlwall*, ed. J. J. Stewart Perowne (London: Daldy, Isbidster, 1878), vol. 3, pp. 1–57; Samuel Taylor Coleridge, *Lectures and Notes on Shakspere and Other English Poets* (London: Bell, 1883, rpt. 1895); Josef Budde, *Zur romantischen Ironie bei Ludwig Tieck* (Bonn, 1907). For Karl Solger and others, see *German Aesthetic and Criticism: The Romantic Ironists and Goethe,*

ed. Kathleen Wheeler (Cambridge: Cambridge University Press, 1984). On the Socratic, German Romantic, and other forms of irony, see Hart *Theater and World*, esp. 1–7, 223–31.

41. William Shakespeare, *Hamlet*, in *Mr. William Shakespeares comedies, histories, & tragedies. Published according to the true original copies. London, Printed by Isaac Iaggard, and Ed. Blount, 1623. Facsimile Reproduction.* ed. Charlton Hinman (New York: W. W. Norton, 1968); all quotations from Shakespeare, except for the sonnets and passages from quartos, like *Hamlet* and *Troilus and Cressida*, are from this work.

42. William Shakespeare, *The Tragicall Historie of Hamlet Prince of Denmarke. By William Shakespeare. Newly imprinted and enlarged to almost as much againe as it was, according to the true and perfect Coppie* (London, 1604).

43. Anne Barton, Introduction to *Love's Labor's Lost* in William Shakespeare, *The Riverside Shakespeare,* 2nd ed., ed. G. Blakemore Evans (Boston, MA: Houghton Mifflin, 1997), 209.

44. See Barton, 212.

45. Hart, "A Comparative Pluralism," 320–45.

46. Plato, *Republic*; Aristotle (see also Longinus), [Greek and English] *The Poetics / Aristotle On the sublime / "Longinus". On style / Demetrius*; Longinus (see entry for Aristotle); Thomas Aquinas, *Aristotle: On interpretation. Commentary by St. Thomas and Cajetan (Peri hermenias),* trans. from the Latin with an intro. by Jean T. Oesterle (Milwaukee, WI: Marquette University Press, 1962).

Chapter 7

1. Jonathan Hart, *Representing the New World: The English and French Uses of the Example of Spain, 1492–1713* (New York: Palgrave, 2001).

2. Daniel Castillo Durante, *Du stéréotype à la literature* (Montréal: XYZ, 1994). My thanks to the editors and to the Canadian Comparative Literature Association for permission to include a revised version of "The Paradox of Stereotype: A New Theory of Literature," *Canadian Review of Comparative Literature/Revue Canadienne de la Littérature Comparée [CRCL/RCLC]* 21 (1994), 705–16. Some recent books on stereotyping take different approaches. For a psychological approach that also discusses culture and includes Walter Lippmann's introduction of the term "stereotype" in *Public Opinion* (1922) and Adorno's research on authoritarian personalities and stereotyping, see Perry Roy Hinton, *Stereotypes, Cognition and Culture* (Hove: Psychology Press, 2000), esp. 8–9, 151–56. For a discussion of the positive as well as negative aspects of stereotyping (for stereotypes are central to our understanding), see Craig McGarty, Vincent Y. Yzerbyt, and Russell Spears, "Social, Cultural and Cognitive Factors in Stereotype Formation," *Stereotypes as Explanations: The Formation of Meaningful Beliefs about Social Groups,* ed. Craig McGarty, Vincent Y. Yzerbyt, and Russell Spears (Cambridge: Cambridge University Press, 2002), 3–7. In defending generalizations and categories by which to make decisions rather than particulars,

Frederick F. Schauer argues that not all stereotypes and profiles are desirable and he sees them as helping people to decide based on statistics and thinking actuarially. See Frederick Schauer, *Profiles, Probabilities, and Stereotypes* (Cambridge, MA: Harvard University Press, 2003, rpt. 2006), ix–x, 1–10. On a practical level and in relation to education in the United States, Andrew J. Fuligni has put together a collection whose authors explore the idea "that persistent disparities in educational opportunities and achievement are often created and sustained by academic stereotypes that are ascribed to different social groups by the larger society and its institutions." See Andrew J. Fuligni, "Introduction," *Contesting Stereotypes and Creating Identities: Social Categories, Social Identities, and Educational Participation*, ed. Andrew J. Fuligni (New York: Russell Sage Foundation, 2007), 1. From these few volumes, it is readily apparent that stereotypes are still controversial.

3. Castillo Durante, 15. See Roland Barthes, *Le Plaisir du texte* (Paris: Éditions du Seuil, 1973).

4. Castillo Durante, 18–19. See Aristotle, *The Complete Works of Aristotle: The Revised Oxford Translation*, ed. Jonathan Barnes (Princeton, NJ: Princeton University Press, 1984).

5. Castillo Durante, 66.

6. See Bertolt Brecht, *Brecht on Theatre: The Development of an Aesthetic*, ed. and trans. John Willett (New York: Hill and Wang, 1964). See also Jonathan Hart, "Alienation, Double Signs with a Difference: Conscious Knots in *Cymbeline* and *The Winter's Tale*," *CIEFL Bulletin* (New Series) 1 (1989), 58–78 and a revised version in *Shakespeare and His Contemporaries* (New York: Palgrave Macmillan, 2011), 169–85, 235–38.

7. See Jonathan Hart, *Northrop Frye: The Theoretical Imagination* (London: Routledge, 1994). See also Louis Althusser, *Pour Marx* (Paris: François Maspero, 1969); Raymond Williams, *The Country and the City* (Oxford: Oxford University Press, 1973); Terry Eagleton, *The Ideology of the Aesthetic* (Oxford: Basil Blackwell, 1990); Paul Ricoeur, *La Métaphore vive* (Paris: Seuil, 1975); Northrop Frye, *Myth and Metaphor: Selected Essays, 1974–1988*, ed. Robert D. Denham (Charlottesville: University Press of Virginia, 1990).

8. Castillo Durante, 22n1.

9. Castillo Durante, 37–41. See Søren Kierkegaard, *Repetition: An Essay in Experimental Psychology*, trans. Walter Lowrie (New York: Harper, 1964).

10. Castillo Durante, 41–45.

11. Castillo Durante, 45–52.

12. Castillo Durante, 52–56. See Jean-Jacques Rousseau, *Les Confessions* (Paris: Garnier-Flammarion, 1968).

13. Castillo Durante, 56–60. See Julia Kristeva, *Séméiotikè: Recherches pour une sémanalyse* (Paris: Seuil, 1969).

14. Castillo Durante, 61–62.

15. Castillo Durante, 62–68.

16. Castillo Durante, 77.

17. Castillo Durante, 79–80.
18. Castillo Durante, 82.
19. Castillo Durante, 82, 83. See Pierre Bourdieu, *Ce Que parler veut dire: L'Économie des échanges linguistiques* (Paris: Fayard, 1982) and Stephen Greenblatt, *Shakespearean Negotiations: The Circulation of Social Energy in Renaissance England* (Berkeley: University of California Press, 1988).
20. Castillo Durante, 82–89.
21. Castillo Durante, 89–96.
22. Castillo Durante, 96–101; see Althusser; Jacques Lacan, *Écrits II* (Paris: Seuil, 1971); Michel Pêcheux, *Les Vérités de la Palice* (Paris: François Maspero, 1975); Jacques Derrida, *Psyché: Inventions de l'autre* (Paris: Galilée, 1987). There are many important discussions of cultural stereotyping. One particularly consequential discourse is that of colonialism, how in the cultural exchange between Europe and America in the early modern period stereotyping had significant material implications for the various American and European cultures. One aspect of that debate is the discussion of the other. The question of the other involves many angles of refraction. One angle concerns the European "re-discovery" of America. In Columbus we already find ambivalence in the relation between European and "Other." By the early eighteenth century, Jonathan Swift satirizes the proliferation of travel literature, and by the 1990s, especially in the wake of the commemoration of Columbus's first voyage, we felt even more saturation. Resistance, ambivalence, and indignation in the face of European imperialism occur before it begins. The ambivalence, if not the reluctance, with which the monarchs of Europe, even Ferdinand and Isabella, received Columbus's enterprise of the Indies represents an opposition from within before the encounter with the other that Todorov, de Certeau, and Greenblatt discuss. See Tzvetan Todorov, *La Conquête de l'Amérique* (Paris: Seuil, 1982); Michel de Certeau, "Montaigne's 'Of Cannibals': The Savage 'I,'" *Heterologies: Discourse on the Other*, trans. Brian Massumi (Minneapolis: University of Minnesota Press, 1986), 67–79 and his "Travel Narratives of the French to Brazil: Sixteenth to Eighteenth Centuries," *Representations* 33 (1991), 221–26; Stephen Greenblatt, *Marvelous Possessions: The Wonder of the New World* (Chicago: University of Chicago Press, 1991). During the encounter between the Spanish and the Natives in 1492, this ambivalence over the American enterprise continues, even within the "Columbus" texts, and soon after a horror over its excesses is felt within Europe itself. For a discussion of textual instabilities, ambivalence, and stereotyping in the "Columbian" texts, see "Images of the Native in Renaissance Encounter Narratives," *Ariel* 25 (October 1994), 55–76. Castillo Durante's theory of stereotyping differs from Todorov's and might have some interesting applications in the early modern period (even before Rabelais). Deborah Root offers a perceptive critique of Todorov's influential theory of the other in the conquest of America. See Deborah Root, "The Imperial Signifier: Todorov and the Conquest of Mexico," *Cultural Critique* 9 (1988), 197–219.

23. Castillo Durante, 101–02.
24. Castillo Durante, 102.
25. Castillo-Durante, 104, 111–19; see Theodor W. Adorno, *The Jargon of Authenticity*, trans. Knut Tarnowski and Frederic Will (London: Routledge, 1973).
26. Castillo Durante, 111. See Martin Heidegger, *Being and Time*, trans. John Macquarrie and Edward Robinson (New York: Harper, 1962).
27. Castillo Durante, 130.
28. Castillo Durante, 119–25.
29. Castillo Durante, 126–29.
30. Castillo Durante, 129–45, esp. 140.
31. Castillo Durante, 145.
32. William Shakespeare, *The Riverside Shakespeare*, textual ed. G. Blakemore Evans (Boston, MA: Houghton Mifflin, 1974). See Jonathan Hart, *Theater and World: The Problematics of Shakespeare's History* (Boston, MA: Northeastern University Press, 1992).
33. See Pierre Klossowski, *Sade, mon prochain* (Paris: Seuil, 1947).
34. See Ernst Kantorowicz, *The King's Two Bodies: A Study in Mediaeval Political Theology* (Princeton, NJ: Princeton University Press, 1957).
35. Castillo Durante, 145–51. See Klossowski.
36. See Fredric Jameson, *The Prison-House of Language: A Critical Account of Structuralism and Russian Formalism* (Princeton, NJ: Princeton University Press, 1972) and Richard Waswo, *Language and Meaning in the Renaissance* (Princeton, NJ: Princeton University Press, 1987).
37. Jonathan Hart, *Northrop Frye: The Theoretical Imagination* (London and New York: Routledge, 1994).
38. Terry Eagleton, *After Theory* (New York: Basic Books, 2003). Many thanks to the editor, Pamela McCallum, for permission to include here a revised version of my contribution to *Ariel* 37 (April-July 2006), 240–41. Although Eagleton speaks about being after theory, perhaps in both senses of "after," books about theory are still being written and courses still being taught in literary theory. For recent books on theory that I have not noted in other chapters, see *Literary Theory: An Anthology*, ed. Julie Rivkin and Michael Ryan (Oxford: Blackwell, 2004); Mary Klages, *Literary Theory: A Guide for the Perplexed* (London: Continuum, 2006); David Ayers, *Literary Theory: A Reintroduction* (Oxford: Blackwell, 2008).
39. Eagleton, *After Theory*, 1.
40. Eagleton, *After Theory*, 1.
41. Eagleton, *After Theory*, 5.
42. Eagleton, *After Theory*, 95.
43. Eagleton, *After Theory*, 138.
44. Eagleton, *After Theory*, 208.
45. Eagleton, *After Theory*, 221.
46. Eagleton, *After Theory*, 228.
47. See, for instance, Derrida's *Psyché*.

Chapter 8

1. Rather than repeat my earlier views on the relation between history and fiction and on Shakespeare's history plays, I refer the reader to Jonathan Hart, *Theater and World: The Problematics of Shakespeare's History* (Boston, MA: Northeastern University Press, 1992). See also Jonathan Hart, *Shakespeare: Poetry, History and Culture* (New York: Palgrave Macmillan, 2009) and *Shakespeare and His Contemporaries* (New York: Palgrave Macmillan, 2011). I wrote an earlier version of this chapter in the 1990s, and it was published in 2002. Thanks to the editors and to the Canadian Comparative Literature Association for permission to include here a revised version of "Between History and Poetry: The Making of the Past," *Canadian Review of Comparative Literature/Revue Canadienne de Littérature Comparée [CRCL/RCLC]* 29 (2002), 568–88. There are a number of books about poetry and history that are of interest. See, for instance, A. W. Gomme, *The Greek Attitude to Poetry and History* (Berkeley: University of California Press, 1954); Emery Edward Neff, *The Poetry of History: The Contribution of Literature and Literary Scholarship to the Writing of History since Voltaire* (New York: Octagon Books, 1979); Nicolas Saul, *History and Poetry in Novalis and in the Tradition of the German Enlightenment* (London: University of London, Institute of Germanic Studies, 1984); Cynthia Jane Brown, *The Shaping of History and Poetry in Late Medieval France* (Birmingham, AL: Summa Publications, 1985); Lionel Gossman, *Between History and Literature* (Cambridge, MA: Harvard University Press, 1990). Gossman's work has made an important contribution in the field. For an assessment of Gossman's contribution, see Stephen Bann, "Review: Gossman, Lionel. 'The Empire Unpossess'd. An Essay on Gibbon's Decline and Fall,'" *History and Theory* 22 (1983), 199–207; Frank Ankersmit, "Review: Gossman, Lionel. *Between History and Literature*," *Clio* 21 (1992), 173–85; Ann Rigney, "Review: Gossman, Lionel. *Between History and Literature*." *History and Theory*. XXI (1992), 208–22. For more recent work, see Blair Worden, "Historians and Poets," *The Uses of History in Early Modern England*, ed. Paulina Kewes (San Marino, CA: Huntington Library/University of California Press, 2006), 69–90. The other essays in the collection also contribute to the debate on history and historiography. See also *Tropes for the Past: Hayden White and the History/Literature Debate*, ed. Kuisma Korhonen (Amsterdam: Rodopi, 2006). Although all the essays in the collection are germane, see especially Kuisma Korhonen, "General Introduction: The History/Literature Debate," 9–20, and Hayden White, "Historical Discourse and Literary Writing," 25–33.

Carlo Ginzburg relates the work of the historian to that of the inquisitor and anthropologist and, in doing so during the 1980s, he showed how the marginal had become central to the study of history. His advocacy of careful attention to texts is something I have also tried to do:

> A close reading of a relatively small number of texts, related to a possibly circumscribed belief, can be more rewarding than the massive accumulation of

repetitive evidence, as anthropologists do, and as inquisitors did. But for the interpretation of this evidence they have something to learn from both. (164)

Each field has its advantages and each can learn from other endeavors. The same is true for poetry, history, and philosophy, so that a ranking of them, while provocative, may be less useful now than it was for Aristotle. See Carlo Ginzburg, "The Inquisitor as Anthropologist," Clues, Myths, and the Historical Method, trans. John and Anne Tedeschi (Baltimore, MD: Johns Hopkins University Press, 1989). The original appeared as *Miti emblemi spie: morfologia e storia* (Torino: Giulio Einaudi editore, 1986). Derek Walcott explores the relation between past and present, the flawed nature of being human, and the way the muse of history turns more to myth in time:

> The method by which we are taught the past, the progress from motive to event, is the same by which we read narrative fiction. In time every event becomes an exertion of memory and is thus subject to invention. The further the facts, the more history petrifies into myth. (37)

Method, memory, and myth are all within the chain of history. The petrification of facts creates a fossil, a geological record that we craft and interpret, and that rock formation may not be entirely positive. There are human beings in this petrified story, living in time, acting as people in a past that leads to the present. To burn up history can consume responsibility, emotion, and engaging with those who went before. See Derek Walcott, "The Muse of History," *What the Twilight Says: Essays* (New York: Farrar, Straus and Giroux, 1998). In a history of the Russian Revolution, Orlando Figes shifts the paradigm from a study of structures and abstract forces to a narrative of lives of individuals well known and not:

> In following the fortunes of these figures, my aim has been to convey the chaos of these years, as it must have been felt by ordinary men and women. I have tried to present the revolution not as a march of abstract social forces and ideologies but as a human event of complicated individual tragedies. It was a story, by and large, of people, like the figures in this book, setting out with high ideals to achieve one thing, only to find out later that the outcome was quite different. This, again, is why I chose to call the book *A People's Tragedy.* (xix)

Figes's work, a good example of the "return" to narrative in history that I am discussing here, shares characteristics of the novel, involves a reincorporation of rhetoric that "scientific" history has tried to occlude, and is a topos where Russian history meets Dostoevsky. See Orlando Figes, *A People's Tragedy: The Russian Revolution 1891–1924* (1996, London: Pimlico, 1997).

2. See Michael Murrin, *History and Warfare in Renaissance Epic* (Chicago, IL: University of Chicago Press, 1994).
3. Murrin, 1.
4. Murrin, 2.
5. Murrin, 8.

6. Murrin, 9.
7. Murrin, 21.
8. Murrin, 38.
9. Murrin, 39.
10. Murrin, 40.
11. Murrin, 55.
12. Murrin, 57.
13. Murrin, 74–75.
14. Murrin, 79.
15. Murrin, 102.
16. Murrin, 103.
17. Murrin, 104–05.
18. Murrin, 118.
19. Murrin, 119.
20. Murrin, 123; see J. R. Hale, "Gunpowder and the Renaissance: An Essay in the History of Ideas," *From the Renaissance to the Counter-Reformation*, ed. Charles H. Carter (New York: Random House, 1965), 113–44.
21. Murrin, 137.
22. Murrin, 138–39.
23. Murrin, 158–59.
24. Murrin, 162–78.
25. Murrin, 179f.
26. Murrin, 186.
27. Murrin, 196.
28. Murrin, 199.
29. Murrin, 215.
30. Murrin, 216–17.
31. Murrin, 223–24.
32. Murrin, 225–28.
33. Murrin, 231–32.
34. Murrin, 238.
35. Murrin, 239–40.
36. Murrin, 241.
37. Murrin, 244–45.
38. Peter Burke, "History of Events and the Revival of Narrative History," *New Perspectives on Historical Writing*, ed. Peter Burke (University Park: Pennsylvania State University Press, 1992), 234; see Lawrence Stone, "The Revival of Narrative," *Past and Present* 85 (1979), 3–24, and Simon Schama, *Citizens: A Chronicle of the French Revolution* (New York: Knopf, 1989).
39. Burke, 235–36.
40. Burke, 237; Mark Phillips, "On Historiography and Narrative," *University of Toronto Quarterly* 53 (1983–84), 149–65.
41. Burke makes a convincing case for using the novelistic techniques of modernists like Joyce and Woolf, such as the breakdown of the continuity of time, and for

seeking new literary forms, such as multiple points of view, as found in the work of Aldous Huxley, William Faulkner, and Lawrence Durrell (237–38; see G. Wilson, "Plots and Motives in Japan's Meijii Restoration," *Comparative Studies in Society and History* 25 (1983), 407–27). I assume that the logic of Burke's argument would also make postmodernist fictional techniques, or any that are useful, available to the historian. He also refers to Bahktin's heteroglossia, so that there is also a cross-fertilization between literary theory and historiography (239). See also Hayden White, *Metahistory: The Historical Imagination in Nineteenth-Century Europe* (Baltimore, MD: Johns Hopkins University Press, 1973).

42. Although rhetoric is something history and poetry share, neither is entirely rhetorical, especially as the one relates to fact and the other to the making of patterned rhythms that are not predictable, mechanical, or necessarily continuous. See Burke 241–45; William R. Siebenschuh, *Fictional Techniques and Factional Works* (Athens: University of Georgia Press, 1983); Marshall Sahlins, *Historical Metaphors and Mythical Realities* (Ann Arbor: University of Michigan Press, 1981).

43. Not wishing to repeat myself, I refer the reader to some of my work on the relation of fiction and fact and my comments on New Historicism in Jonathan Hart, *Theater and World: The Problematics of Shakespeare's History* (Boston, MA: Northeastern University Press, 1992) and *Northrop Frye: The Theoretical Imagination* (London and New York: Routledge, 1994) as well as to the bibliographies in both volumes. See also chapter 5 in this book, *Literature, Theory, History*. Burke's insight into the ways in *Gate of Heavenly Peace* (1973) and *The Death of the Woman Wang* (1978) that Jonathan Spence sets up an analogy between private and public, above and below, may be applied to the important work of New Historicists like Stephen Greenblatt, but in Greenblatt's work the intellectual daring and perceptive interpretations depend in large part on the yoking of public and private, central and marginal, high and low in the same essay or book (something I have discussed in "Stephen Greenblatt's Shakespearean Negotiations," *Textual Practice* 5 (1991), 429–48).

44. Burke, 245–46.

45. Elizabeth Ermarth, *Sequel to History: Postmodernism and the Crisis of Representational Time* (Princeton, NJ: Princeton University Press, 1992), xi. Elizabeth Ermarth, for instance, speaks about the challenge of postmodernism to history, but history is as much narrative history, which includes microhistory, as structural history, which aspires more to the kind of "totalization" postmodernist theorists so often attack (7–8). She does note with André Breton that aspects of postmodernist movements, like surrealism, can be found in Romanticism. Ermarth outlines the high stakes, political and otherwise, in not resisting or coming to terms with postmodernism in the empirical domain of the Anglo-American world while also recognizing that she cannot give up history even as she challenges what she takes to be its hegemony (something Aristotle and Philip Sidney would not admit in their respective advocacies of

philosophy and poetry). Instead of the Cartesian *cogito*, she advocates rhythmic time, which takes the dictum, "I swing therefore I am," from chapter 16 of Julio Cortázar's *Hopscotch* (1963) and qualifies or throws off dialectics, transcendence, neutrality, and teleology of historical time (9–16). Postmodernism can, then, open up new possibilities in history: while history is, like any verbal discipline, textual, it is not, in my view, the same as saying that history is entirely textual. There are facts and actions in the world that are soon interpreted and disputed in verbal constructs, but the pursuit of the question—what happened?—is, hard as it might be, important to pursue.

46. Ermarth, 3.
47. See Alain Robbe-Grillet, "Note sur la notion d'itinéraire dans *Lolita*," *L'Arc* 24 (1964), 37–38.
48. See Ermarth.
49. See Umberto Eco, *Lector in Fabula*: Pragmatic Strategy in a Metanarrative Text," *The Role of the Reader: Explorations in the Semiotics of Texts* (Bloomington: Indiana University Press, 1979), 200–66.
50. For related comments on Fuentes's novel, see Brian McHale, *Postmodernism* (New York: Methuen, 1987), 17.
51. McHale, *Postmodernism*, 96; see 92.
52. For a discussion of this kind of "historiographic metafiction," see Linda Hutcheon *A Poetics of Postmodernism: History, Theory, Fiction* (New York: Routledge, 1988) and Brian McHale, *Constructing Postmodernism* (London and New York: Routledge, 1992), 152–53. McHale says that Eco claims that when his readers praise him for historical accuracy, they do so when citing a modern passage, and when they dispraise him for anachronism, they point to a passage he has quoted from a fourteenth-century text; see also Umberto Eco, *The Name of the Rose* (1980. New York: Warner, 1984), 74–77 and *Postscript to The Name of the Rose*, trans. William Weaver (San Diego, CA: Harcourt Brace Jovanovich, 1984). Eco's novel does not necessarily borrow any more characters from other texts than Shakespeare does (Falstaff, after his name is changed from Oldcastle, perhaps for political reasons, echoes the name of a historical figure and is a different character in the *Henry VI* plays) and it is not necessarily any more polyglot than that supreme modernist fiction, Joyce's *Finnegans Wake* (1941), not to mention Rabelais's Panurge (McHale recognizes this debt). Postmodernism may, then, represent a different concentration and reconfiguration of these narrative techniques and literary conventions in a later historical period.
53. Harry Levin's study of five French realists, *The Gates of Horn* (New York: Oxford University Press, 1963), shows how the notion of reality in fiction was quite different in the nineteenth century than it was to become. Like Erich Auerbach, Levin is interested in the ever-expanding notion of reality and the techniques available to make the reader aware of that expansion. See Erich Auerbach, *Mimesis: The 'Representation of Reality in Western Literature*, trans. Willard R. Trask (Princeton, NJ: Princeton University Press, 1953).
54. Ginzburg, *Clues*, 159–60.

55. Auerbach, 285.
56. For a discussion of Hegel and Auerbach, including Auerbach's use of Shakespeare, see Suzanne Gerhardt, *The Interrupted Dialectic: Philosophy, Psychoanalysis, and Their Tragic Other* (Baltimore, MD: Johns Hopkins University Press, 1992), 133–38.
57. Louis O. Mink, "History and Fiction as Modes of Comprehension," *Historical Understanding*, ed Brian Fay, Eugene Golob, and Richard Vann (Ithaca, NY: Cornell University Press, 1987), 55.
58. Bernard Bailyn, *On the Teaching and Writing of History: Responses to a Series of Questions*, ed. Edward Connery Lathem (Hanover, NH: Dartmouth College and University Press of New England, 1994), 7–8.
59. Timothy Bahti has an interesting discussion of Hegel and the understanding of history in which he draws on Paul de Man. Timothy Bahti, *Allegories of History: Literary Historiography after Hegel* (Baltimore, MD: Johns Hopkins University Press, 1992), 77. If the literary and allegorical are equivalents, as Bahti assumes, then there is a gap between historical understanding and historical events; then, as I have also argued, history's truth to itself would be a difficult matter, and historians might not necessarily decide the same thing about historical truth that literary historians would (see Bahti, 291).
60. Bahti, 291–92.
61. Bahti, 293. See Paul de Man, "Sign and Symbol in Hegel's *Aesthetics*," *Critical Inquiry* 8 (1982), 761–75.
62. Bahti, 293, see Hart, *Northrop Frye*.
63. See Northrop Frye, *Anatomy of Criticism* (1957. Princeton, NJ: Princeton University Press, 1973).
64. Jerome Bruner, *Actual Minds, Possible Worlds* (Cambridge, MA: Harvard University Press, 1986), 42–43.
65. Charles Taylor, *Sources of the Self: The Making of the Modern Identity* (Cambridge, MA: Harvard University Press, 1989), 204.
66. Thomas Pavel discusses the possibility of transhistorical communication, something Northrop Frye saw as being at the foundation of literature even as it grew out of its own history; see Thomas Pavel, *Fictional Worlds* (Cambridge, MA: Harvard University Press, 1986), 129–31.
67. See R. G. Collingwood, *The Idea of History* (1946; London: Oxford University Press, 1948, rpt. 1966).
68. Richard Lanham, *The Motives of Eloquence: Literary Rhetoric in the Renaissance* (New Haven, CT: Yale University Press, 1976), 19–20.
69. See Lanham 191–93.
70. A. J. Woodman, *Rhetoric in Classical Historiography: Four Studies* (Portland, OR: Areopagitica Press, 1988), ix; R. F. Atkinson, *Knowledge and Explanation in History: An Introduction to the Philosophy of History* (London: Macmillan, 1978).

Chapter 9

1. My thanks to the editors, Santa Arias and Eyda M. Merediz, for inviting the original essay and for granting permission, along with the Modern Language

Association of America, to reprint this revised version of "Las Casas in French and Other Languages," *Approaches to Teaching the Writings of Bartolomé de Las Casas,* ed. Santa Arias and Eyda M. Merediz (New York: Modern Language Association of America, 2008), 224–34. Since I wrote that essay, which took a while to come into production, some other work has appeared. See, for instance, Daniel Castro, *Another Face of Empire: Bartolomé de Las Casas, Indigenous Rights, and Ecclesiastical Imperialism* (Durham, NC: Duke University Press, 2007), and Lawrence A. Clayton, *Bartolomé de las Casas and the Conquest of the Americas* (Oxford: Wiley-Blackwell, 2010). This last book is designed largely for students.

2. A good resource for all teachers of Las Casas and other writers representing the New World is *European Americana: A Chronological Guide to Works Printed in Europe Relating to the Americas, 1493–1776,* ed. John Alden, vols. 1–5 (New York: Readex, 1980–97). See also Jonathan Hart, *Representing the New World: English and French Uses of the Example of Spain* (New York: Palgrave, 2001).

3. *Tyrannies et cruautez des Espagnols,* trans. Jacques de Miggrode (Antwerp: François de Ravelenghien, 1579; Paris: Guillaume Julien, 1582; Rouen: Jacques Cailloué, 1630; Rouen, 1642).

4. "Je confesse n'avoir jaimais gueres aimé la nation en general, à cause de leur orgueil insupportable; com-bien que ie ne laisse de Louër & aimer aulcuns excellens personages qu'il y a entre eux" (*2r–v). This quotation comes from the French-language edition published in 1579 in Antwerp, available online through Gale (http://galenet.galegroup.com) and now the most available copy. (My thanks to Stephen Ferguson, curator of Rare Books at Princeton, for pointing this out to me.) In general, references to the *Tyrannies* in this essay are, unless otherwise noted, to the 1582 Paris edition, because that was the volume to which I originally had access. This 1582 edition, printed by Guillaume Julien, is based on (and has the same title as) the 1579 Antwerp edition, which translated the original Spanish edition of 1552 (published in Seville as *Brevíssima relación*). Other editions appear as *Histoire admirable des horribles insolences, cruautez, et tyrannies exercees par les Espagnoles és Indes Occidentales*: probably Geneva, 1582; Lyons, 1594. Saint-Lu identifies the 1594 Lyons edition, noting that it included the canceled title page of the 1582 edition and was based on the 1579 Antwerp translation (André Saint-Lu, *Las Casas indigeniste: Études sur la vie et l'œuvre du défenseur des Indiens* (Paris: L'Harmatten, 1982), 164). All translations are mine, unless otherwise indicated.

5. Las Casas, trans. Miggrode, *ii recto–*ii verso.

6. Las Casas, Bartolomé de, *A Short Account of the Destruction of the Indies,* ed. and trans. Nigel Griffith, intro. Anthony Pagden (New York: Penguin, 1992), 96.

7. Saint-Lu, *Las Casas indigeniste,* 162–63.

8. See, for instance, book 1, chapter 17 of the edition of 1618 in the accessible Grant translation of Marc Lescarbot, *The History of France,* trans. W. L. Grant, 3 vols. (Toronto: Champlain Society, 1907–14), 1: 125–30. Lescarbot uses a rhetorical flourish to highlight not simply the vast numbers of dead but also the number of incidents of cruelty in Las Casas's text: "This good bishop, unable to

endure all these cruelties and a hundred thousand others, made remonstrances and complaints thereon to the King of Spain." Moreover, Lescarbot claims, "what I have said is a small parcel of the contents of the book of this author," whom, he emphasizes, the Spaniards themselves cite (1: 30).

9. André Thevet, *Les singularitez de la France antarctique* (Paris: Chex les héritiers de Maurice de la Porte, 1558), 16–24.

10. *Le miroir de la tyrannie espagnole* (the Amsterdam edition of 1620) composes part 2 of Johannes Gysius, *Le mirroir de la cruelle, et horrible tyrannie espagnole perpetree au Pays Bas . . . On a adjoinct la deuxiesme parties de les tyrannies commise aux Indes Occidentales par les Espagnoles.* The next version is *Tyrannies et cruautez des Espagnols* (published in Rouen by J. Cailloué in 1630). The French edition of 1620 is translated from the two-part Dutch edition of the same year—*Den spiegel der Spaensche tijrannijegeschiet in West-Indien* (published in Amsterdam by J. E. Cloppenburg). The French edition transposes the two parts. Part 2, by Las Casas, has a special title page with the title *Le miroir de la tyrannie perpetree aux Indes Occidentales.* Gysius's work includes a reference to the massacre of the French in Florida by the Spaniards and also to the Spanish treatment of the Indians. In other words, the French reverses the two parts, which are as follows in the Dutch edition: part 1 was first published in Dutch in Antwerp in 1578 under the title *Seer cort verhael vande destructie van d' Indien . . . uyte Spaensche overgeset.* This was a translation of the edition of Las Casas's *Brevíssima relación* published in Seville in 1552. Part 2 has the title *Tweede deel van de spieghel der Spaensche tyrannye* and is an abridged version of Johannes Gysius's *Oorsprong en voortgang der Nederlandtschen bercertin,* published in Leyden in 1616.

11. See also Saint-Lu, *Las Casas indigeniste,* 159–70.

12. Bartolomé de Las Casas, *Tyrannies et cruautez des Espagnols commises es Indes Occidentales qu'on dit le Nouveau Monde,* trans. Jacques de Miggrode (Rouen, 1642), Ã2r.

13. Las Casas, trans. Miggrode (1642), Ã3r.

14. Las Casas (1642), Ã4r, Ã4v.

15. Las Casas (1642), Ã4v.

16. Chauveton's 1579 volume also included Nicolas Le Challeux's *Discours . . . de la Floride* (first published in Dieppe in 1566), an account of the Spanish massacre of the French in Florida. The 1565 massacre was one of the events that turned the rhetoric of the Huguenots against Spain.

17. André Thevet, *André Thevet's North America: A Sixteenth-Century View,* ed. Roger Schlesinger and Arthur Stabler (Kingston, ON: McGill-Queen's University Press, 1986), 161.

18. Richard Hakluyt, *A Particular Discourse* (1584), ed. David B. Quinn and Alison Quinn (London: Hakluyt Society, 1993), 111; see also the Quinns' "Commentary" in Hakluyt's book, 186–87.

19. See the foreword by the anonymous editor of the March of America Facsimile Series reprint of *The Spanish Colonie.* Foreword, Q2r.

20. Bartolomé de Las Casas, *Tears of the Indians*, trans. John Phillips (London: Nath, Brook, 1656), A4v–A6r. Edward Leigh's Latin *Treatise of Religion and Learning, and of Religious and Learned Men* (London: A. M[iller] for C. Admas, 1656) relayed Las Casas's account of the destruction of the Indies, and in 1658, the king of Spain's cabinet discussed the cruelties of the Spaniards in America (*The King of Spain's Cabinet Divulged; or, A Discovery of the Prevarications of the Spaniard's* [London: J. H. for J. S., 1658]).

21. The intertextuality of translations related to the French versions of Las Casas's *Brevissima relacion* can be seen through the following thread. The 1579 French translation of the 1552 Spanish original was used for the English translation of 1583. Theodor de Bry Latin version of 1598 (*Narratio*), with the now famous illustrations, was based on that French translation of 1579. But there were other later French translations of this text by Las Casas. The 1620 French translation of Gysius (which contained Las Casas) was from the Dutch edition of 1620 (*Tweede* [based on the Dutch original of 1616 (*Oorsprong*)]). The 1697 French translation (*La decouverte*) translated only six of the nine books from Las Casas and was the basis for the English translation of 1699. In this chapter about early French translations of this text by Las Casas, we can see that there are three books, two that spawn other translations and one that is from the Dutch. See *Narratio regionem indicarum per hispanos quosdam devastatarum verissima*, trans. and illus. Theodor de Bry and Jean Israêl de Bry (Frankfurt am Main: Hispali, Hispanicè, 1598); Johannes Gysius, *Oorsprong en voortgang der Nederlandtschen becerten* [Leyden, 1616] and his *Tweede deel van de spieghel der Spaenishe tyrannye* (Amsterdam: J. E. Cloppenburg, 1620); Bartolomé de Las Casas, *La decouverte des Indes Occidentales, par les Espagnols,* trans. J. B. M. Morvan de Bellegarde (Paris: André Pralard, 1697).

22. Las Casas, *La decouverte des Indes Occidentales, par les Espagnols,* trans. J. B. M. Morvan de Bellegarde (Paris: André Pralard, 1697). Bellegarde's version was reprinted with *Relation curieuse des voyages du Sieur de Montauban* in Amsterdam in 1698. It was also translated as *A Relation of the First Voyages and Discoveries Made By Spaniards in America* (London: D. Brown and A. Bell, 1699). Saint-Lu, *Las Casas indigeniste* 168–69; A. F. Allison, *English Translations from the Spanish and Portuguese to the year 1700: An Annotated Catalogue of the Extant Printed Adaptations, Excluding Dramatic Adaptations* (London: Dawson of Pall Mall, 1974), 42; Colin Steele, *English Interpreters of the Iberian New World from Purchas to Stevens: A Bibliographical Study, 1603–1726* (Oxford: Dolphin, 1975), 107–08, 175–76.

23. Peter Burke, *Montaigne* (Oxford: Oxford University Press, 1981), 46.

24. Michel de Montaigne, *Essais de Michel Seigneur de Montaigne* (Paris, 1588), rpt. as *Les Essais de Montaigne*, 3 vols. Paris: Imprimerie Nationale, 1906–31), 3: 399. All citations from the *Essais* are from the 1588 edition, unless otherwise indicated.

25. *Montaigne's Essays*, trans. John Florio, ed. J. I. M. Stewart, 2 vols. (London: Nonesuch, 1931), 2: 314. Montaigne's sentence ends simply after "mechaniques

victoirs" (*Essais* 3: 399). This original is now available online at Gallica from the Bibliothèque nationale de France in Paris (http://gallica.bnf.fr). My thanks to Stephen Ferguson for calling my attention to this electronic version.

26. Montaigne, *Essais* 3: 399.

27. Montaigne, *Essais* 3: 401.

28. *Montaigne's Essays*, trans. John Florio, 2: 317.

29. "Nous tenons d'eux-meſmes ces narrations, car ils ne les aduoent pas ſelement, ils les preſchent & publient" (*Essais* 3: 401). For "aduouent" in this sentence, in another translation I have used "confess," and I might well take "preſchent" as "preach" to continue this religious theme, but I have chosen not to be as literal here, as it makes the English more idiomatic. See Hart, *Representing the New World*, 119.

30. Montaigne, *Essais* 3: 401–02.

31. William Shakespeare, *The Tempest*. ed. Frank Kermode (London: Methuen, 1958).

32. Kermode, *The Tempest*, 145–47n62; Carl Orwin Sauer, *Sixteenth-Century North America: The Land and the People as Seen by the Europeans* (Berkeley: University of California Press, 1971), 13, 15.

Chapter 10

1. Harry Levin, "English, American, and Comparative Literature," *Grounds for Comparison* (Cambridge, MA: Harvard University Press, 1972), 71, see 72–73. Many thanks to the editors and to the Canadian Comparative Literature Association for permission to include here a revised version of "Reviewing Comparative Reviews," *Canadian Review of Comparative Literature/Revue Canadienne de Littérature Comparée* [CRCL/RCLC] 14 (1987), 351–67. At the journal, I would like to thank Paul Robberecht, an editor there at the time, and the research assistants, Mila Bongco for Zhang Benzi, and Sharon Ryan.

2. See Hayden White, "The Question of Narrative in Contemporary Historical Theory," *History and Theory* 23 (1984), 1–33.

3. This is something that Horst Steinmetz suggests in "Weltliteratur: Umriß eines literaturgeschichtlichen Konceptz," *Arcadia* 20 (1985), 2–19.

4. See Edward Said, *Orientalism* (New York: Vintage Books, 1978); "Islam, Philology, and French Culture: Renan and Massignon," *The World, the Text, and the Critic* (Cambridge, MA: Harvard University Press, 1983), 268–89; *Covering Islam: How the Media and the Experts Determine How We See the Rest of the World* (New York: Pantheon Books, 1981).

5. See Lisa Lowe, "The Orient as Woman in Flaubert's *Salammbô* and *Voyage en Orient*," *Comparative Literature Studies* 23 (1986), 44–58.

6. Earl E. Fitz, "The First Inter-American Novels: Some Choices and Some Comments," *Comparative Literature Studies* 22 (1985), 362–76.

7. See Craig Randall, "Plato's *Symposium* and the Tragicomic Novel," *Studies in the Novel* 17 (1985), 158–73.
8. Texts yield many meanings for writers and readers: see Dietrich Meutsch and Siegfried J. Schmidt, "On the Role of Conventions in Understanding Literary Texts," *Poetics* 14 (1985), 551–74.
9. Steven Mailloux, "Rhetorical Hermeneutics," *Critical Inquiry* 11 (1985), 620–39.
10. See Kevin E. McClearey, "Summons, Protorhetoric and Rhetoric," *Neophilologous* 69 (1985), 490–500.
11. See Marshall W. Alcorn and Mark Bracher, "Literature, Psychoanalysis, and the Re-Formation of the Self: A New Direction for Reader-Response Theory," *PMLA* 100 (1985), 342–54.
12. Paul B. Armstrong, "Reading Figures: The Cognitive Powers of Metaphor," *University of Hartford Studies in Literature* 17 (1985), 49–67.
13. Joanne M. Golden, "Interpreting a Tale: Three Perspectives on Text Construction," *Poetics* 14 (1985), 503–24.
14. Reed J. Hoyt, "Reader-Response and Implication-Realization," *Journal of Aesthetics and Art Criticism* 43 (1985), 281–90.
15. Victoria Kahn, "The Figure of the Reader in Petrarch's *Secretum*," PMLA 100 (1985), 154–66.
16. See Joëlle Mertes-Gleize, "Lectures romanesques," *Romantisme* 47 (1985), 107–18; Lance Olsen, "Zombies and Academics: The Reader's Role in Fantasy," *Poetics* 15 (986), 279–85. For the difficulty of defining fantasy and the fantastic, see Eric S. Rabkin, *The Fantastic in Literature* (Princeton, NJ: Princeton University Press, 1976), esp. 3–41.
17. Kaja Silverman, *The Subject of Semiotics* (New York: Oxford University Press, 1983), esp. 243, 246.
18. Roland Barthes, "La mort de l'auteur," *Manteia* 5 (1968), 142–48.
19. Jonathan Culler, *The Pursuit of Signs: Semiotics, Literature, Deconstruction* (Ithaca, NY: Cornell University Press, 1981), vii. See Keir Elam, *The Semiotics of Theatre and Drama* (London: Methuen, 1980), 1.
20. Maja Bošković-Stulli, "Darstellerische Aspekte des Erzählens," *Fabula* 26 (1985), 58–71.
21. David Robey, "Literary Theory and Critical Practice in Italy: Formalist, Structuralist and Semiotic Approaches to the *Divine Comedy*," *Comparative Criticism* 7 (1985), 73–103.
22. Elizabeth Gülich and Uta M. Quasthoff, eds., "Narrative Analysis: An Interdisciplinary Dialogue," *Poetics* 15 (1986), 1–241.
23. Cees J. Van Rees, "Implicit premises on text and reader in Genette's study of narrative mood," *Poetics*, 14 (1985), 445–64.
24. See Harold Bloom, *The Anxiety of Influence* (New Haven, CT: Yale University Press, 1973) and his *A Map of Misreading* (New Haven, CT: Yale University Press, 1975).

25. Peter Hunt, "Necessary Misreadings: Directions in Narrative Theory for Children's Literature," *Studies in the Literary Imagination* 18 (1985), 107–21.

26. Peter Brooks, "Constructions psychanalytiques et narratives," *Poétiques* 61 (1985), 63–74; Lynne Layton, "From Oedipus to Narcissus: Literature and the Psychology of Self," *Mosaic* 18 (1985), 97–105.

27. David Novitz, "Metaphor, Derrida, and Davidson," *Journal of Aesthetics and Art Criticism* 44 (1985), 101–14.

28. Gerald Prince, "The Narrative Revisited," *Style* 19 (1985), 299–303; Gerald Prince, "Thématiser," *Poétique* 64 (1985), 425–33.

29. Claude Bremond, "Concept et thème," *Poétique* 64 (1985), 414–23; in the same issue: Menachem Brinker, "Thème et Interprétation," 435–43; Peter Cryle, "Sur la critique thèmatique," 505–16; Shlomith Rimmon-Kenan "Qu'est-ce qu'un theme?" 397–405; see Lubomír Doležel, "Le triangle du double: un champ thèmatique," 463–72. Doležel argues for aesthetic dimension of theme.

30. Siegfried J. Schmidt, ed. "On Writing Histories of Literature," *Poetics* 14 (1985), 191–363; Schmidt himself (195–98) explains how German literary scholars have, since the 1960s, made a contribution to literary history and historiography.

31. For a discussion of figures and tropes and the continuity between poetry and history, see Jacques Bompaire, "La place du genre historique dans le traité 'Du Sublime,'" *Revue d'Histoire Littéraire de la France* 86 (1986), 6–14 and, in the same issue, Paulette Carrive, "Le sublime dans l'esthétique de Kant," 71–85. Carrive analyzes the connections among the spirit, reason, and imagination in Kant's theory of the sublime in *The Critique of Pure Reason*. In the same issue, Marie-Claire Banquart discusses the shift from a Romantic notion of the sublime to the medical idea of sublimation in France, in the age of decadence from 1880 to 1900—"Une mise en cause du sublime à la fin du XIXᵉ siècle: sublime, sublime, sublimation," 109–11; on the sublime in nature and artistic creation, see Michel Delon, "Le Sublime et l'idée d'énegergie: de la théologie au matérialisme," 62–70; on the rhetoric of the ineffable and mystical transparence, see Alain Michel, "Sublime et parole de Dieu: de Saint Augustin à Fénelon," 52–61; on the difference in the use of classical models in relation to the marvelous and the sublime, see Daniel Poiron, "Théorie et practique au style au Moyen Age: Le sublime et la merveille," 15–32.

32. In a different context, David B. Morris sees the Gothic sublime as a movement from a view of the sublime in the eighteenth century to one that is Romantic and takes into account terror; see his "Gothic Sublimity," *New Literary History* 16 (1985), 299–319. See also, in the same issue, Charles Altieri, "Plato's Performative Sublime and the Ends of Reading," 251–73; on the role of rhetoric in the sublime, see Suzanne Guerlac, "Longinus and the Subject of the Sublime," 275–89.

33. Jean Weisgerber, " Rénouver l'histoire: Le problème des avant-gardes littéraires," *Komparatistische Hefte* 11 (1985), 21–33.

34. Yuri B. Vipper, "National Literary History in History of World Literature: Theoretical Principles of Treatment," *New Literary History* 16 (1985), 545–58.

35. Hans Ulrich Gumbrecht, "History of Literature—Fragment of a Vanished Totality?" *New Literary History* 16 (1985), 467–79.
36. David J. Langston, "Temporality, Knowledge, and the Social Dimension of Metaphor," *University of Hartford Studies in Literature* 17 (1985), 13–27.
37. Peter J. Rabinowitz, "Circumstantial Evidence: Musical Analysis and Theories of Reading," *Mosaic* 18 (1985), 159–73.
38. J. Russell Reaver, "How Musical Is Literature?" *Mosaic* 18 (1985), 1–10 and, in the same issue, W. John Rempel and Ursula M. Rempel, "Introduction," v–xi.
39. Garrett Stewart, "Singer Sung: Voice as Avowal in Streisand's *Yendtl*," *Mosaic* 18 (1985), 135–58.
40. Rose A, Zak, "*L'Histoire du soldat:* Approaching the Musical text," *Mosaic* 18 (1985), 101–07.
41. Jack F. Stewart, "Cubist Elements in *Between the Acts*," *Mosaic* 18 (1985), 65–89.
42. See E, Heier, "Schiller's Die Räuber in the Light of Tolstoj's Concept of Art," *Canadian Review of Comparative Literature/Revue Canadienne de Littérature Comparée* [*CRCL/RCLC*] 13 (1986), 531–47; Elmar Jansen, "Poetische Gemälde und Bildersprache: Zum Verständnis von Dichtung und Malerei in Philipp Otto Runges hinterlassenen Schriften," *Goethe Jahrbuch* 102 (1985), 215–25; Marlene Kadar, "Partisan Culture in the Thirties: *Partisan Review*, the Surrealists and Leon Trotsky," *Canadian Review of Comparative Literature/Revue Canadienne de Littérature Comparée* [*CRCL/RCLC*] 13 (1986), 373–423; Carol Wootton, "Literary Portraits of Mozart," *Mosiac* 18 (1985), 77–84; Juliette Spering, "Richard Wagner—ein Leitmotiv in Prousts *Recherche*?" *Arcadia* 20 (1985), 252–72; Sara Zimmerman Steinman, "Discovering the Nature and Function of the Image in Photography: Toward a Methodology," *Yearbook of Comparative and General Literature* 33 (1984), 37–44; Jorge H. Valdés, "Cardenal's Poetic Style: Cinematic Parallels," *Revista Canadiense de Estudios Hispánicos* 11 (1986), 119–29; Patricia Dunlavy Valenti, "The Frozen Art of the Ethereal Domain: Hawthorne's Concept of Sculpture," *Studies in Short Fiction* 22 (1985), 323–30; Martin M. Winkler, "Classical Mythology and Western Film," *Comparative Literature Studies* 22 (1985), 516–40; Bryan J. Wolf, "A Grammar of the Sublime, or Intertextuality Triumphant in Church, Turner, and Cole," *New Literary History* 16 (1985), 322–41.
43. Luiz Costa Lima, "Social Representation and Mimesis," *New Literary History* 16 (1985), 447–66.
44. The work on literary translation and translation theory is vast. On translation, see, for example, the special issue "Literary Translation and Literary System," *New Comparison* 1 (1986); Kwanshang Chen, "Random Notes on Translation," *Waiguoyu* 6 (1983), 11–14, 47; Mary Ann Caws, "Literal or Liberal: Translating Perception," *Critical Inquiry* 13 (1986), 49–63; Georges-Arthur Goldschmidt, "Écriture, traduction, liberté," *Revue d'Esthétique* 12 (1986), 159–64; Eugene A. Nida, "A Functional Approach to Problems of Translating," *Waiyu Jiaoxue Yu Yanjiu* 3 (1986), 25–31; Rainer Schulte, "Translation and Reading," *Gestus* 2 (1986), 13–16; *The World of Translation* (1970; New York: PEN American

238 • Notes to Pages 176–7

Center, 1987). The journal, *Waiguoyu*, contains articles in Chinese on translation in the following issues: March 1983, March and September 1985,
and January 1986. Alan Bass, Barbara Johnson, Jacques Derrida, and others have contributed essays in a volume on translation theory: see *Difference
in Translation*, ed. Joseph F. Graham (Ithaca, NY: Cornell University Press,
1985), esp. 102–48, 165–248. Another comprehensive volume on translation
theory is *Der Übersetzer und seine Stellung in der Öffentlichkeit/Translators and
Their Position in Society/Le Traducteur et sa place dans la société*, ed. Hildegrund
Buhler (Vienna: Wilhelm Branmuller, 1985). This collection touches on translation in Africa and Asia in addition to many other topics about literary and
nonliterary translation. See also *The Manipulation of Literature: Studies in
Literary Translation*, ed. Theo Hermans (New York: St. Martin's, 1985), esp.
103–35 and Paul de Man, "'Conclusions' on Walter Benjamin's 'The Task of
the Translator,'" *Yale French Studies* 69 (1985), 25–46. For an article with a
few references to translation in Canada, see Milan V. Dimić, "Comparative
Literature in Canada," *Neohelicon* 12 (1985), 59–74.

45. Laurel B. Boone, "The Relationship between *The Owl and the Nightingale*
    and Marie de France's *Lais* and *Fables*," *English Studies in Canada* 11 (1985),
    157–77.

46. W. Rothwell, "Stratford atte Bowe and Paris," *Modern Language Review* 80
    (1985), 39–54.

47. Virgil Nemoianu, "Picaresque Retreat: From Xenophon's *Anabasis* to Defoe's
    Singleton," *Comparative Literature Studies* 23 (1986), 91–102.

48. Rosemary M. Nielson and Robert H. Soloman, "Horace and Housman:
    Twisting Conventions," *Canadian Review of Comparative Literature/Revue
    Canadienne de Littérature Comparée* [*CRCL/RCLC*] 13 (1986), 325–49.

49. H. B. Nisbet, "Lucretius in Eighteenth-Century Germany: With a Commentary
    on Goethe's 'Metamorphose der Tiere,'" *Modern Language Review* 81 (1986),
    97–115; Norbert Oellers, "Goethes Novelle 'Die pilgernde Thörinn' und ihre
    französische Quelle," *Goethe Jahrbuch* 102 (1985), 88–104.

50. Reginald Gibbons, "Poetic Form and the Translator," *Critical Inquiry* 11 (1985),
    654–71.

51. Joseph Pivato, "Italian-Canadian Women Writers Recall History," *Canadian
    Ethnic Studies* 18 (1986), 79–88.

52. Carla Fratta, "Traduzioni italiane di testi letterari quebecchesi," *Il Veltro* 3–4
    (1985), 303–12.

53. Sandra M. Gilbert and Susan Gubar, "Sexual Linguistics: Gender, Language,
    Sexuality," *New Literary History* 16 (1985), 515–43.

54. Jack Corzani, "Problèmes méthodologiques d'une 'Histoire Littéraires des
    Caraïbes,'" *Komparatistische Hefte* 11 (1985), 49–67.

55. Tijani El-Miskin, "Disclaiming Authorial Originality: The Negotiation of
    Textuality in Two African Texts," *Comparative Literature Studies* 22 (1985),
    252–64.

56. Norbert Hopster and Ulrich Nassen, "Nationalsozialistische koloniale
    Jugendliteratur: Kolonialismus Zwischen Imperialismus und Exotismus,"

Komparatistische Hefte 12 (1985), 5–16; Pierrette Herzberger-Fofana, "La Littérature enfantine et pour la jeunesse en Afrique noire: le cas du Sénégal," *Komparatistische Hefte* 12 (1985), 39–49.

57. Mineke Schipper, "Toward a Definition of Realism in the African Context," *New Literary History* 16 (1985), 559–75.

58. Said, *The World*, 20–23, 90–110; and Jameson, *The Political Unconscious: Narrative as a Socially Symbolic Act* (Ithaca, NY: Cornell University Press, 1981), 151–69.

59. Mohammad Shaheen, "Tayeb Salih and Conrad," *Comparative Literature Studies* 22 (1985), 156–71.

60. Aritha Van Herk, "An(other) Third World: Girls in Children's Literature," *Komparatistische Hefte* 12 (1985), 33–37.

61. Richard Bjornson, "Nationalliteratur und Nationale Identität in Afrika: Kamerun als Beispiel," *Komparatistische Hefte* 12 (1985), 69–97.

62. Roberto Ventura, "Literature, Anthropology, and Popular Culture in Brazil: From José de Albencar to Darcy Ribeiro," *Komparatistische Hefte* 12 (1985), 35–47.

63. Adele King, "*Le temps de Tamango*: Eighteen Hundred Years of Solitude," *Komparatistische Hefte* 12 (1985), 77–89.

64. For studies on imperialism in Africa, see Walter Rodney, *How Europe Underdeveloped Africa* (Washington, DC: Howard University Press, 1974), George Padmore's *Africa, Britain's Third Empire* (1949; Greenwood: Negro University Press, 1970), and Basil Davidson's *Africa in Modern History: The Search for a New Society* (London: Allen Lane, 1978). I would like to thank Edward Said for his seminar course on colonialism and imperialism at Dartmouth College in 1988.

65. Francis Bacon, *Of the Proficience and Advancement of Learning, Human and Divine, The Works of Francis Bacon*, 10 vols. (London, 1824), 1: 147, and James Boswell, *Life of Johnson*, ed. R. W. Chapman (Oxford, 1980), 929, 984–85, quoted and cited in Zhang Longxi, "The Myth of the Other: China in the Eyes of the West," *Critical Inquiry* 15 (1988), 119, 122. Zhang's discussion is perceptive, especially in his view of language and of trying to accept China as it is; he also calls attention to the important work of Qian (esp. 118, 127–31). Zhang admits a debt to the following articles by Qian Zhongshu [Ch'ien Chung-shu]: "China in the English Literature of the Seventeenth Century," *Quarterly Bulletin of Chinese Bibliography* 1 (1940), 361–84; "China in the English Literature of the Eighteenth Century (I)," and "China in the English Literature of the Eighteenth Century (II)," *Quarterly Bulletin of Chinese Bibliography* 2 (1941), 7–48, 113–52. For the quotation below, see "De L'Experience," *Les Essais de Michel de Montaigne*, ed. Pierre Villey (Paris: Librairie Félix Alcan, 1931), III: 576.

66. The original reads: "En la Chine, duquel royaume la police et les arts, sans commerce et cognoissance des nostres, surpassent nos exemples en plusieurs parties d'excellence, et duquel l'histoire m'apprend combien le monde est plus ample et plus divers que ny les anciens ny nous ne penetrons, les officiers [...]

punissent ceux qui malversent en leur charge, [et] ils remunerent [...] ceux qui s'y sont bien portez [...]." (Montaigne, III: 576). I thank Philip J. Ford for his advice and suggestions for improving my translation and on the textual state of the original. See the Montaigne Project at http://artfl.uchicago.edu/cgi-bin/philologic/getobject.pl?c.0:4:12:0:1.montaigne.3331472.

67. Zhang, 126–27. See Zhang's "The Tao and the Logos: Notes on Derrida's Critique of Logocentrism," *Critical Inquiry* 11 (1985), 385–98. Zhang cites Henri Cordier, "Chinese Language and Literature," in Alexander Wylie, *Chinese Researches* (Shanghai, 1897), 195; George Steiner, *After Babel: Aspects of Language and Translation* (Oxford, 1975), 357; Jacques Derrida, *Of Grammatology*, trans. Gayatri C. Spivak (Baltimore, MD: Johns Hopkins University Press, 1976), 90. For an extensive discussion of Chinese language and poetry, see James J. Y. Liu, *The Art of Chinese Poetry* (Chicago, IL: University of Chicago Press, 1962). See also Ernest Fenellosa, *The Chinese Written Character as a Medium for Poetry*, ed. Ezra Pound (San Francisco, CA: City Lights Books, 1936). For other discussions of literary relations between China and the West, see Yuan Heh-hsiang and Dong Xiangxiao, trans., "East-West Comparative Literature: An Inquiry into the Possibilities," *Waiguoyu* 3 (1982), 55–60 (in Chinese); Yuan Haoyi, "Survey of Current Developments in the Comparative Literature of China," *Cowrie* 1 (1983), 81–125; John J. Deeney, "Chinese-English Comparative Literature Studies: A Poetics of Contrast?" in *Proceedings of the xth Congress of the International Comparative Literature Association/ Actes du xe congres de l'Association internationale de littérature comparée* (Vol. 2 *Comparative Poetics / Poétiques Comparées*), ed. Anna Balakian (New York: Garland, 1985), III: 602–07; Cecile Chu-Chin Sun, "Problems of Perspective in Chinese-Western Comparative Literature Studies," *Canadian Review of Comparative Literature/Revue Canadienne de Littérature Comparée* [CRCL/RCLC] 13 (1986), 531–47; Michelle Yeh, "Metaphor and Bi: Western and Chinese Poetics," *Comparative Literature* 39 (1987), 237–54.

68. *The Iliad of Homer*, trans. Richmond Lattimore (Chicago, IL: University of Chicago Press, 1951), 55, and *Plautus: Three Comedies: The Braggart Soldier, The Brothers Menaechmus, The Haunted House*, trans. Erich Segal (New York: Harper and Row, 1969), xvii–xviii.

69. *Stories from a Ming Collection: Translations of Chinese Short Stories Published in the Seventeenth Century*, trans. Cyril Birch (New York: Grove Press, 1958), 7–13; Kai-Yu Hsu, "Introduction," *Twentieth Century Chinese Poetry: An Anthology*, trans. and ed. Kai-Yu Hsu (Ithaca, NY: Cornell University Press, 1970), vii–xiii; *Li Po and Tu Fu: Poems Selected and Translated with an Introduction and Notes*, trans. Arthur Cooper (Harmondsworth: Penguin, 1973), esp. 13–15, 76–88. See also Liu.

70. Kenneth Rexroth, "Introduction," *One Hundred Poems from the Japanese* (New York: New Directions, 1964), ix–xx. See also *The Upanishads*, trans. Juan Mascaro (Hamondsworth: Penguin, 1965), 45–46; *Folk Tales from Korea*, trans. Zong In-Sob (New York: Grove Press, 1979), xviii–xix. See A. H. Qureshi, "Guy Amirthanayagam, Asian and Western Writers in Dialogue: New Cultural

Identities," *Canadian Review of Comparative Literature/Revue Canadienne de Littérature Comparée* [CRCL/RCLC] 10 (1983), 298–302. See also Peter Nagy, "National Literature—World Literature—Comparative Literature," *Neohelicon* 10 (1983), 97–106, and Anne Paolucci, "Regrouping Literatures and Languages: A Global View," *New Literary Continents* (Whitestone, NY: Griffon House, 1984), 6–15.

71. Masauki Ayiyama, "James and Nanboku: A Comparative Study of Supernatural Stories in the East and West," *Comparative Literature Studies* 22 (1985), 43–52.

72. Margaret Berry, "Almanzor and Coxinga: Drama West and East," *Comparative Literature Studies* 22 (1985), 97–109.

73. Matoshi Fujisawa, "A Survey of Japanese Immigrant-Emigrant literature," *Comparative Literature Studies* 22 (1985), 9–22.

74. Yoshinobu Hakutani, "Yone Noguchi's Poetry: From Whitman to Zen," *Comparative Literature Studies* 22 (1985), 67–79.

75. Yukinori Iwaki, "Iskikawa Takuboku and the Early Russian Revolutionary Movement," *Comparative Literature Studies* 22 (1985), 34–42.

76. Yoshiko Takita, "Wakamatsu Shizuko and *Little Lord Fauntleroy*," *Comparative Literature Studies* 22 (1985), 1–8.

77. Jaishree Odin, "Suggestiveness—Poe's Writing from the Perspective of Indian *Rasa* Theory," *Comparative Literature Studies* 22 (1985), 295–309.

78. Uwanda H. J. Sugunasiri, "The Literature of Canadians of South Asian Origins: An Overview," *Canadian Ethnic Studies* 17 (1985), 1–21.

79. Gloria Bien, "Baudelaire in China," *Comparative Literature Studies* 22 (1985), 121–35.

80. Carolyn T. Brown, "Creative Imitation: Hung Shen's Translation of Eugene O'Neill's *The Emperor Jones*," *Comparative Literature Studies* 22 (1985), 147–55.

81. Patricia J. Howard, "Hermann Hesse's 'Der Dichter': The Artist/Sage as Vessel Dissolving Paradox," *Comparative Literature Studies* 22 (1985), 110–20.

82. Dore J. Levy, "The Trojan and the Hegemon; or, the Culture Hero as Slave of Duty," *Comparative Literature Studies* 22 (1985), 136–46.

83. Ingrid Schuster, "Goethe und der 'chinesche Geschmack': Zum Landschaftgarten als Abbild der Welt," *Arcadia* 20 (1985), 164–78.

84. Thomas Schoonover, *Uncle Sam's War of 1898 and the Origins of Globalization* (Lexington: University Press of Kentucky, 2003). My thanks to the editors and publisher, Wiley, for permission to reprint a revised edition of my contribution on "*Uncle Sam's War of 1898 and the Origins of Globalization* by Thomas Schoonover" in *The Historian*, 67.2 (2005), 335–36. See Jonathan Hart, *Comparing Empires: European Colonialism from Portuguese Expansion to the Spanish-American War* (New York: Palgrave Macmillan, 2003). See also G. J. A. O'Toole, *The Spanish War: An American Epic—1898* (1984; New York: W. W. Norton, 1986).

85. Schoonover, 3.

86. Schoonover, 52.
87. Schoonover, 87.
88. Schoonover, 101.
89. Schoonover, 118.
90. Schoonover, 122.
91. David Day, *Conquest: How Societies Overwhelm Others* (Oxford: Oxford University Press, 2008). Many thanks to the editors and publisher for permission to reprint a revised edition of my contribution on "David Day, *Conquest: How Societies Overwhelm Others*," *European History Quarterly* 40 (2009). See also Anthony Pagden, *Peoples and Empires: A Short History of European Migration, Exploration, and Conquest, from Greece to the Present* (New York: The Modern Library, 2001); Jonathan Hart, *Empires and Colonies* (Cambridge: Polity Press 2008).
92. Day, 178.

Chapter 11

1. Ezra Pound, *Selected Prose, 1909–1965* (New York: New Directions, 1973), 192, quoted in Harry Levin, *Memories of the Moderns* (London: Faber and Faber, 1981), 20; *Literary Essays of Ezra Pound*, ed. T. S. Eliot (London: Faber and Faber, 1954), 24–25, quoted in Levin, 20.
2. Gertrude Stein, 19. *The Autobiography of Alice B. Toklas* (New York: Random House, 1933), 246, quoted in Levin, 19.
3. See Tom Conley, *Cartographic Cinema* (Minneapolis: University of Minnesota Press, 2007), 2–3. For Conley's reference to Borges, see Jorge Luis Borges, *Dreamtigers*, trans. Mildred Boyer and Harold Morland (Austin: University of Texas Press, 1964), 90.
4. J. Hillis Miller, *For Derrida* (New York: Fordham University Press, 2009), 55–56. Derrida makes this remark in *Mémoires pour Paul de Man* (Paris: Galilée, 1988), 27 and in *Memoires for Paul de Man*, trans. Cecile Lindsay, Jonathan Culler, and Eduardo Cadava (New York: Columbia University Press, 1986), 3.
5. See *The Older Sophists: A Complete Translation by Several Hands of the Fragments in Die Fragmente der Vorsokratiker, edited by Diels-Kranz . . . with a New Edition of Antiphon and Euthydemus*, ed. Rosamond Kent Sprague (Columbia: University of South Carolina Press, 1972).
6. There are exceptions. Some school systems, like those in the city of Edmonton in Alberta, allow for many publicly funded bilingual elementary, junior high and high schools in a myriad of languages.
7. *Isocrates*, vol. 2, trans. George Norlin (London: William Heinemann, 1929), 163.
8. See Jonathan Hart, "Stephen Greenblatt's Shakespearean Negotiations," *Textual Practice* 5 (1991), 429–48.
9. Hayden White, *The Fiction of Narrative: Essays on History, Literature, and Theory 1957–2007*, ed. Robert Doran (Baltimore, MD: John Hopkins University Press, 2010), 125.

10. R. G. Collingwood, *Speculum Mentis, or the Map of Knowledge* (Oxford: Clarendon Press, 1924). See White, 30.
11. See, for instance, Jonathan Hart, *Interpreting Culture: Literature, Religion, and the Human Sciences* (New York: Palgrave Macmillan, 2006).
12. White, 50. See Erich Auerbach, *Mimesis: The Representation of Reality in Western Literature*, trans Willard Trask (Princeton, NJ: Princeton University Press, 1953), 17.
13. White, 60–61. See Benedetto Croce, *Storiografia e idealità morale* (Bari: G. Laterza, 1950) and *History as the Story of Liberty*, trans. Sylvia Sprigge (New York: Meridian Books, 1955).
14. Margaret W. Ferguson, *Dido's Daughters: Literacy, Gender and Empire in Early Modern England and France* (Chicago, IL: University of Chicago Press, 2003), 378.
15. E. P. Thompson, *Making History: Writings on History and Culture* (New York: The New Press, 1994), 339.
16. Thompson, 330–32.
17. Plutarch, "On the Study of Poetry," *Classical Literary Criticism*, ed. D. A. Russell and M. Winterbottom (Oxford: Oxford University Press, 1989, rpt. 1991), 194.
18. Plutarch, 194.
19. Plutarch, 195.
20. Plutarch, 201.
21. Plutarch, 211.
22. Theodor W. Adorno, *Aesthetic Theory*, ed. Gretel Adorno and Rolf Tiedeman, trans. Robert Hullot-Kentor (London: Continuum, 2004), 6.
23. Terry Eagleton, *Literary Theory: An Introduction* (Oxford: Basil Blackwell, 1983), 17.
24. Peter Burke, "History of Events and the Revival of Narrative," *New Perspectives on Historical Writing*, ed. Peter Burke (University Park: Pennsylvania State University Press, 1992), 233, 236.
25. Burke, 238. See White, "The Burden of History," *History and Theory* 5, 1966, and Lionel Gossman, "History and Literature," *The Writing of History*, ed. R. H. Canary and H. Kozicki (Madison: University of Wisconsin Press, 1978), 3–39.
26. Burke, 246. See N. Z. Davis, J.-C. Carrière, and D. Vigne, *Le retour de Martin Guerre* (Paris, 1982). An English history book and a French film "translated" this past event in textual and film versions, providing different interpretative forms.
27. Robert Darnton, *The Great Cat Massacre and Other Episodes in French Cultural History* (1984; New York: Vintage Books, 1985), 3.
28. Darnton, 3–4.
29. Darnton, 6.
30. Bernard Bailyn, *On the Teaching and Writing of History* (Hanover, NH: Montgomery Endowment, Dartmouth College, 1994), 8.

Index